IMAGE COMICS, INC.
Robert Kirkman – Chief Operating Officer
Erik Larsen – Chief Financial Officer
Todd McFarlane – President
Marc Silvestri – Chief Executive Officer
Jim Valentino – Vice-President

Eric Stephenson – Publisher
Corey Murphy – Director of Sales
Jeff Boison – Director of Publishing Planning & Book Trade Sales
Jeremy Sullivan – Director of Digital Sales
Kat Salazar – Director of PR & Marketing
Branwyn Bigglestone – Controller
Drew Gill – Art Director
Jonathan Chan – Production Manager
Meredith Wallace – Print Manager
Briah Skelly – Publicist
Sasha Head – Sales & Marketing Production Designer
Randy Okamura – Digital Production Designer
David Brothers – Branding Manager
Olivia Ngai – Content Manager
Addison Duke – Production Artist
Vincent Kukua – Production Artist
Tricia Ramos – Production Artist
Jeff Stang – Direct Market Sales Representative
Emilio Bautista – Digital Sales Associate
Leanna Caunter – Accounting Assistant
Chloe Ramos-Peterson – Library Market Sales Representative
IMAGECOMICS.COM

EAST OF WEST

JONATHAN HICKMAN
WRITER

NICK DRAGOTTA
ARTIST

FRANK MARTIN
COLORS

RUS WOOTON
LETTERS

EAS

W

T

OF

EST

I HAVE COME TO **ABUSE** THE
SKEPTICS, AND SET **FIRE** TO
THE **UNWASHED.**

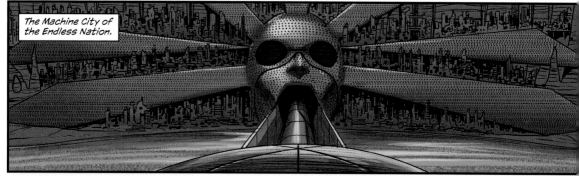

The Machine City of the Endless Nation.

Narsimha...

Narsimha...

Narsimha...

Wake up, Narsimha...

The moon is *waxing*...

And the time is *nigh*...

It's time for you to *choose*.

Are you a *chief* who sacrifices himself for his people...

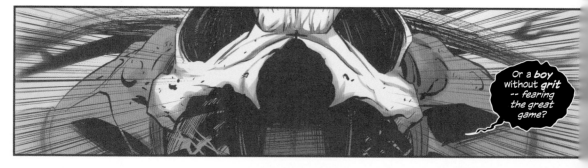

Or a *boy* without *grit* -- fearing the great game?

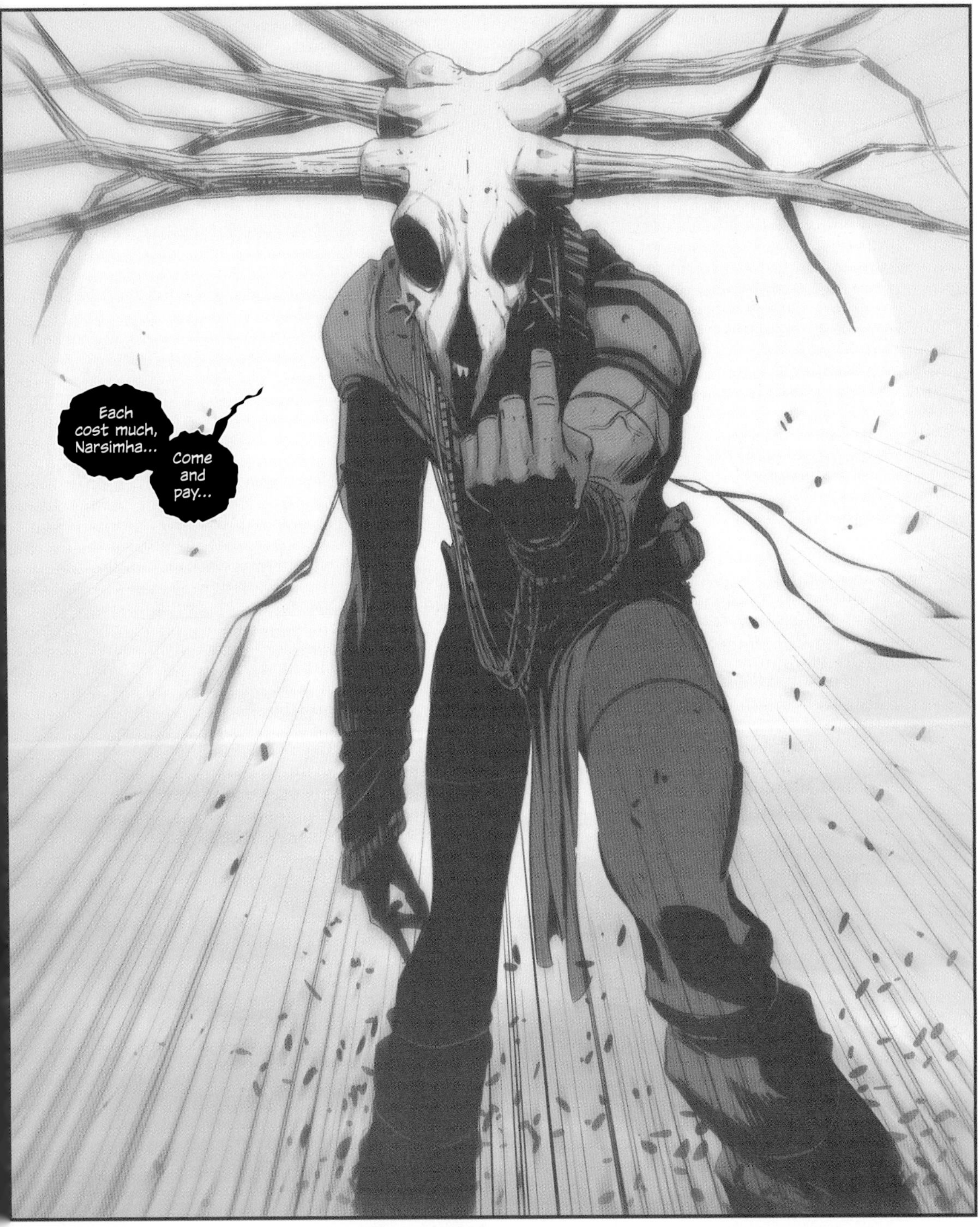
Each cost much, Narsimha...
Come and pay...

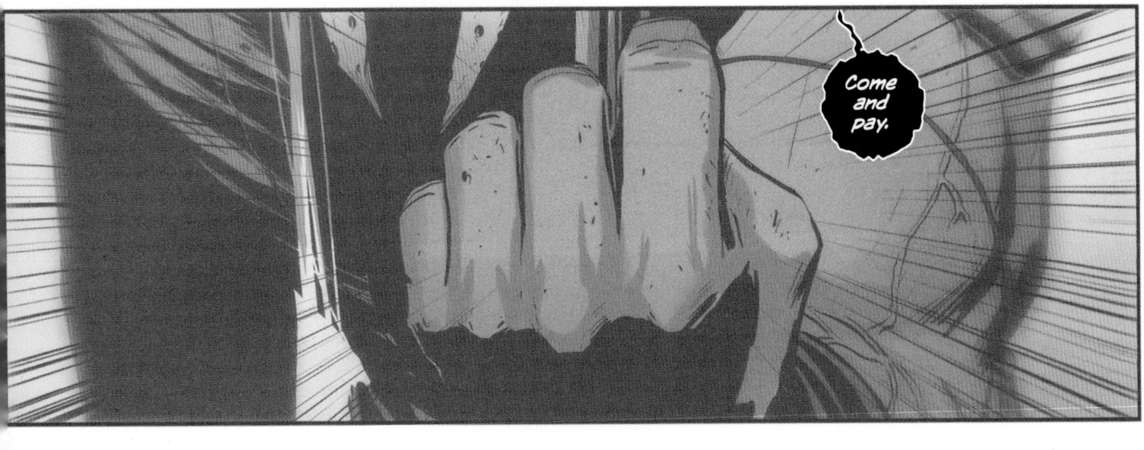
Come and pay.

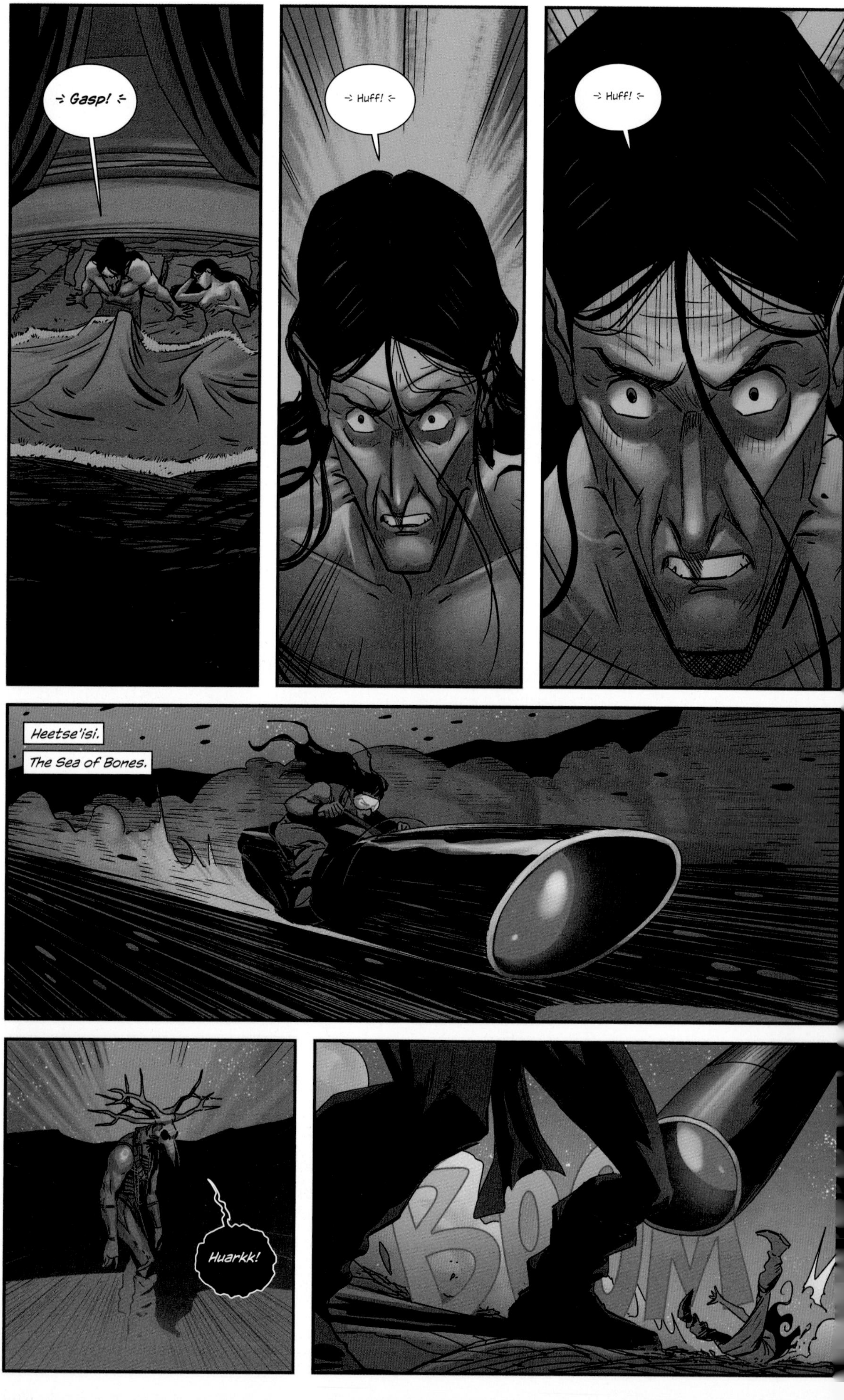
Gasp!
Huff!
Huff!
Heetse'isi.
The Sea of Bones.
Huarkk!
BOOM

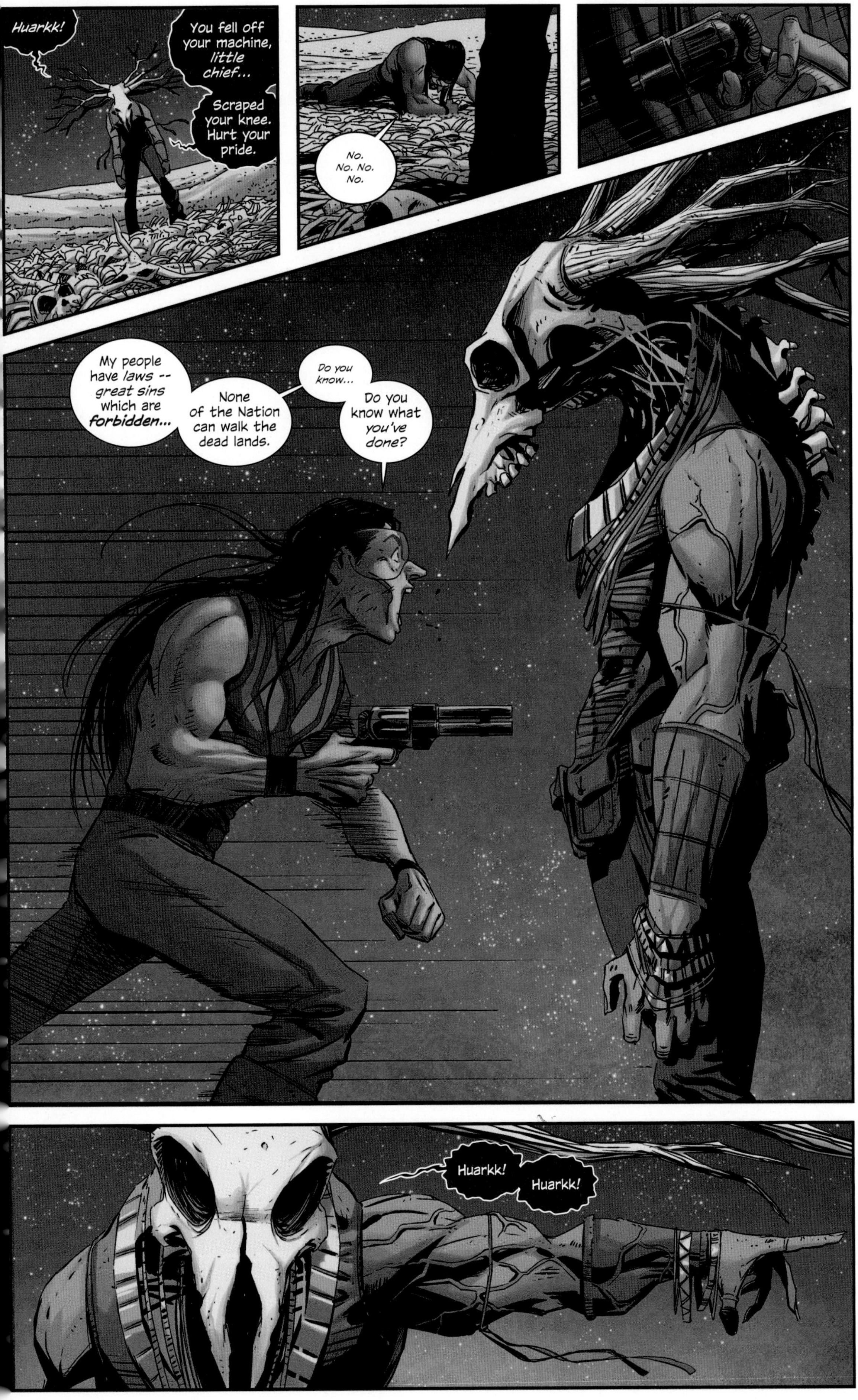
Huarkk!
You fell off your machine, little chief...
Scraped your knee. Hurt your pride.
No. No. No. No.
My people have laws -- great sins which are forbidden...
None of the Nation can walk the dead lands.
Do you know...
Do you know what you've done?
Huarkk!
Huarkk!

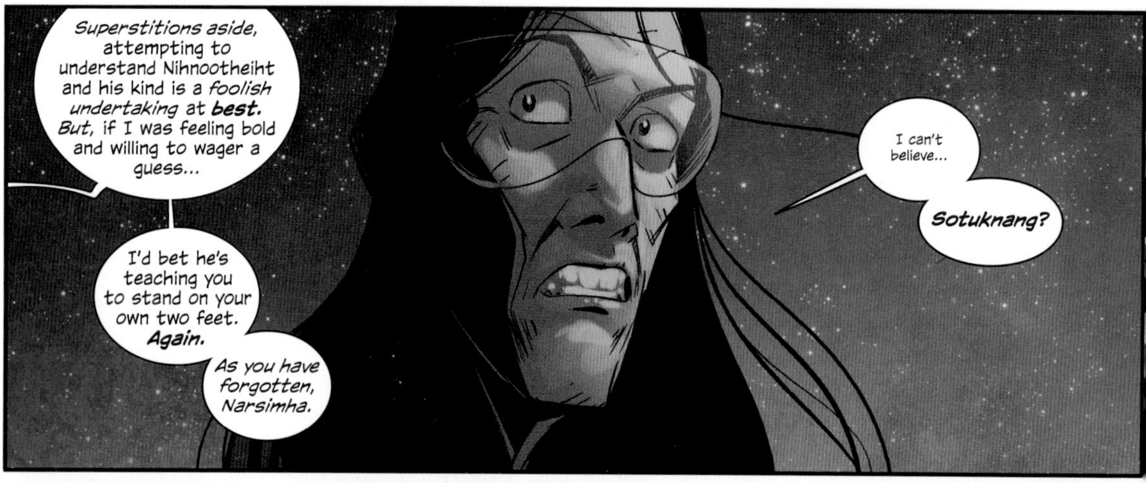
Superstitions aside, attempting to understand Nihnootheiht and his kind is a *foolish undertaking* at ***best.*** *But,* if I was feeling bold and willing to wager a guess...
I'd bet he's teaching you to stand on your own two feet. ***Again.***
As you have forgotten, Narsimha.
I can't believe...
Sotuknang?

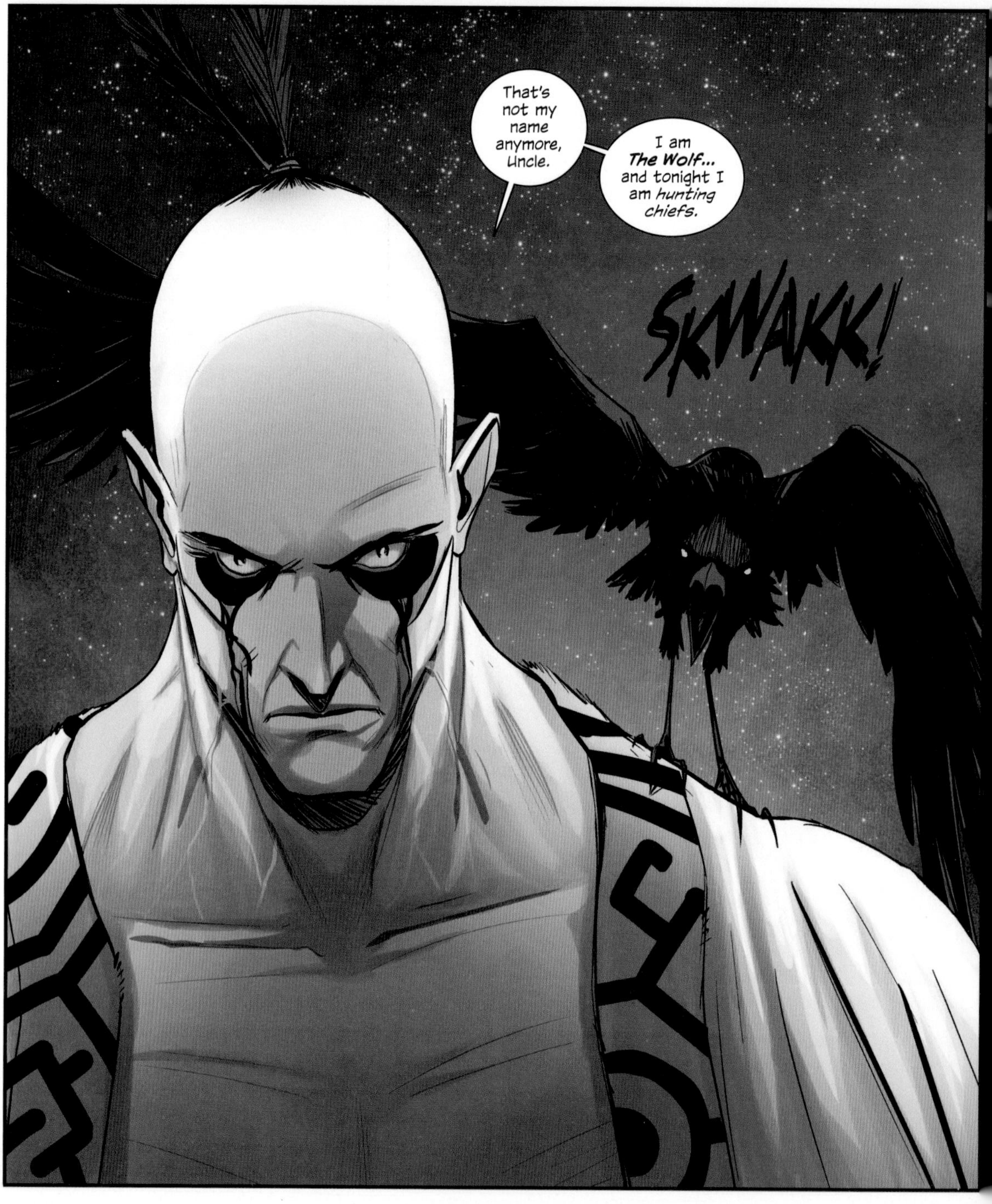
That's not my name anymore, Uncle.
I am ***The Wolf...*** and tonight I am *hunting chiefs.*
SKWAKK!

MY **DISCIPLES** ARE **LEGION**.

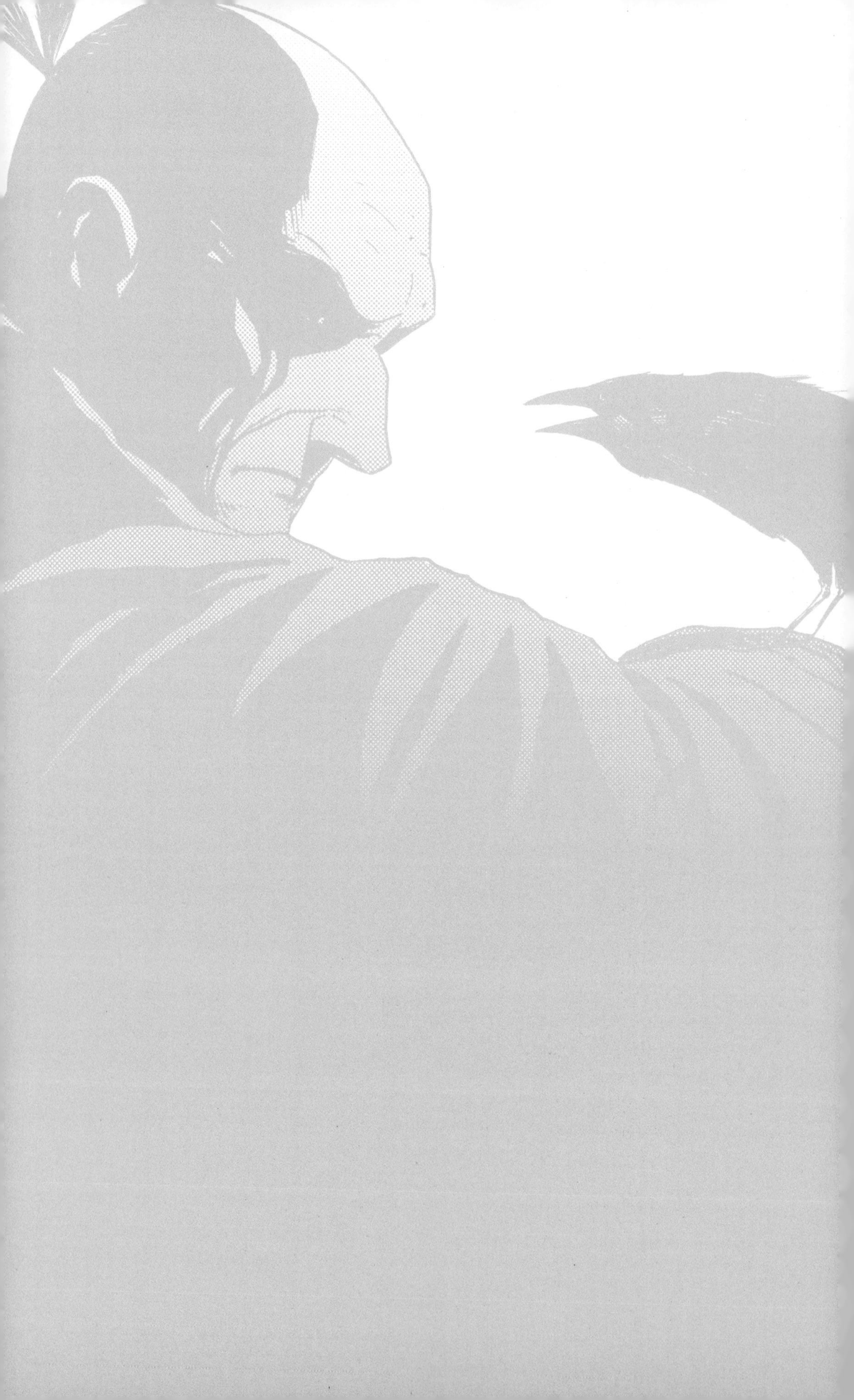

25

TWENTY-FIVE:
CAST OUT ALL
UNBELIEVERS

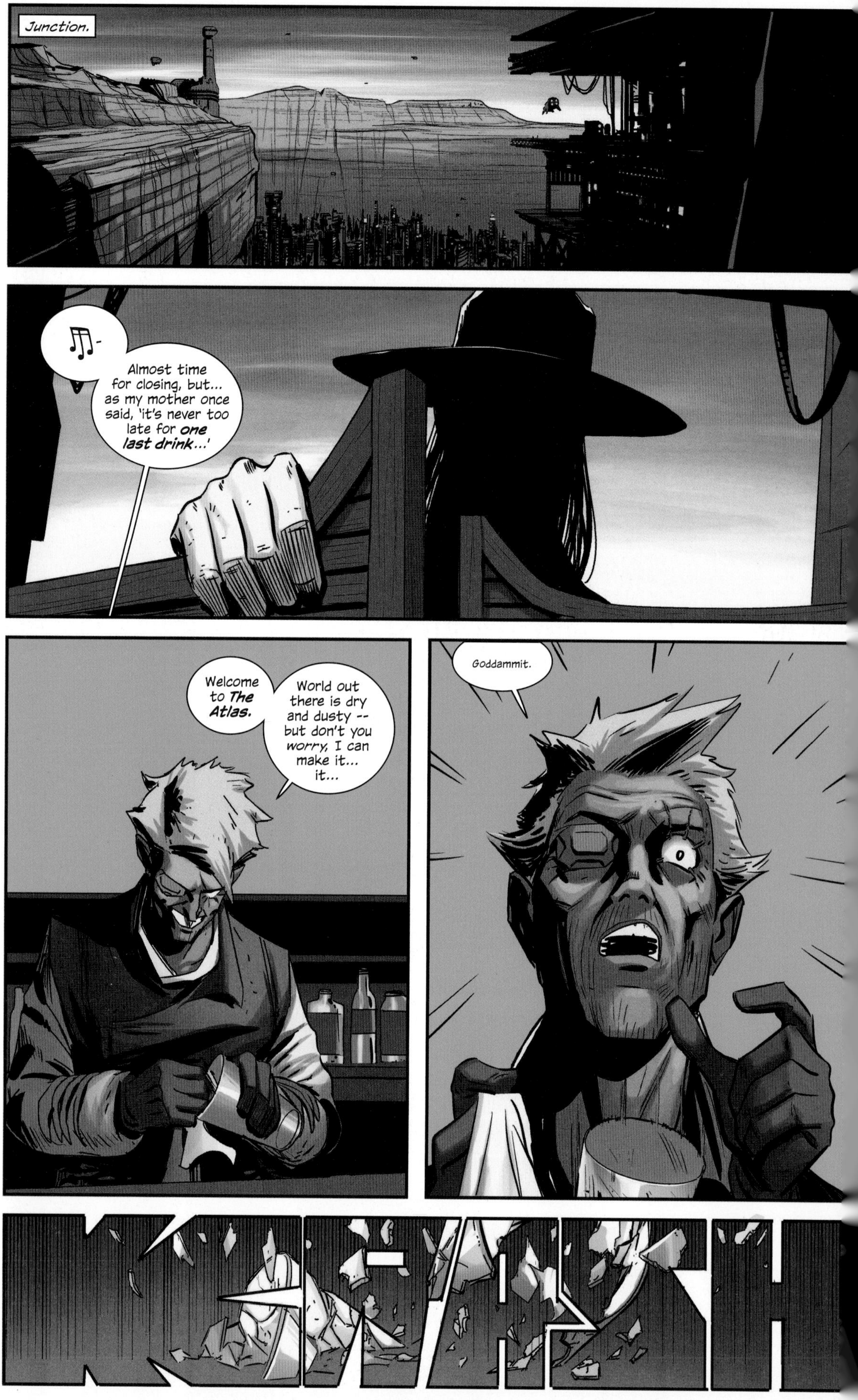
Junction.
♫-
Almost time for closing, but... as my mother once said, 'it's never too late for **one last drink**...'
Welcome to ***The Atlas.***
World out there is dry and dusty -- but don't you *worry,* I can make it... it...
Goddammit.
KSSH-TTTCH

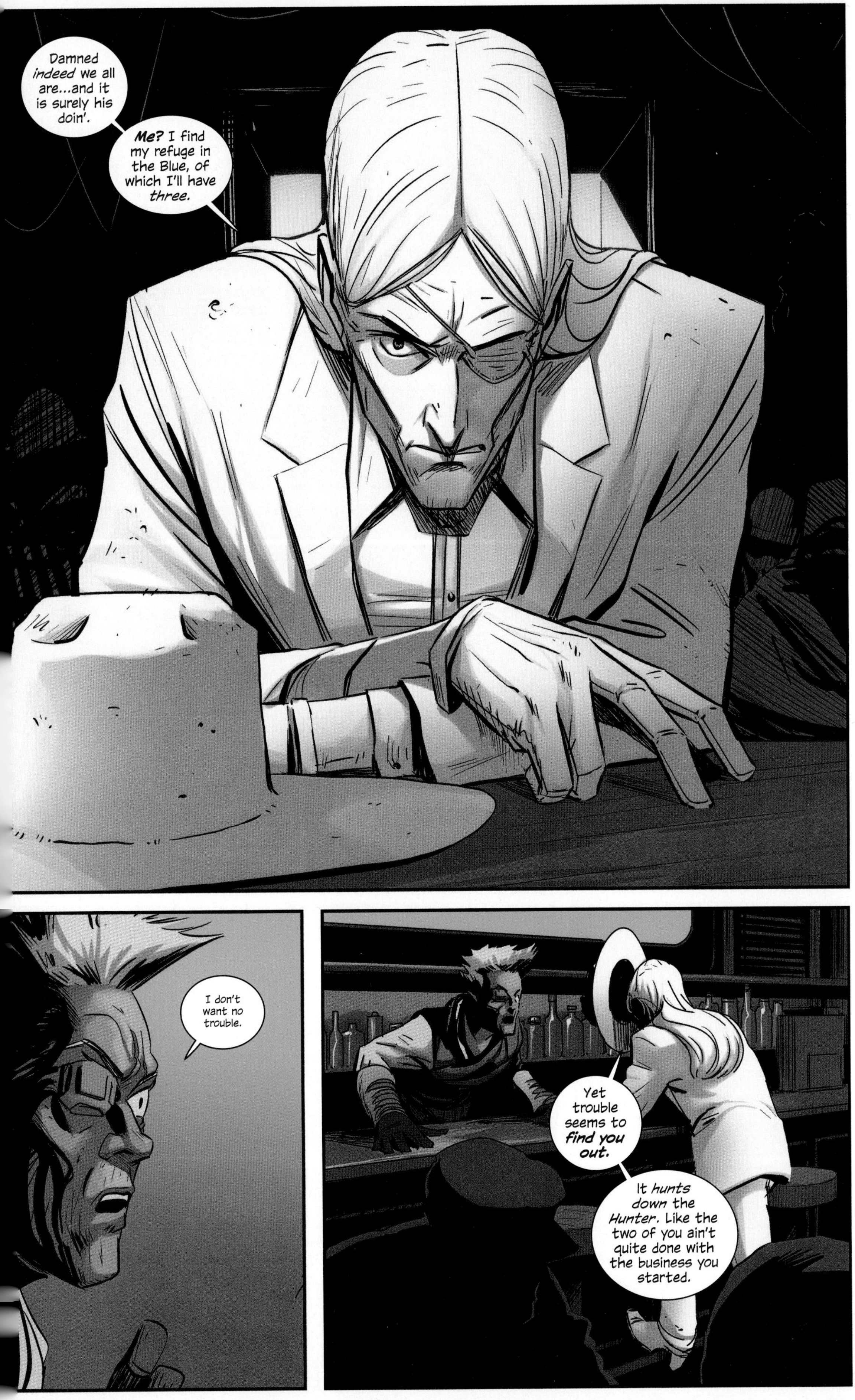
Damned *indeed* we all are...and it is surely his doin'.
Me? I find my refuge in the Blue, of which I'll have *three.*
I don't want no trouble.
Yet trouble seems to ***find you out.***
It *hunts down* the *Hunter*. Like the two of you ain't quite done with the business you started.

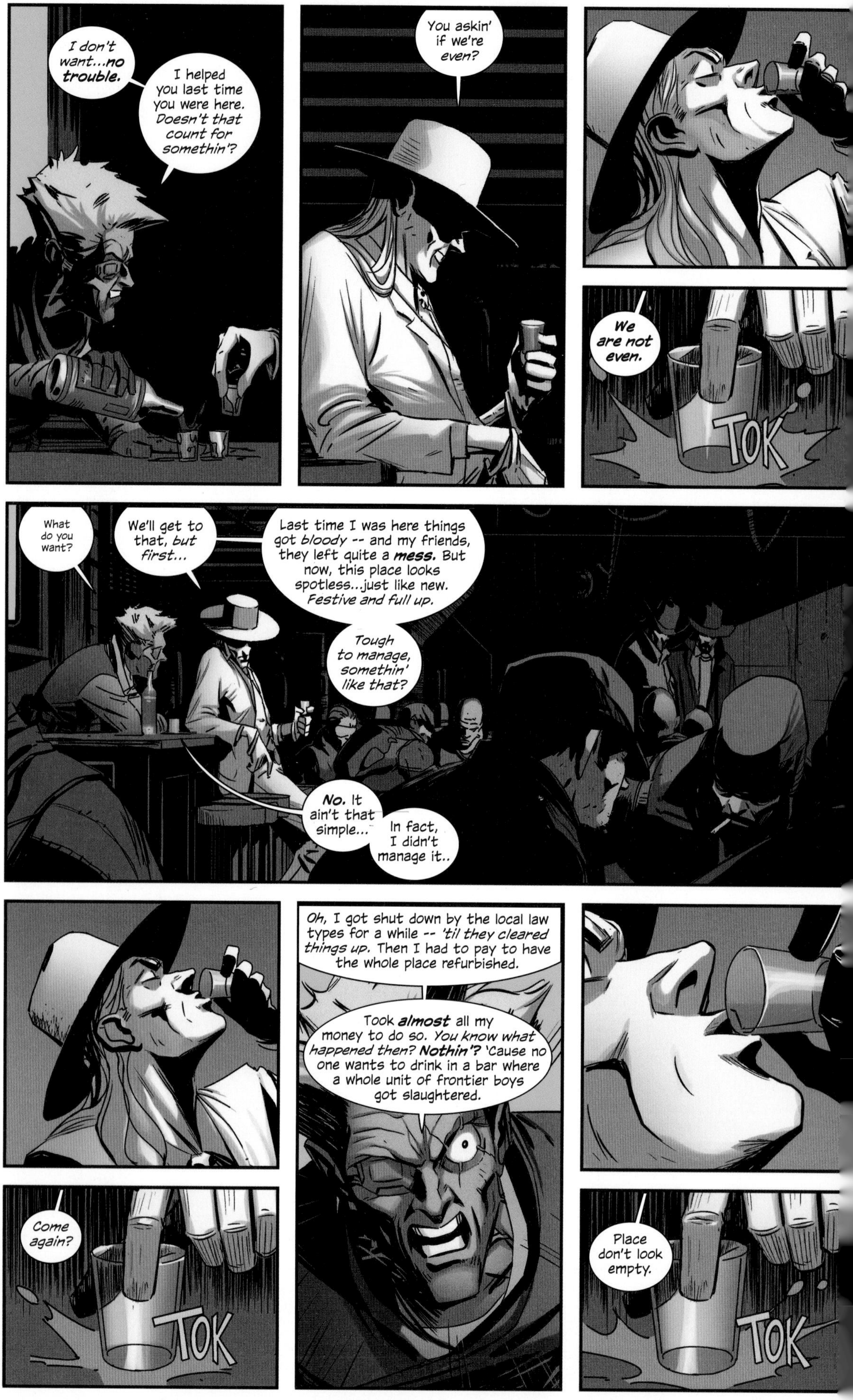
I don't want...**no trouble.**
I helped you last time you were here. *Doesn't that count for somethin'?*
You askin' if we're *even?*
We are not even.
TOK
What do you want?
We'll get to that, *but first...*
Last time I was here things got *bloody* -- and my friends, they left quite a ***mess.*** But now, this place looks spotless...just like new. *Festive and full up.*
Tough to manage, somethin' like that?
No. It ain't that simple...
In fact, I didn't manage it..
Oh, I got shut down by the local law types for a while -- *'til they cleared things up.* Then I had to pay to have the whole place refurbished.
Took ***almost*** all my money to do so. *You know what happened then?* ***Nothin'?*** 'Cause no one wants to drink in a bar where a whole unit of frontier boys got slaughtered.
Come again?
TOK
Place don't look empty.
TOK

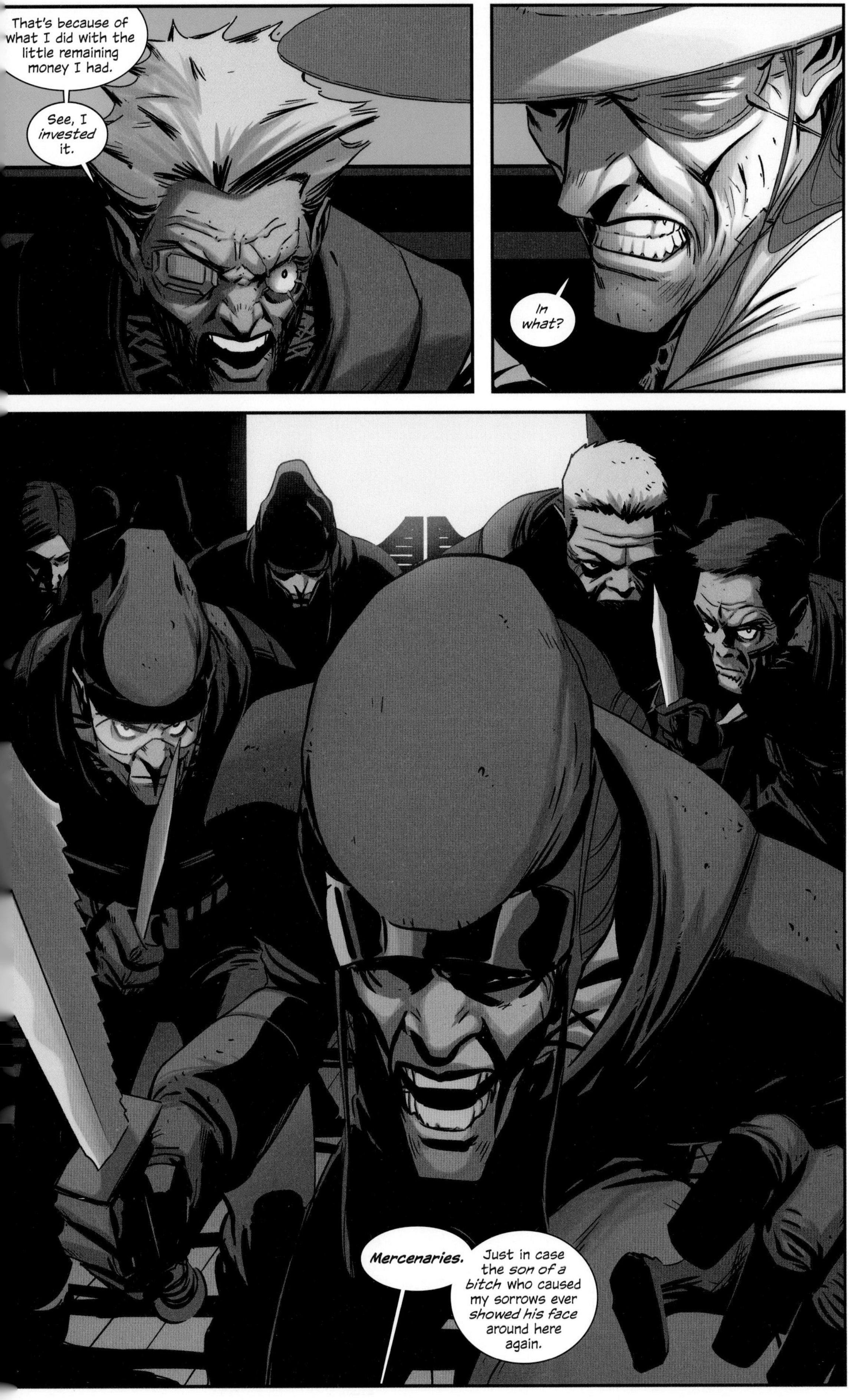
That's because of what I did with the little remaining money I had.
See, I *invested* it.
In what?
Mercenaries.
Just in case the *son of a bitch* who caused my sorrows ever *showed his face* around here again.

All right then...
KRAK
You sit tight, Hunter...
I'll be *back to you* in just a second!

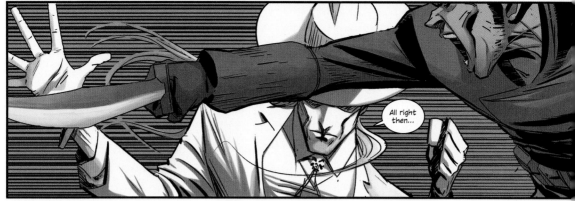

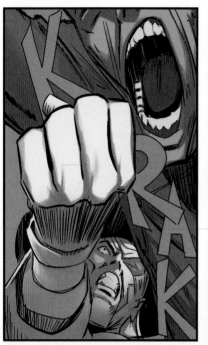

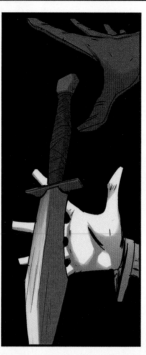

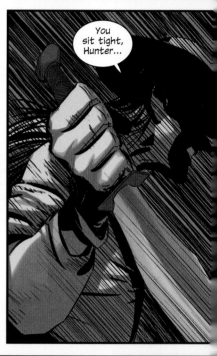

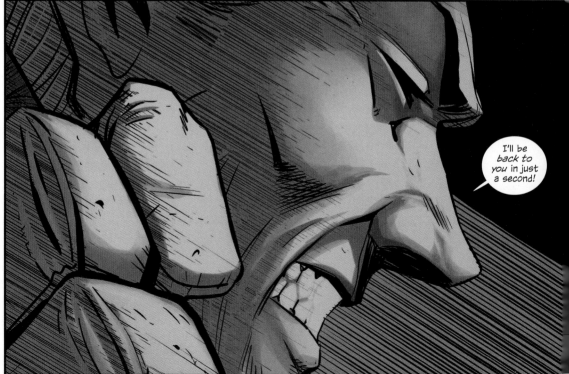

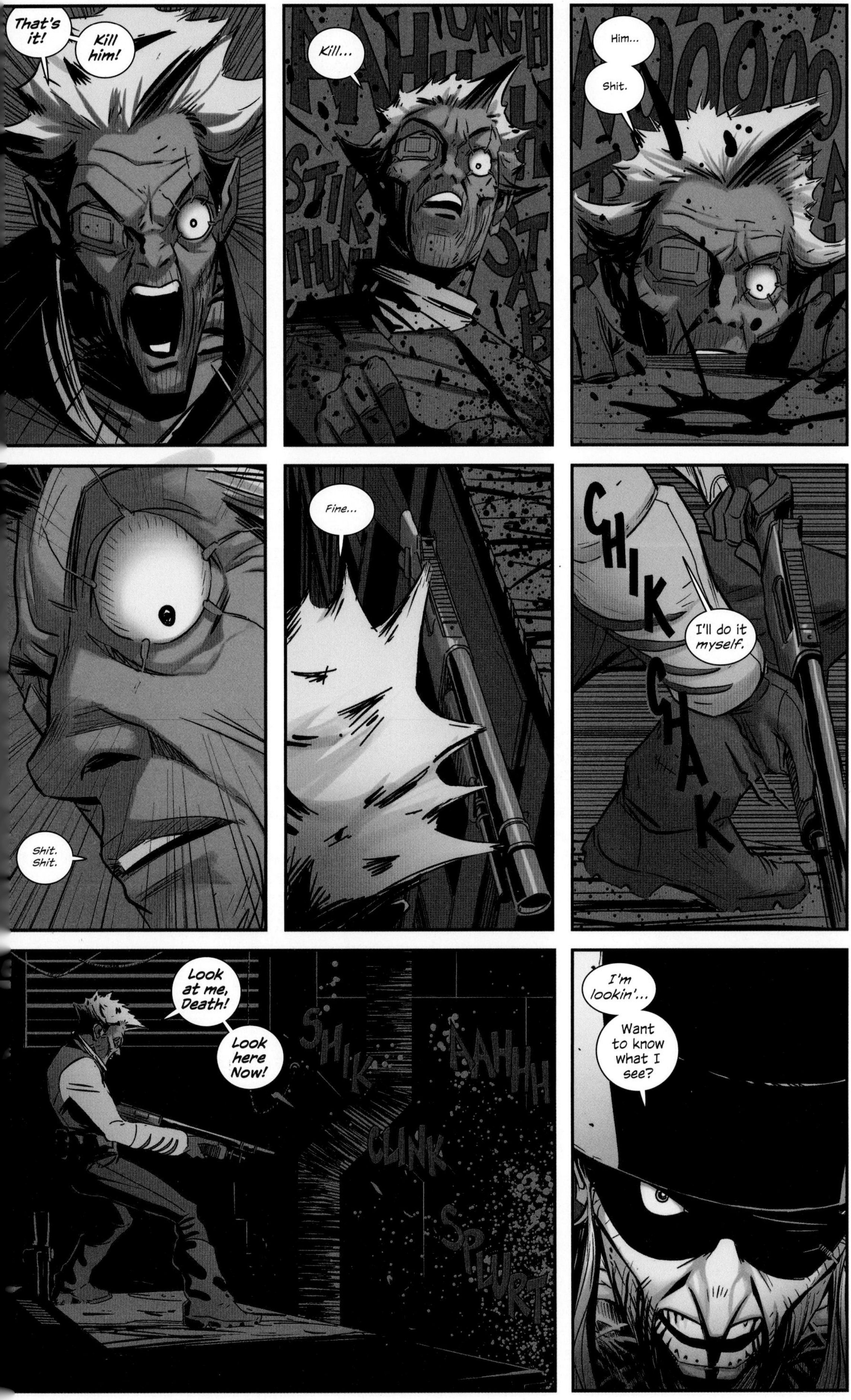

That's it!
Kill him!
Kill...
STIK
THUNK
STAB
Him...
Shit.
Shit.
Shit.
Fine...
CHIK
I'll do it myself.
CHAK
Look at me, Death!
Look here Now!
SHIK
AAHHH
CLINK
SPLURT
I'm lookin'...
Want to know what I see?

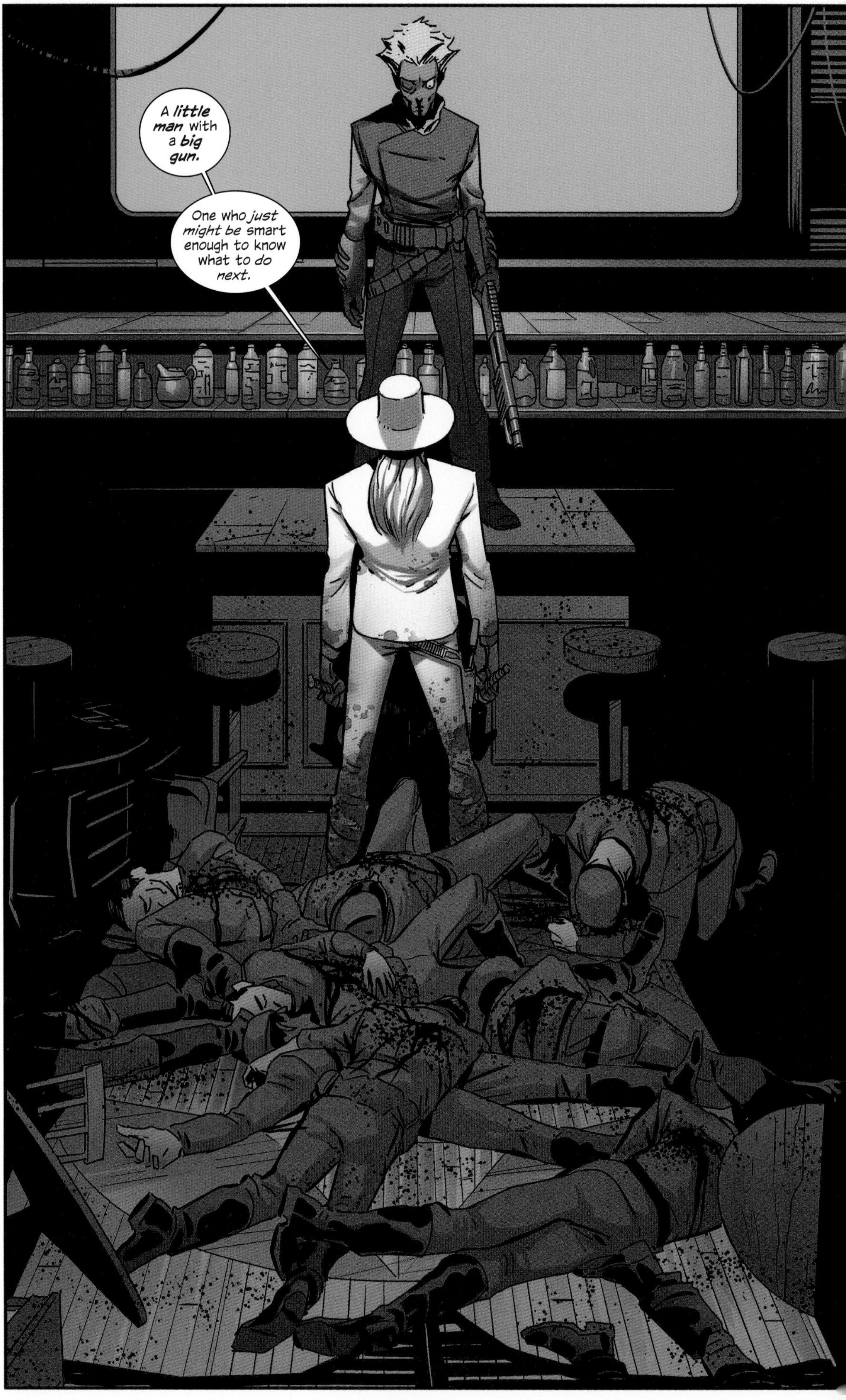
A *little* *man* with a *big* *gun.*
One who *just* *might* be smart enough to know what to *do* next.

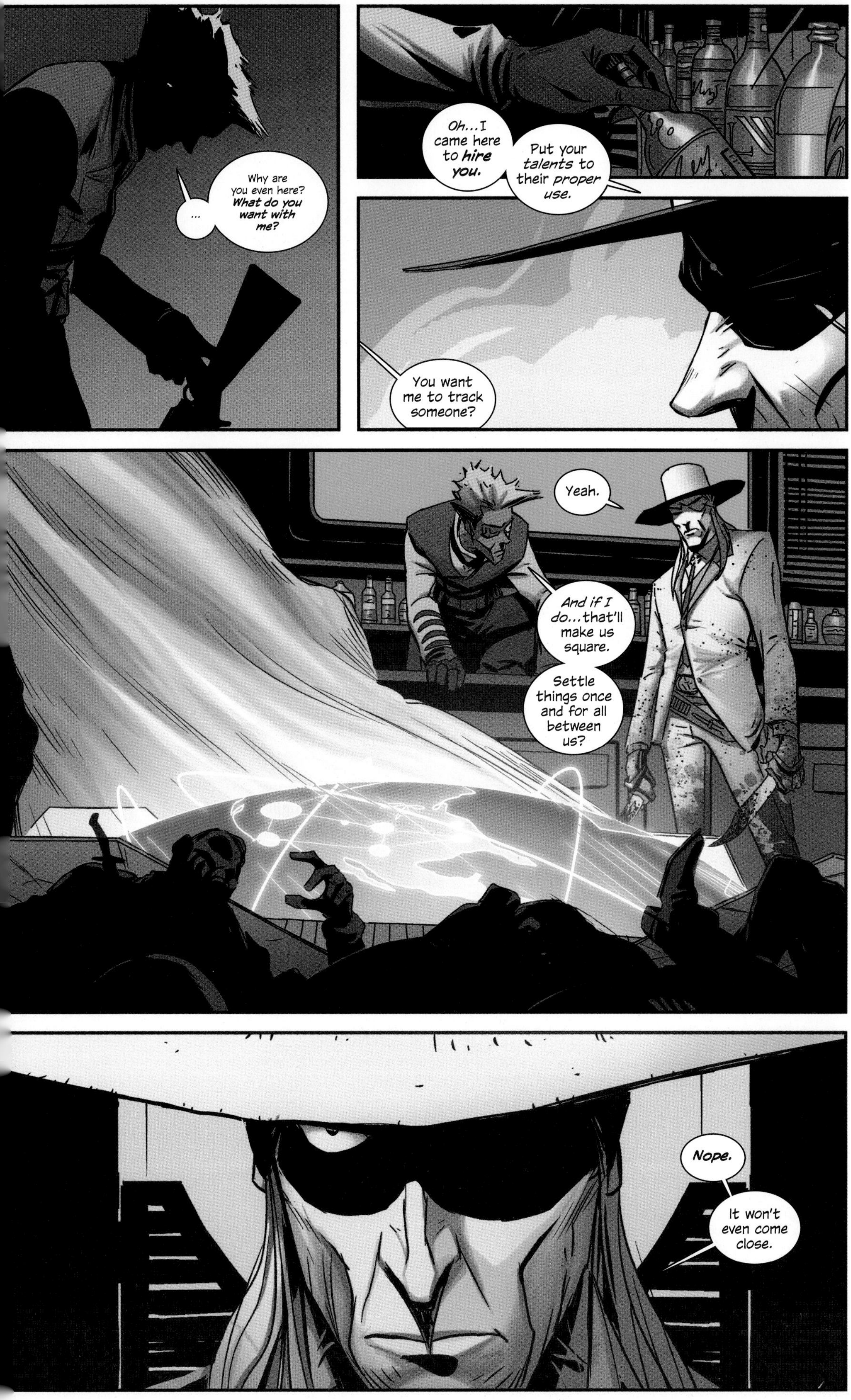

...
Why are you even here? *What do you want with me?*
*Oh...*I came here to ***hire you.***
Put your *talents* to their *proper* use.
You want me to track someone?
Yeah.
*And if I do...*that'll make us square.
Settle things once and for all between us?
Nope.
It won't even come close.

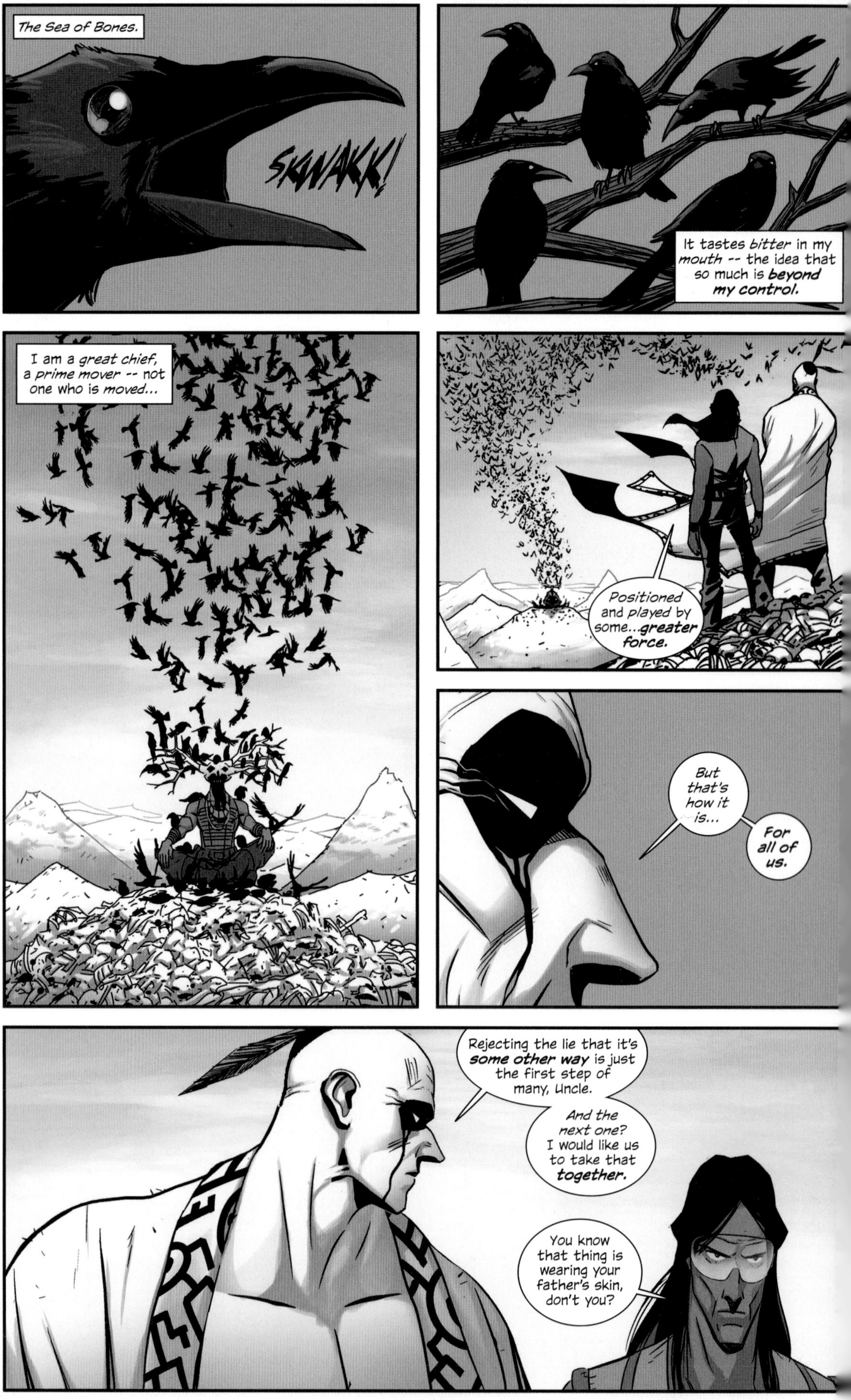
The Sea of Bones.
SKWAKK!
It tastes bitter in my mouth -- the idea that so much is beyond my control.
I am a great chief, a prime mover -- not one who is moved...
Positioned and played by some...greater force.
But that's how it is...
For all of us.
Rejecting the lie that it's some other way is just the first step of many, Uncle.
And the next one? I would like us to take that together.
You know that thing is wearing your father's skin, don't you?

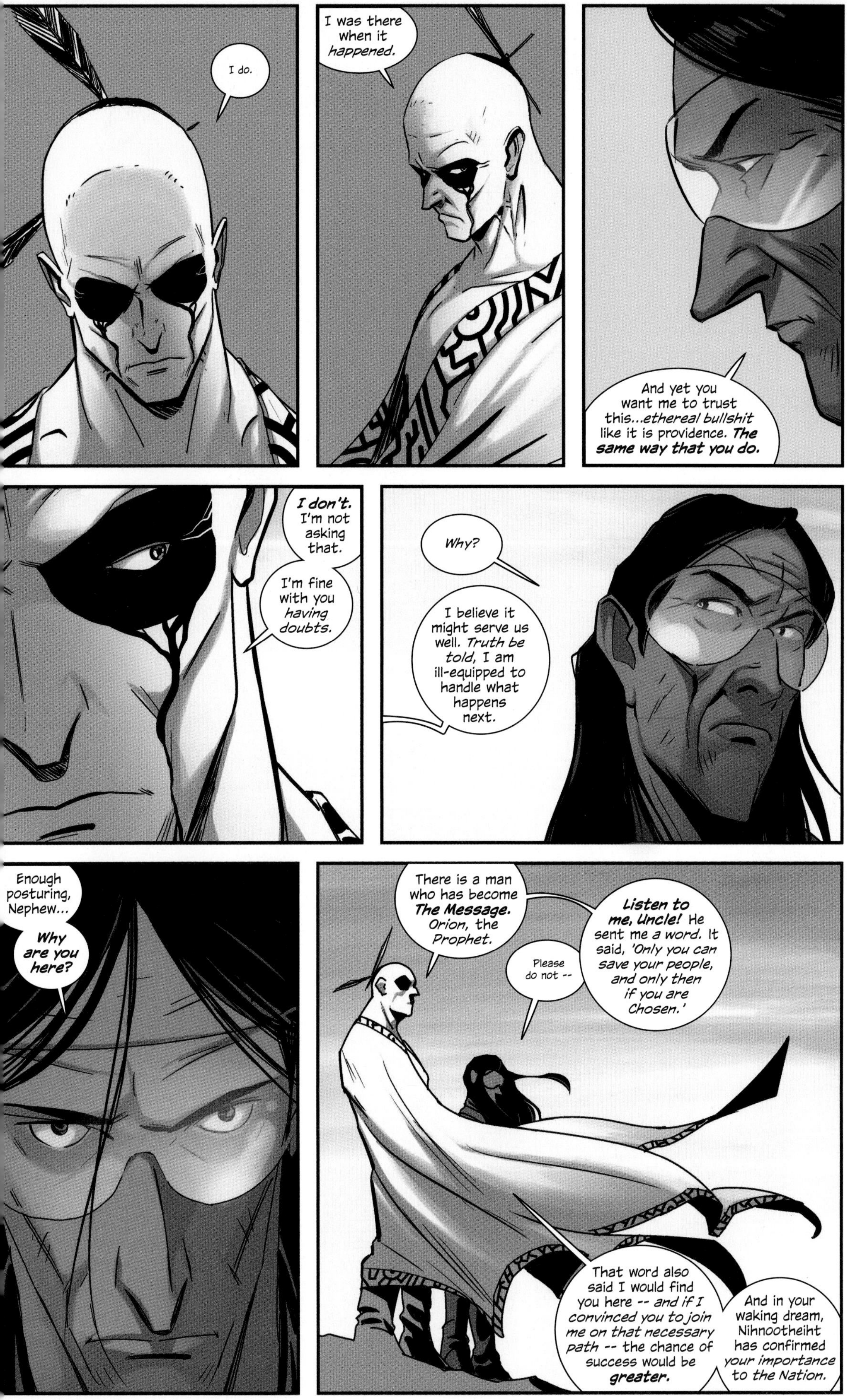

I do.
I was there when it *happened.*
And yet you want me to trust this...*ethereal bullshit* like it is providence. ***The same way that you do.***
I don't. I'm not asking that.
I'm fine with you *having* doubts.
Why?
I believe it might serve us well. *Truth be told,* I am ill-equipped to handle what happens next.
Enough posturing, Nephew...
Why are you here?
There is a man who has become ***The Message.*** *Orion,* the *Prophet.*
Please do not --
Listen to me, Uncle! He sent me a word. It said, *'Only you can save your people, and only then if you are Chosen.'*
That word also said I would find you here -- *and if I convinced you to join me on that necessary path* -- the chance of success would be ***greater.***
And in your waking dream, Nihnootheiht has confirmed *your importance to the Nation.*

I need you, Uncle. As do our people.

My importance to the Nation?..

I am Chief of Chiefs, boy. **What are you?**

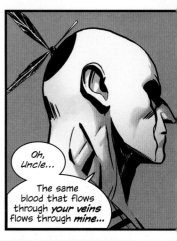

Oh, Uncle...

The same blood that flows through *your veins* flows through *mine...*

You know exactly what I am.

I am Son of Cheveyo. The Chief who walked away... And when he did, *you* took his place.

Now it is time for you to take his place again.

You have been *chosen,* Uncle.

Will you take his seat at the table?

Will you help me *save our people?*

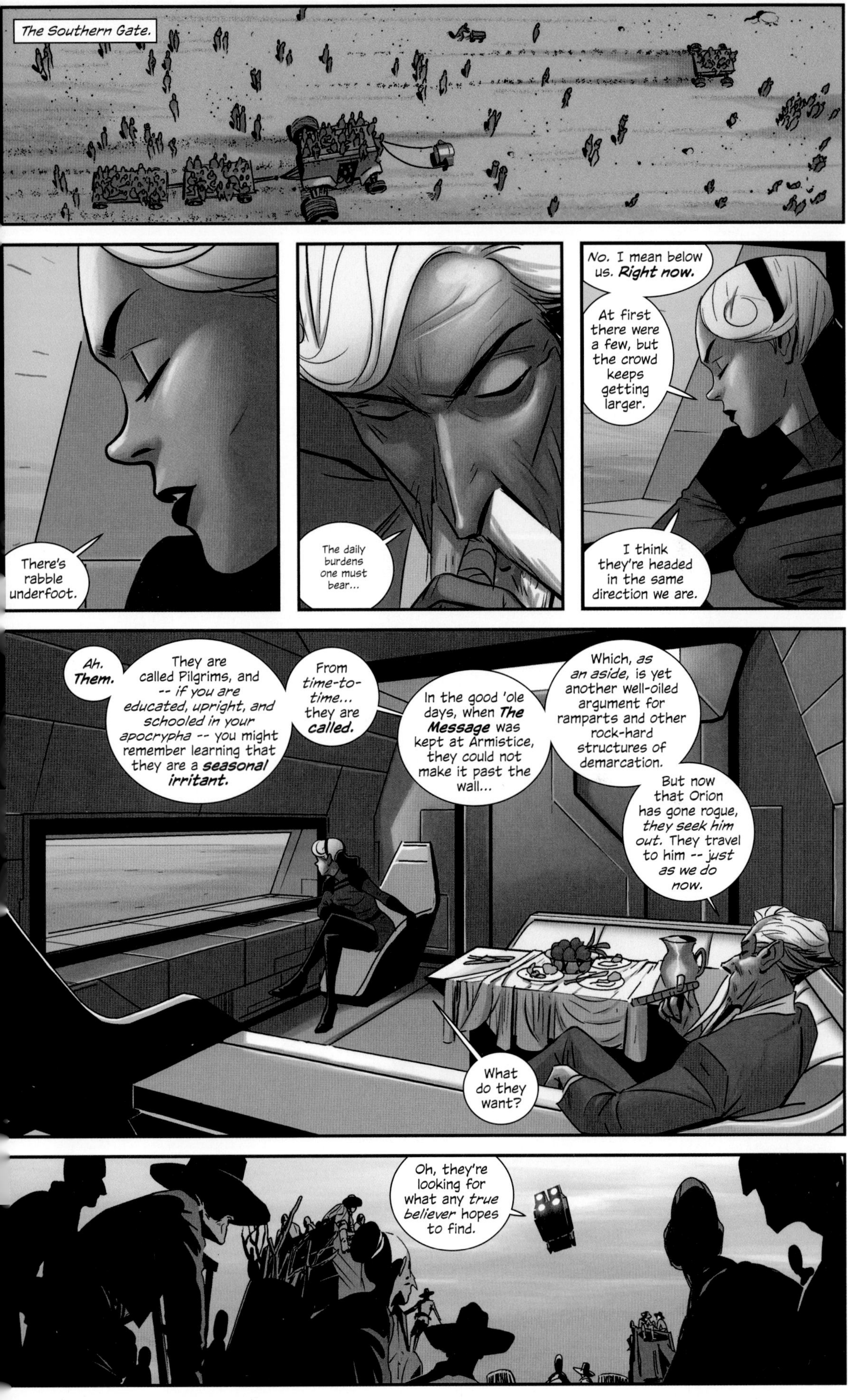

The Southern Gate.
There's rabble underfoot.
The daily burdens one must bear...
No. I mean below us. Right now.
At first there were a few, but the crowd keeps getting larger.
I think they're headed in the same direction we are.
Ah. Them.
They are called Pilgrims, and -- if you are educated, upright, and schooled in your apocrypha -- you might remember learning that they are a seasonal irritant.
From time-to-time... they are called.
In the good 'ole days, when The Message was kept at Armistice, they could not make it past the wall...
Which, as an aside, is yet another well-oiled argument for ramparts and other rock-hard structures of demarcation.
But now that Orion has gone rogue, they seek him out. They travel to him -- just as we do now.
What do they want?
Oh, they're looking for what any true believer hopes to find.

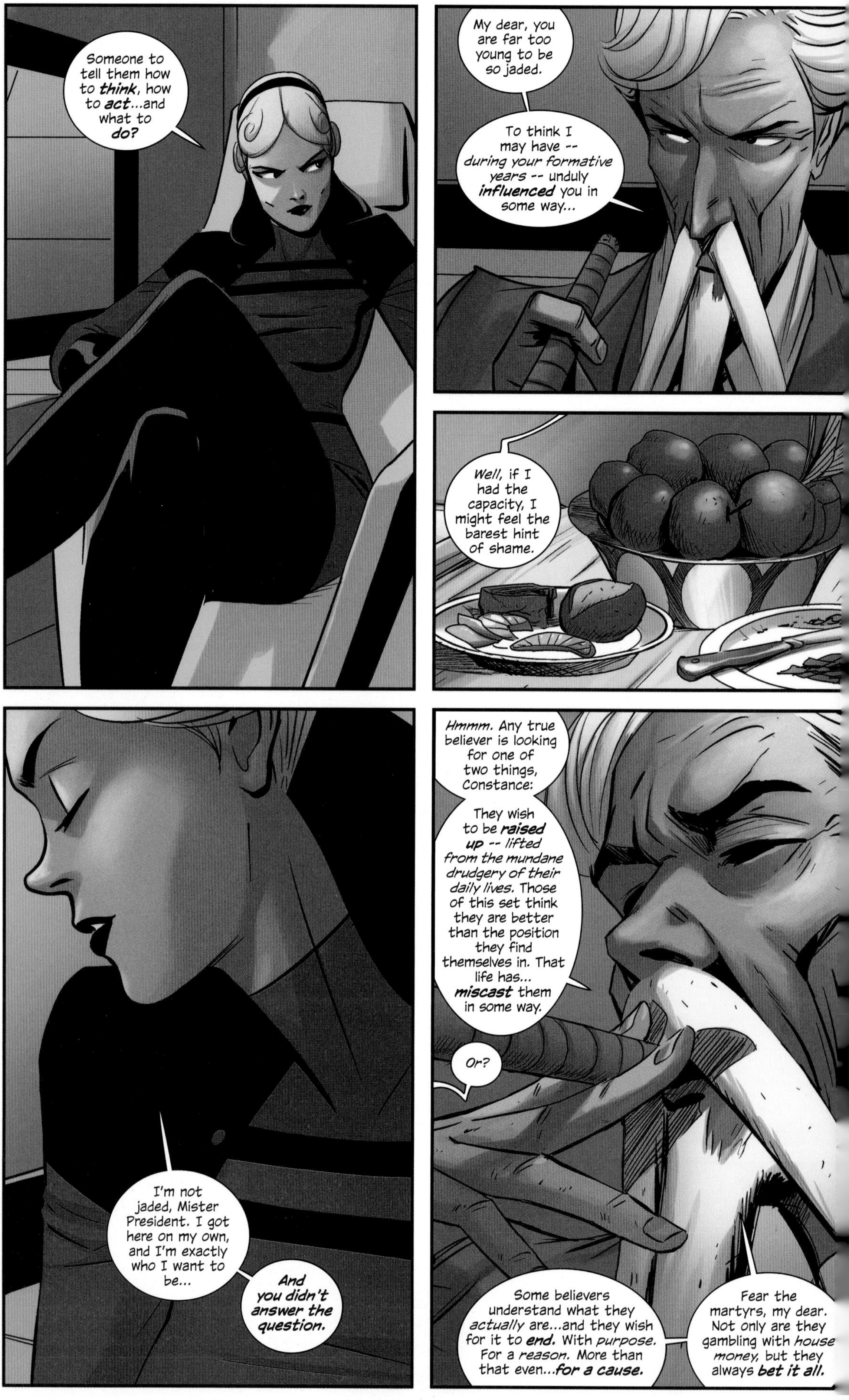
Someone to tell them how to *think*, how to *act*...and what to *do?*
My dear, you are far too young to be so jaded.
To think I may have -- *during your formative years* -- unduly ***influenced*** you in some way...
Well, if I had the capacity, I might feel the barest hint of shame.
I'm not jaded, Mister President. I got here on my own, and I'm exactly who I want to be...
And you didn't answer the question.
Hmmm. Any true believer is looking for one of two things, Constance:
They wish to be ***raised up*** *-- lifted from the mundane drudgery of their daily lives.* Those of this set think they are better than the position they find themselves in. That life has... ***miscast*** them in some way.
Or?
Some believers understand what they *actually* are...and they wish for it to ***end.*** With *purpose.* For a *reason.* More than that even...***for a cause.***
Fear the martyrs, my dear. Not only are they gambling with *house money*, but they always ***bet it all.***

My god. You're **serious,** aren't you?

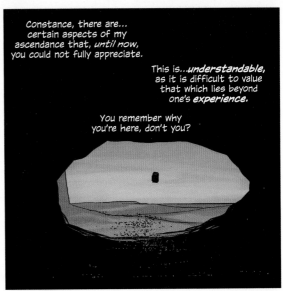

Constance, there are... certain aspects of my ascendance that, *until now,* you could not fully appreciate.

This is...**understandable,** as it is difficult to value that which lies beyond one's **experience.**

You remember why you're here, don't you?

Yes. You need my mind to manage this geopolitical game of chess you're playing. You need me to oversee the **complexities.**

That's right...

And if you are going to truly be useful, then it's time you know all the *variables.* Even the ones that might be offensive to your automaton-like logic.

Like?

Oh, nothing grand...

Just abstractions like the irrational, all-consuming passion one might find in a generational blood feud, or... more than that, the fervor of disciples and acolytes.

Men and women moved by the spirit. You know, *that* **otherworldly shit.**

Uncle, you've never struck me as a believer.

Oh, I find it *tiresome...* but I do **believe.** I have seen too much not to.

Really? Next I suppose you're going to tell me about finding Christ and deliverance from all of Hell's demons.

Well, I don't know anything about **the former...**

~ Gasp! ~

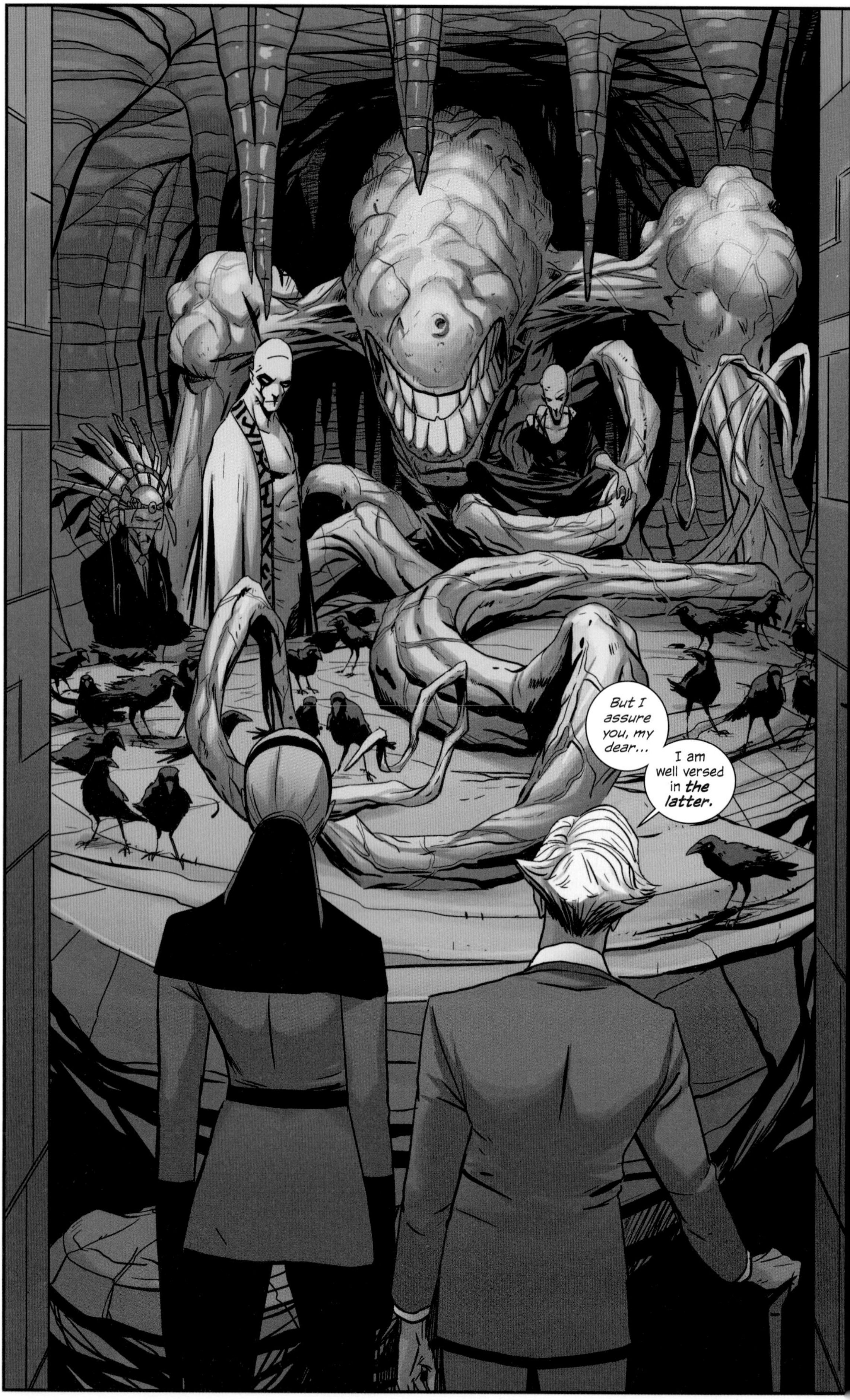
But I assure you, my dear...
I am well versed in **the latter.**

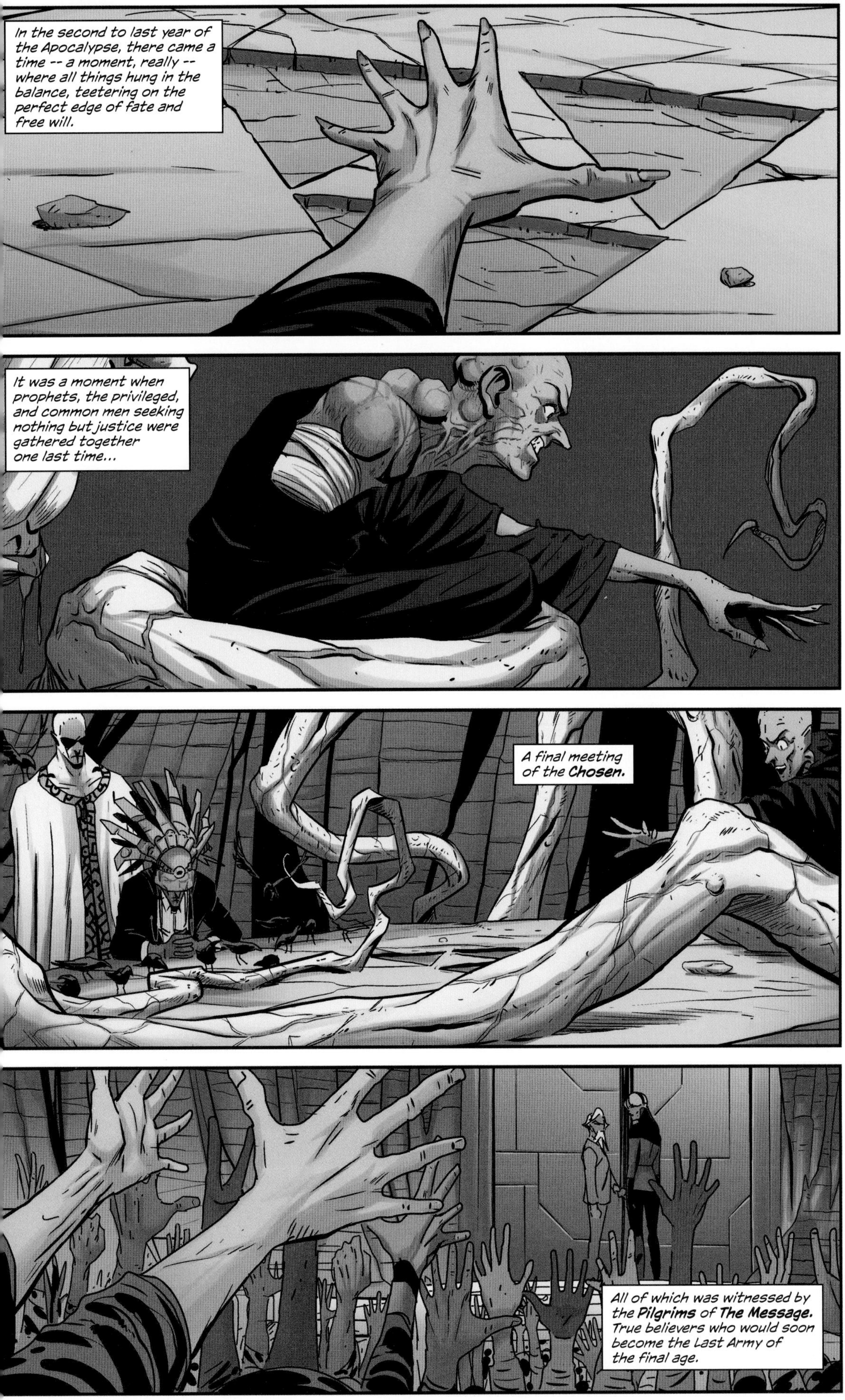
In the second to last year of the Apocalypse, there came a time -- a moment, really -- where all things hung in the balance, teetering on the perfect edge of fate and free will.
It was a moment when prophets, the privileged, and common men seeking nothing but justice were gathered together one last time...
A final meeting of the **Chosen.**
All of which was witnessed by the **Pilgrims** of **The Message.** True believers who would soon become the Last Army of the final age.

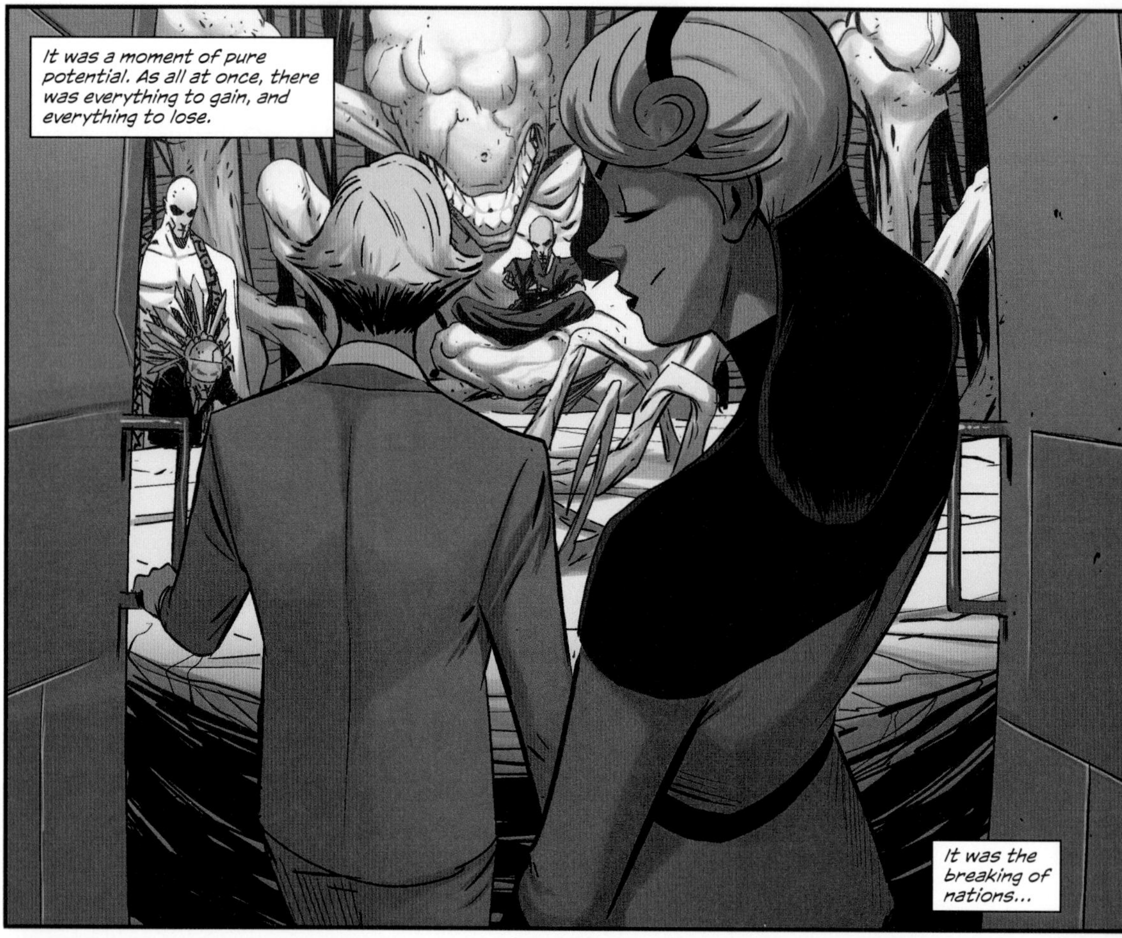
It was a moment of pure potential. As all at once, there was everything to gain, and everything to lose.
It was the breaking of nations...

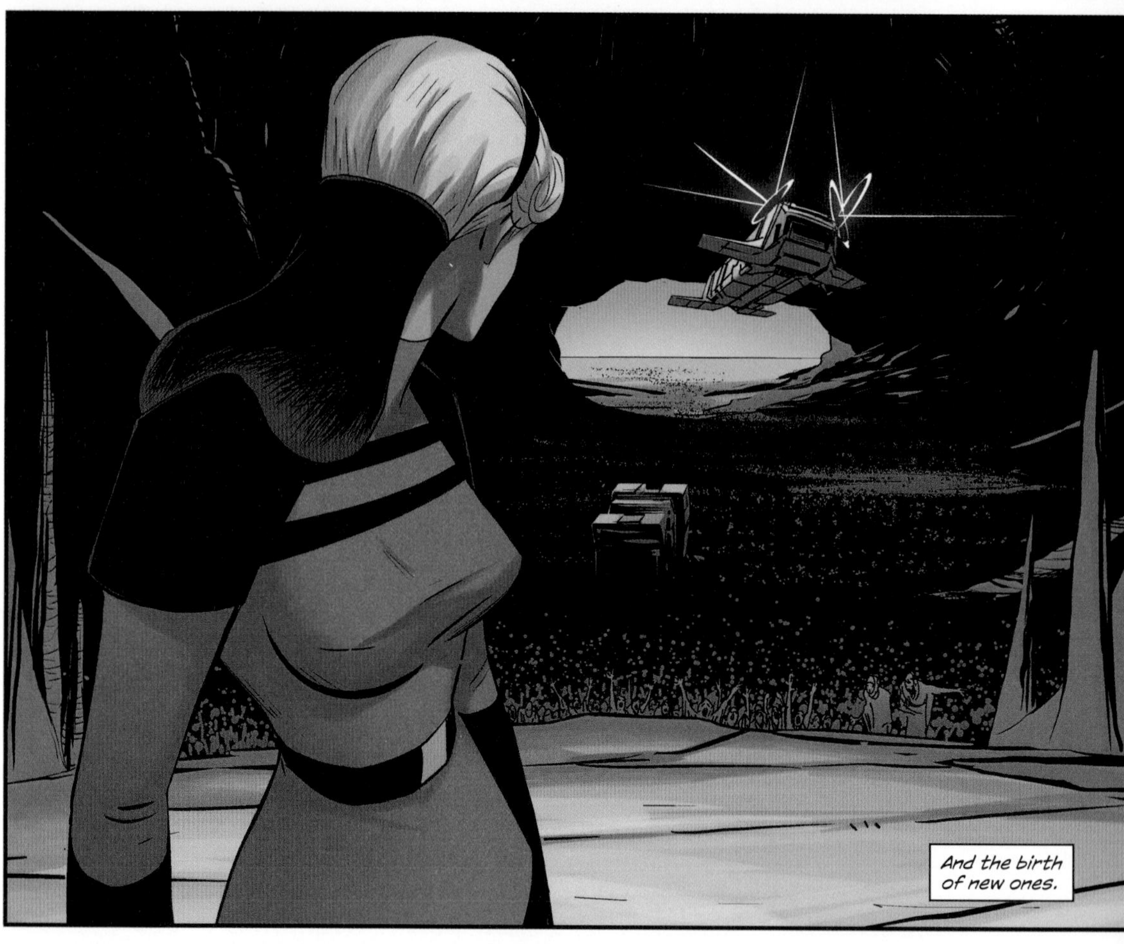
And the birth of new ones.

SEE THE HORIZON, AND THE
ARRIVAL OF **THE CHOSEN.**

LOOK HOW THEY ARE **HOLY.**
LOOK HOW THEY ARE **DAMNED.**

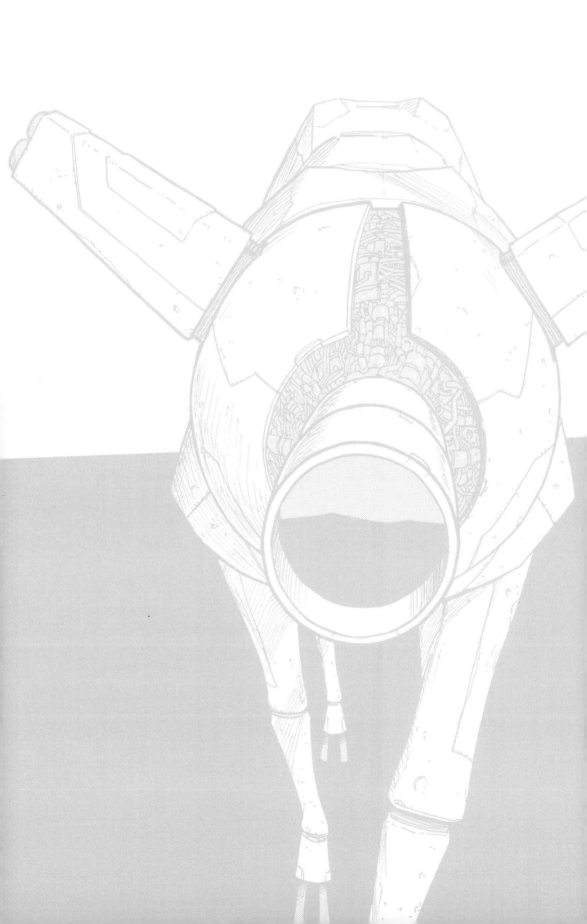

26

 TWENTY-SIX:
SUMMON ALL
CHOSEN

I WARN YOU. FROM HERE TO
THE VERY END OF TIME...

READY YOURSELF FOR **BLOOD.**

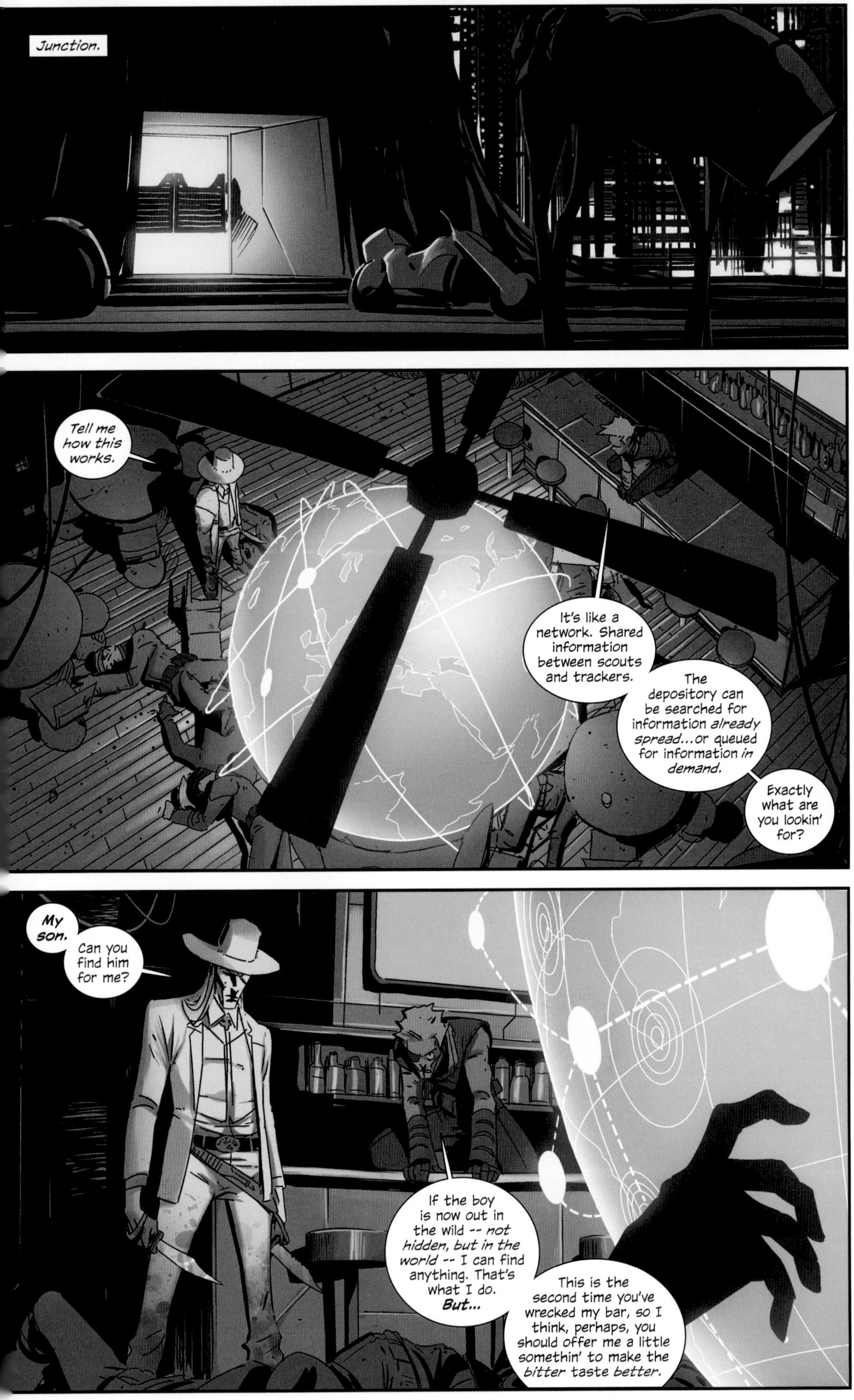
Junction.
Tell me how this works.
It's like a network. Shared information between scouts and trackers.
The depository can be searched for information *already spread*...or queued for information *in demand.*
Exactly what are you lookin' for?
My son.
Can you find him for me?
If the boy is now out in the wild -- *not hidden, but in the world* -- I can find anything. That's what I do. ***But...***
This is the second time you've wrecked my bar, so I think, perhaps, you should offer me a little somethin' to make the *bitter* taste *better.*

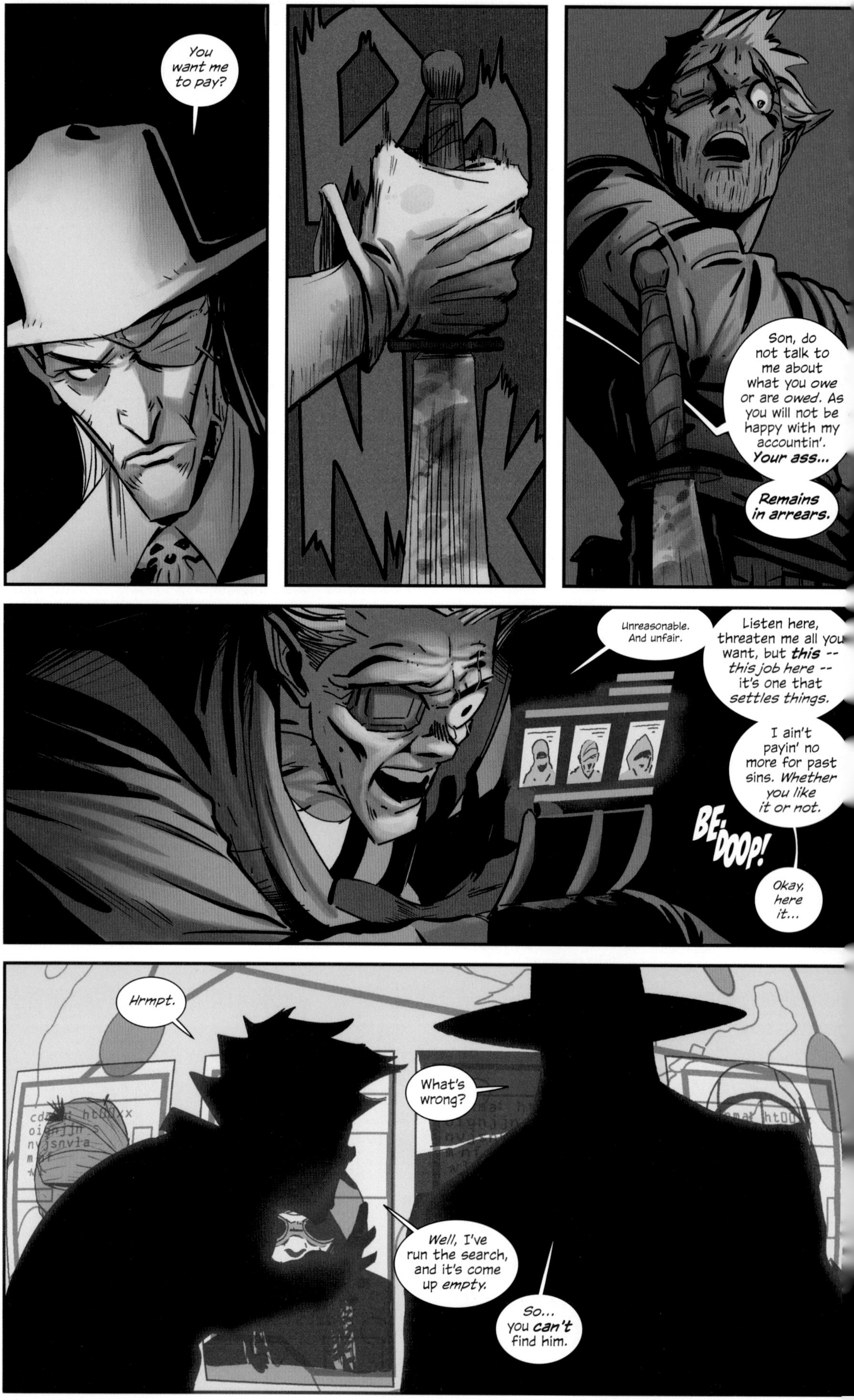
You want me to pay?
Son, do not talk to me about what you *owe* or are *owed*. As you will not be happy with my accountin'. ***Your ass...***
Remains in arrears.
Unreasonable. And unfair.
Listen here, threaten me all you want, but ***this*** -- *this job here* -- it's one that *settles things.*
I ain't payin' no more for past sins. *Whether you like it or not.*
BE-DOOP!
Okay, here it...
Hrmpt.
What's wrong?
Well, I've run the search, and it's come up *empty.*
So... you ***can't*** find him.

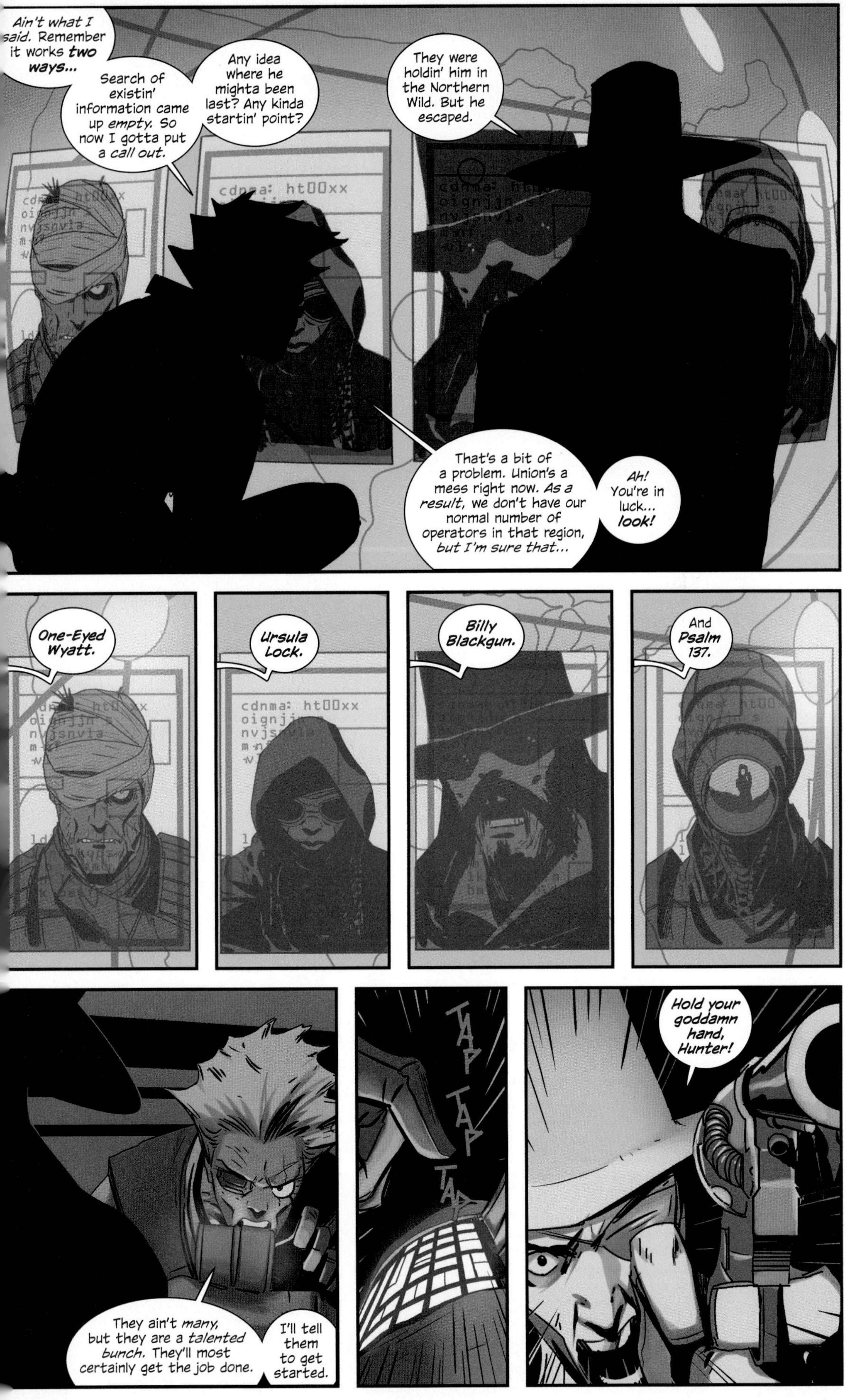
Ain't what I said. Remember it works two ways...
Search of existin' information came up empty. So now I gotta put a call out.
Any idea where he mighta been last? Any kinda startin' point?
They were holdin' him in the Northern Wild. But he escaped.
That's a bit of a problem. Union's a mess right now. As a result, we don't have our normal number of operators in that region, but I'm sure that...
Ah! You're in luck... look!
One-Eyed Wyatt.
Ursula Lock.
Billy Blackgun.
And Psalm 137.
They ain't many, but they are a talented bunch. They'll most certainly get the job done.
I'll tell them to get started.
TAP TAP TAP TAP
Hold your goddamn hand, Hunter!

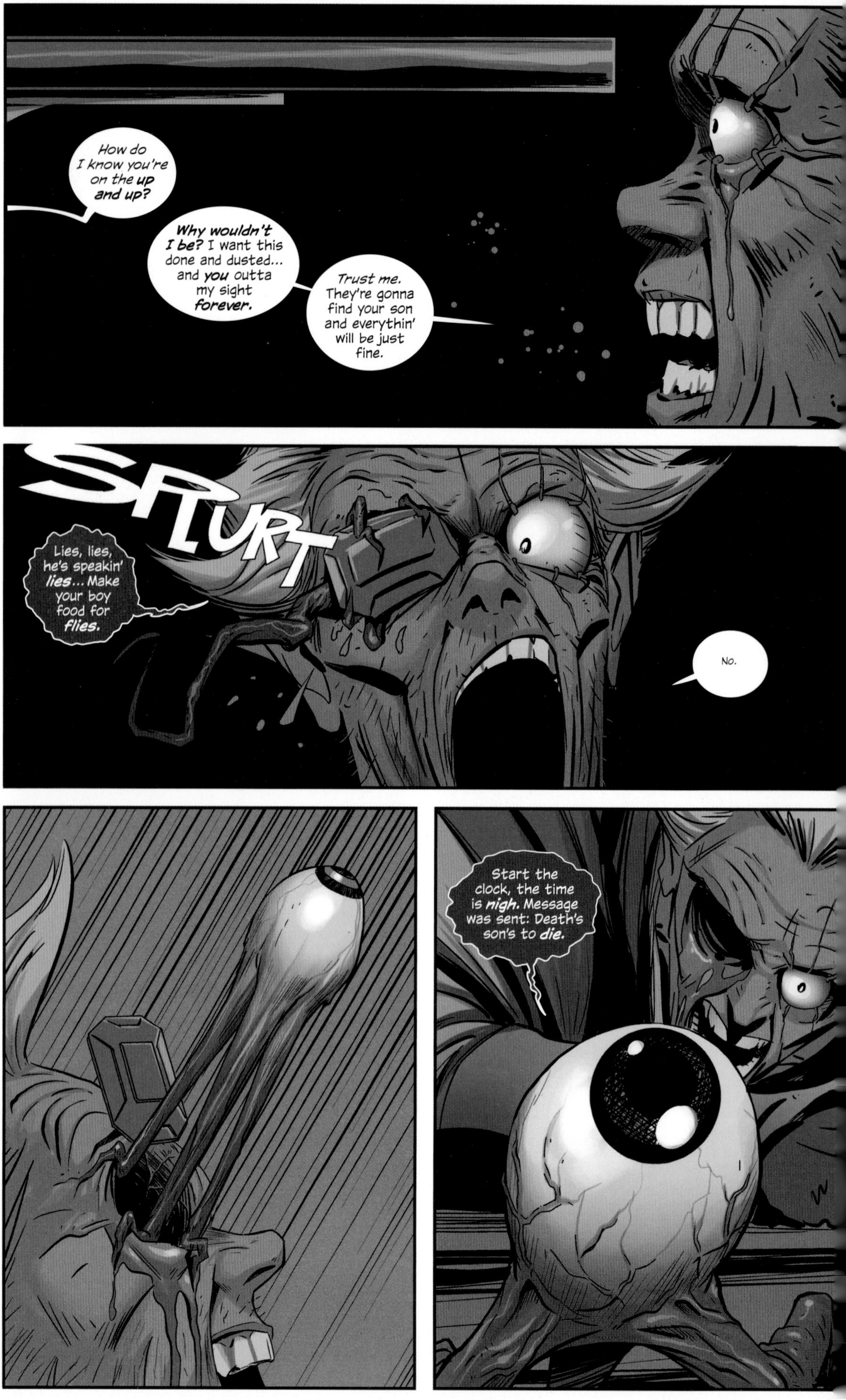
How do I know you're on the **up and up?**
Why wouldn't I be? I want this done and dusted... and ***you*** outta my sight ***forever.***
Trust me. They're gonna find your son and everythin' will be just fine.
SPLURT
Lies, lies, he's speakin' ***lies...*** Make your boy food for ***flies.***
No.
Start the clock, the time is ***nigh.*** Message was sent: Death's son's to ***die.***

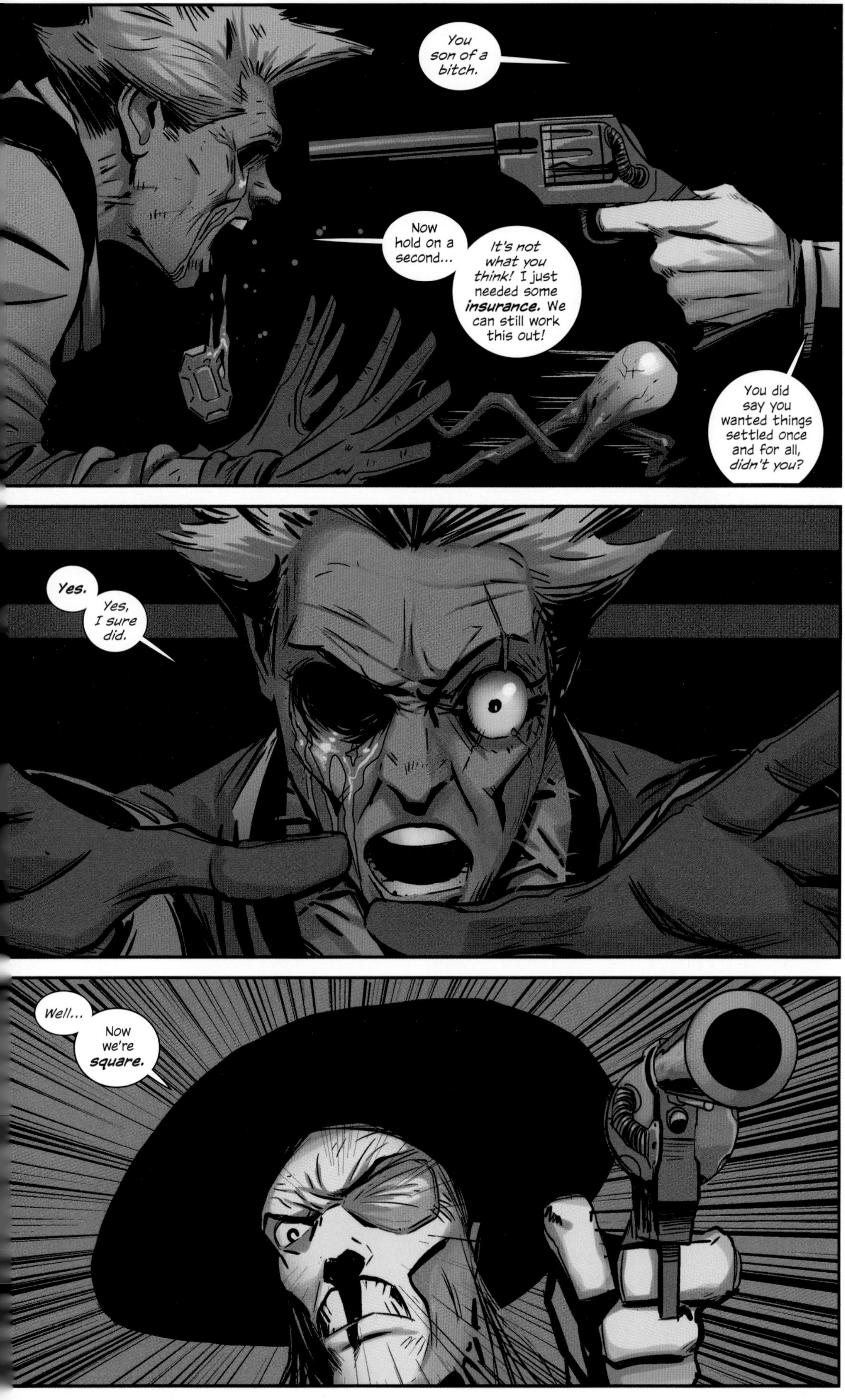
You son of a bitch.
Now hold on a second...
It's not what you think! I just needed some insurance. We can still work this out!
You did say you wanted things settled once and for all, didn't you?
Yes.
Yes, I sure did.
Well...
Now we're square.

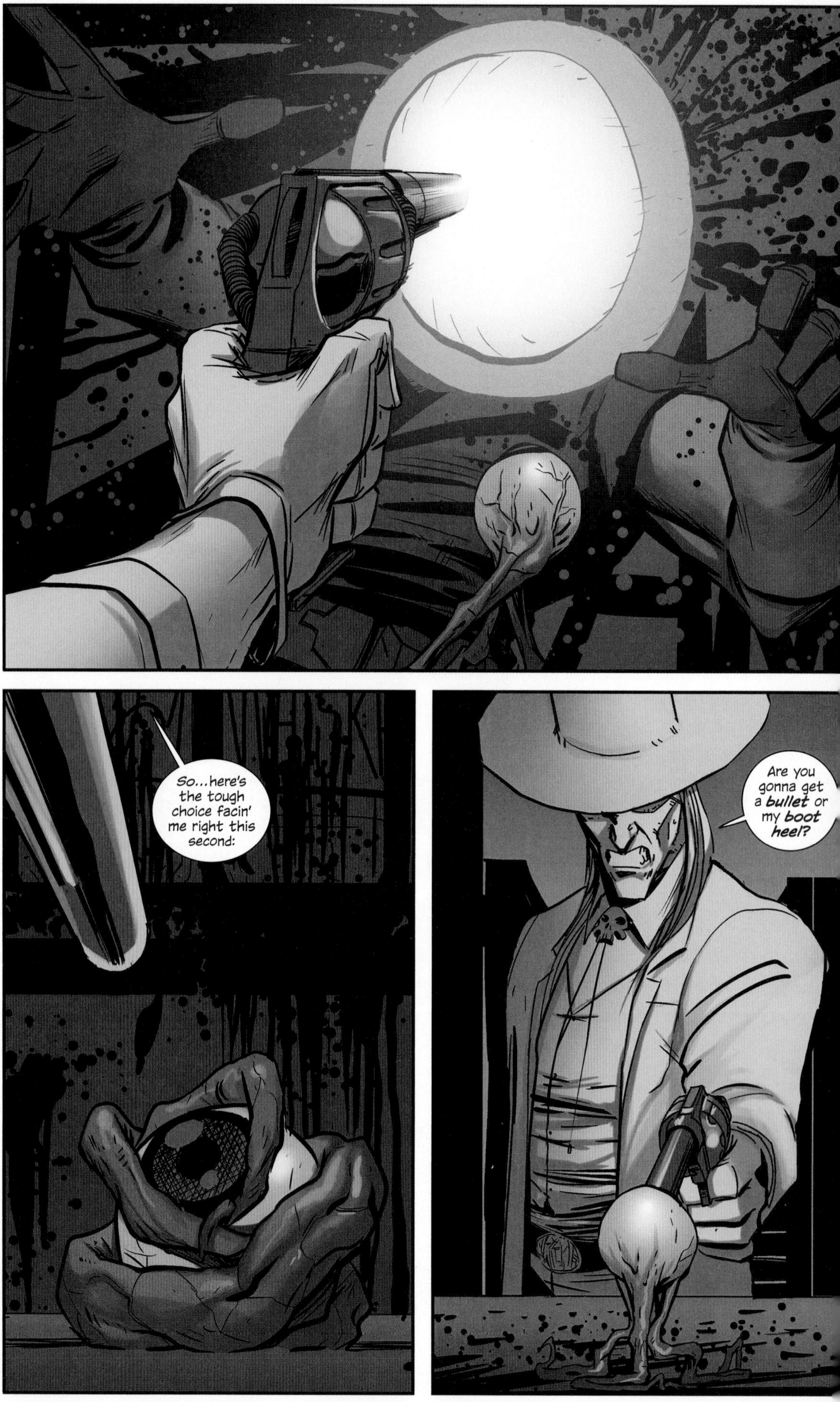
So...here's the tough choice facin' me right this second:
Are you gonna get a **bullet** or my **boot heel?**

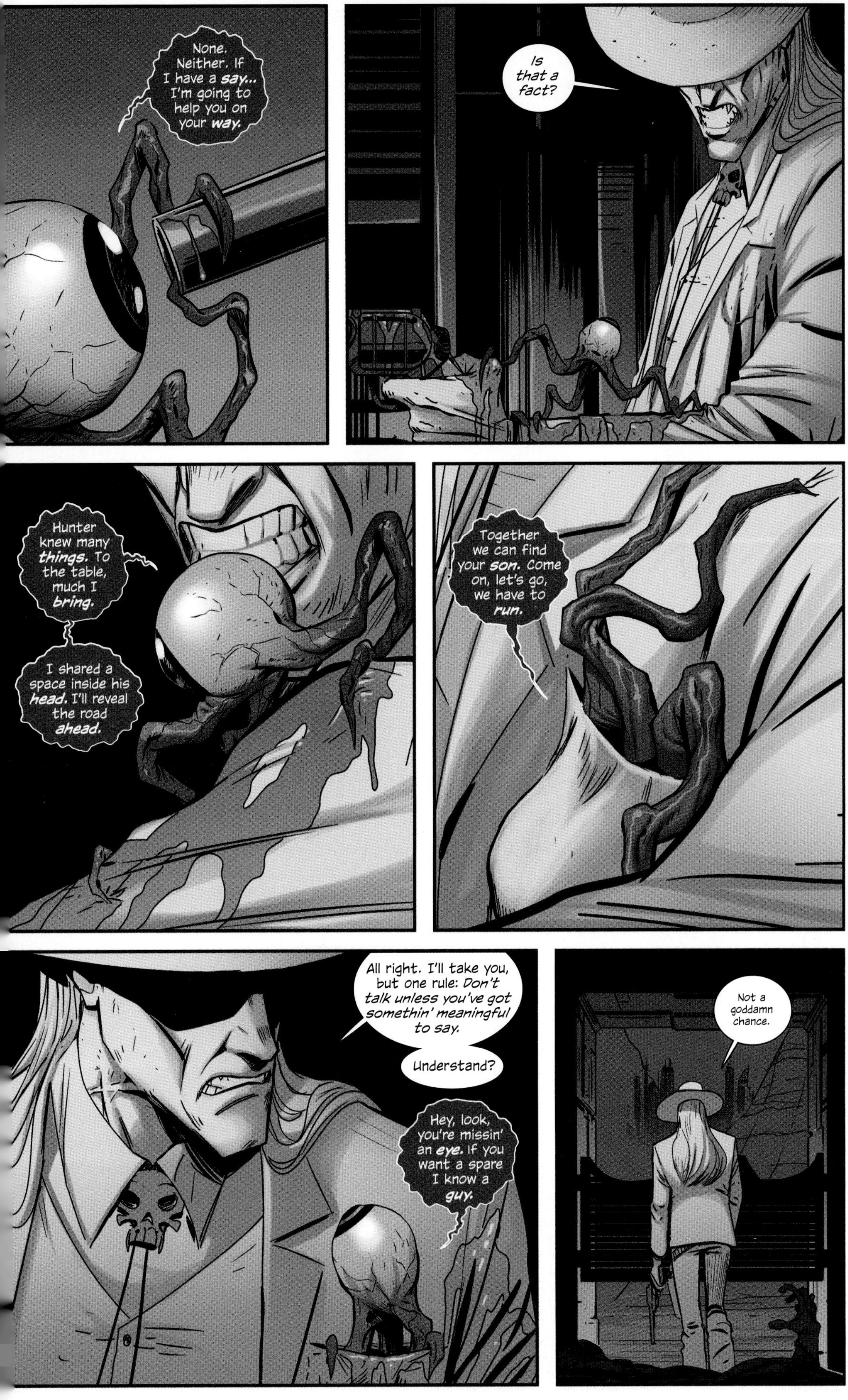
None. Neither. If I have a say... I'm going to help you on your way.
Is that a fact?
Hunter knew many things. To the table, much I bring.
I shared a space inside his head. I'll reveal the road ahead.
Together we can find your son. Come on, let's go, we have to run.
All right. I'll take you, but one rule: Don't talk unless you've got somethin' meaningful to say.
Understand?
Hey, look, you're missin' an eye. If you want a spare I know a guy.
Not a goddamn chance.

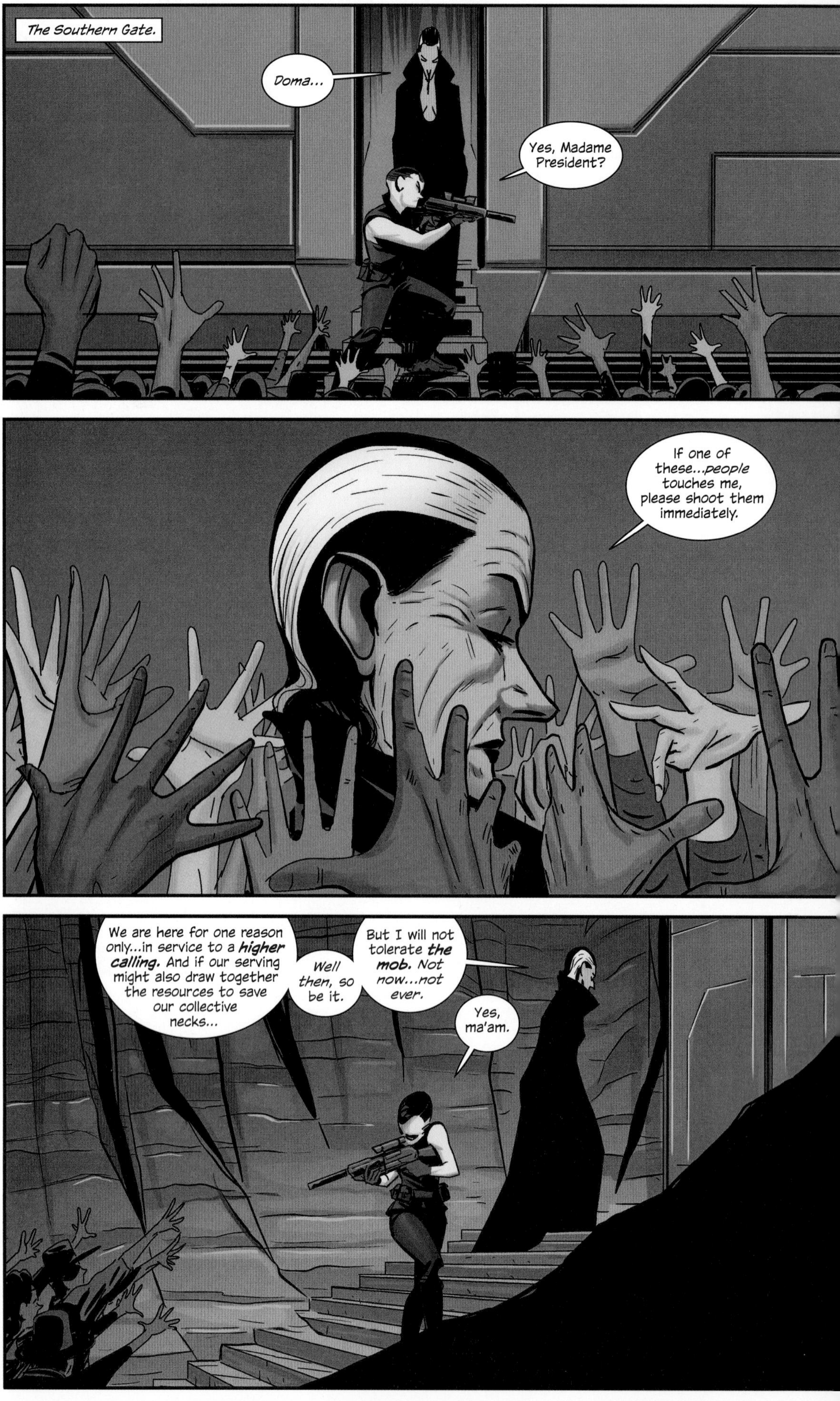
The Southern Gate.
Doma...
Yes, Madame President?
If one of these...*people* touches me, please shoot them immediately.
We are here for one reason only...in service to a ***higher calling.*** And if our serving might also draw together the resources to save our collective necks...
Well then, so be it.
But I will not tolerate ***the mob.*** *Not now...not ever.*
Yes, ma'am.

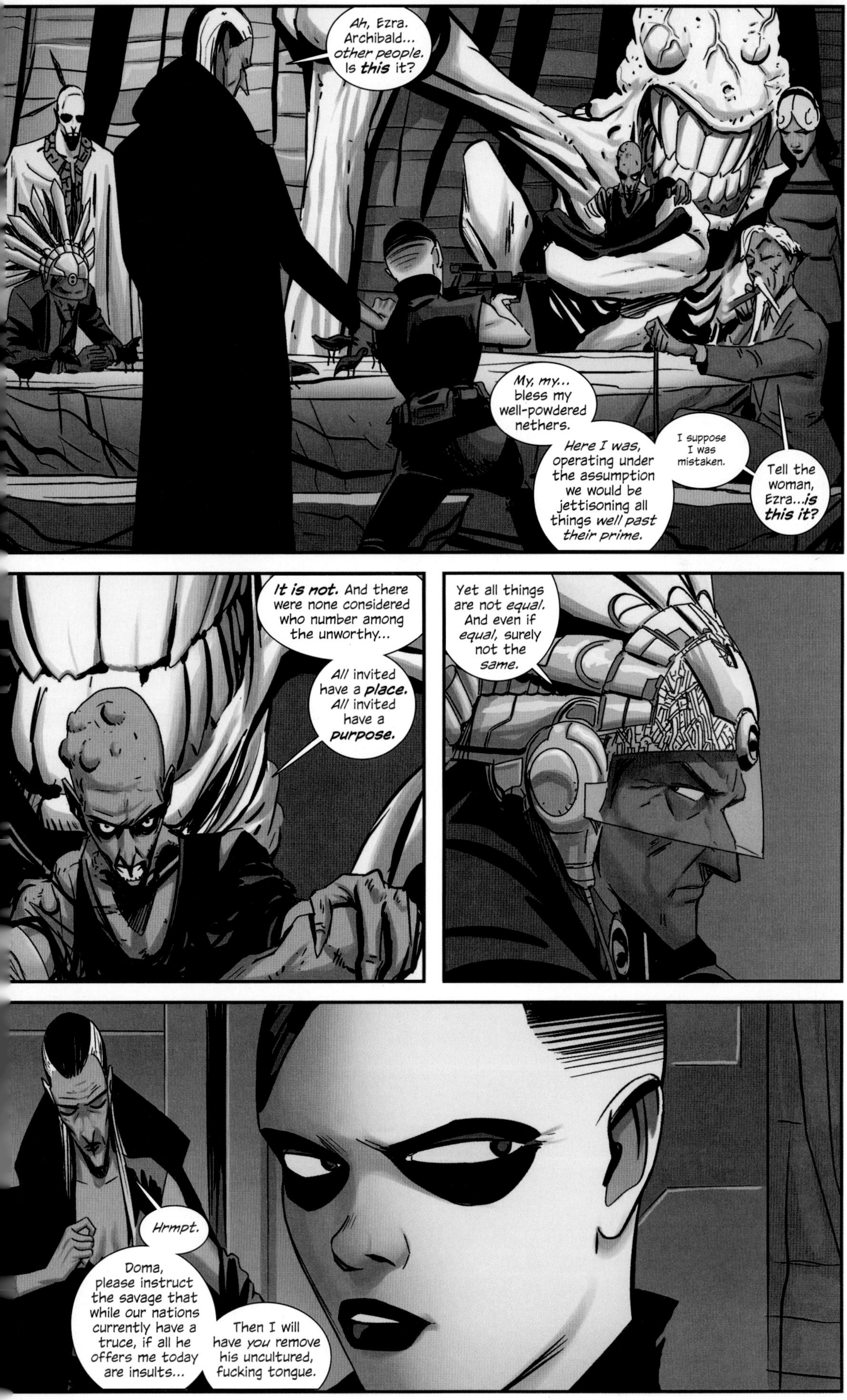

Ah, Ezra. Archibald... other people. Is this it?
My, my... bless my well-powdered nethers.
Here I was, operating under the assumption we would be jettisoning all things well past their prime.
I suppose I was mistaken.
Tell the woman, Ezra...is this it?
It is not. And there were none considered who number among the unworthy...
All invited have a place. All invited have a purpose.
Yet all things are not equal. And even if equal, surely not the same.
Hrmpt.
Doma, please instruct the savage that while our nations currently have a truce, if all he offers me today are insults...
Then I will have you remove his uncultured, fucking tongue.

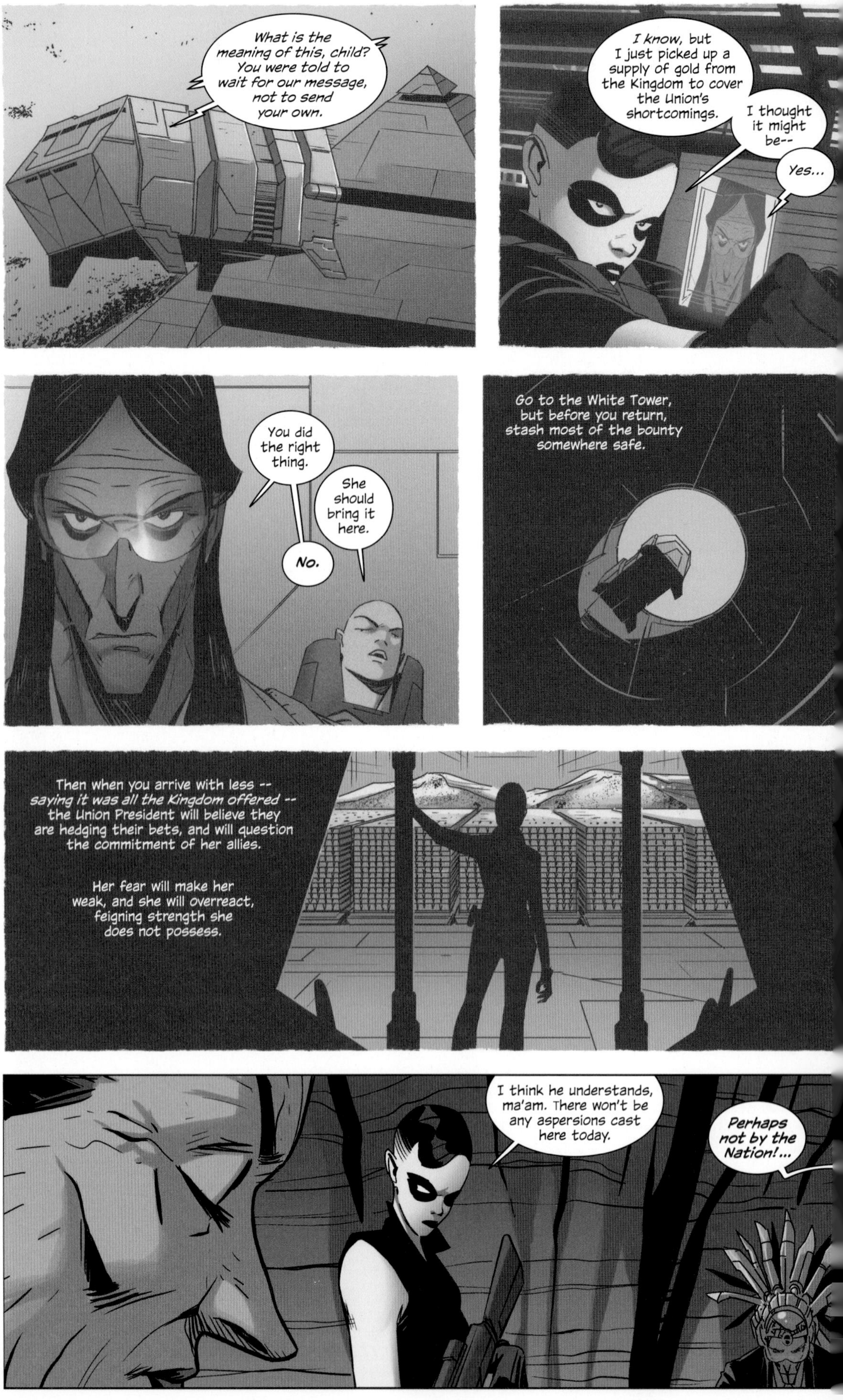
What is the meaning of this, child? You were told to wait for our message, not to send your own.
I know, but I just picked up a supply of gold from the Kingdom to cover the Union's shortcomings.
I thought it might be--
Yes...
You did the right thing.
No.
She should bring it here.
Go to the White Tower, but before you return, stash most of the bounty somewhere safe.
Then when you arrive with less -- saying it was all the Kingdom offered -- the Union President will believe they are hedging their bets, and will question the commitment of her allies.
Her fear will make her weak, and she will overreact, feigning strength she does not possess.
I think he understands, ma'am. There won't be any aspersions cast here today.
Perhaps not by the Nation!...

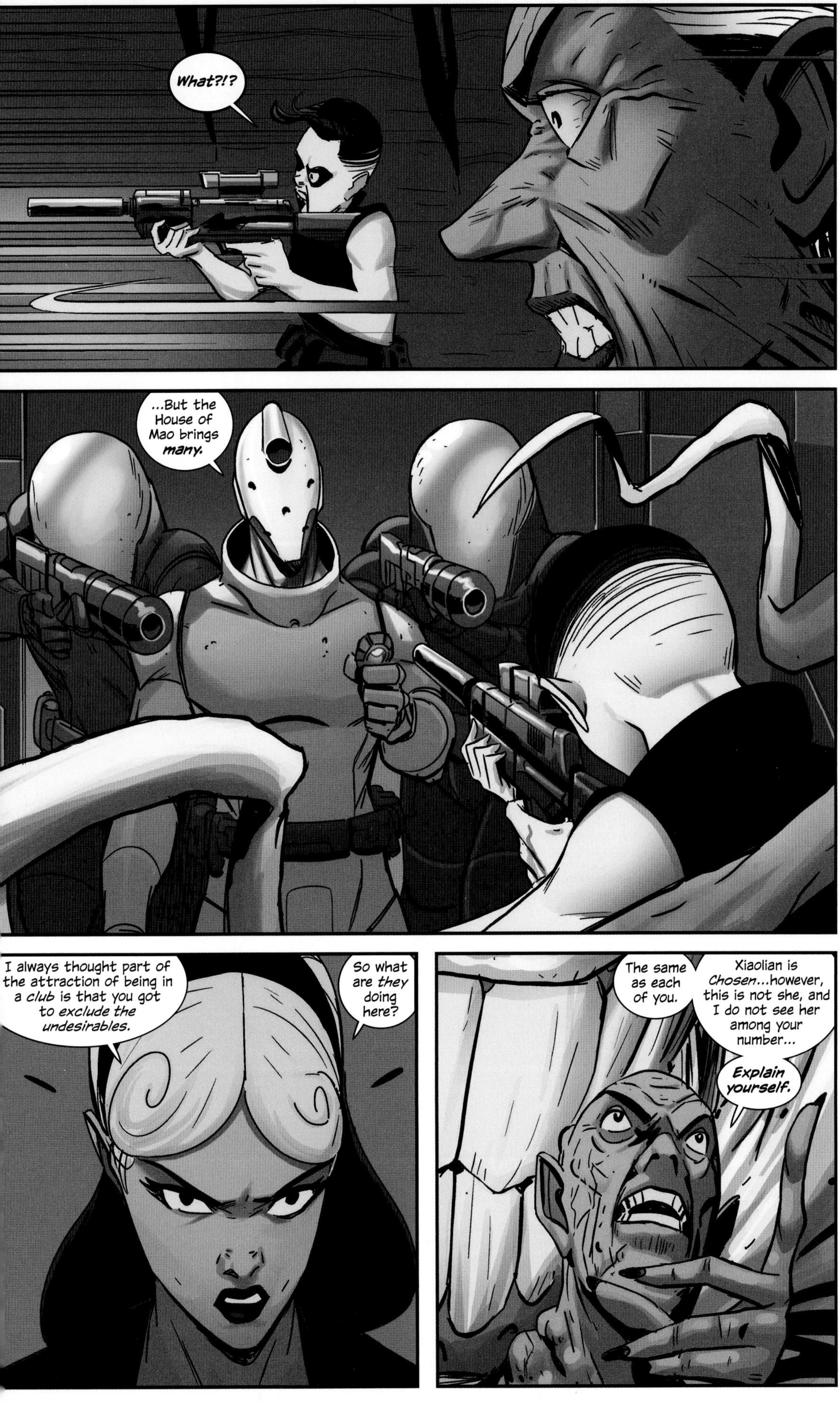
What?!?
...But the House of Mao brings *many.*
I always thought part of the attraction of being in a *club* is that you got to *exclude the undesirables.*
So what are *they* doing here?
The same as each of you.
Xiaolian is *Chosen*...however, this is not she, and I do not see her among your number...
Explain yourself.

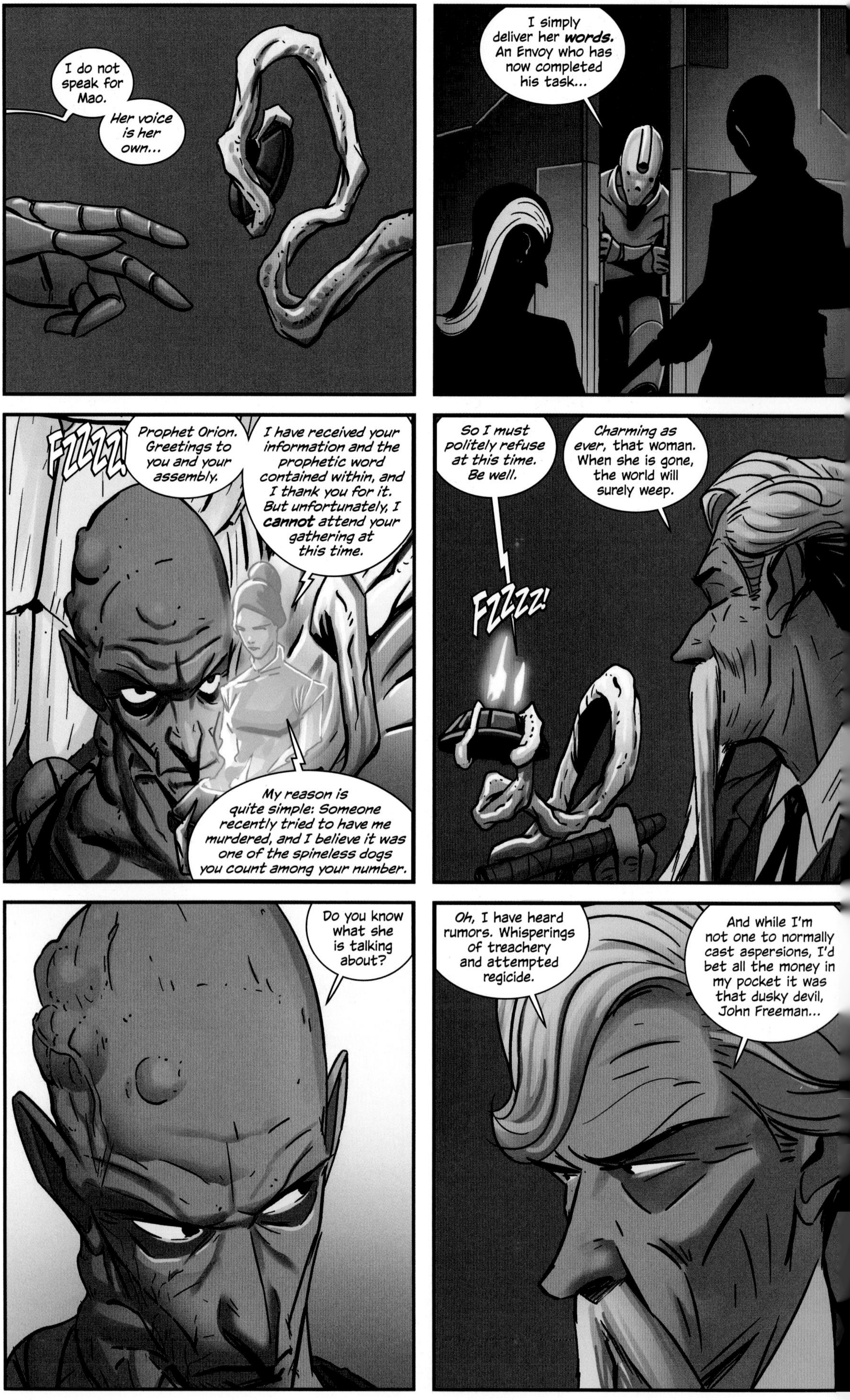
I do not speak for Mao.
Her voice is her own...
I simply deliver her words. An Envoy who has now completed his task...
FZZZZ!
Prophet Orion. Greetings to you and your assembly.
I have received your information and the prophetic word contained within, and I thank you for it. But unfortunately, I cannot attend your gathering at this time.
My reason is quite simple: Someone recently tried to have me murdered, and I believe it was one of the spineless dogs you count among your number.
So I must politely refuse at this time. Be well.
FZZZZ!
Charming as ever, that woman. When she is gone, the world will surely weep.
Do you know what she is talking about?
Oh, I have heard rumors. Whisperings of treachery and attempted regicide.
And while I'm not one to normally cast aspersions, I'd bet all the money in my pocket it was that dusky devil, John Freeman...

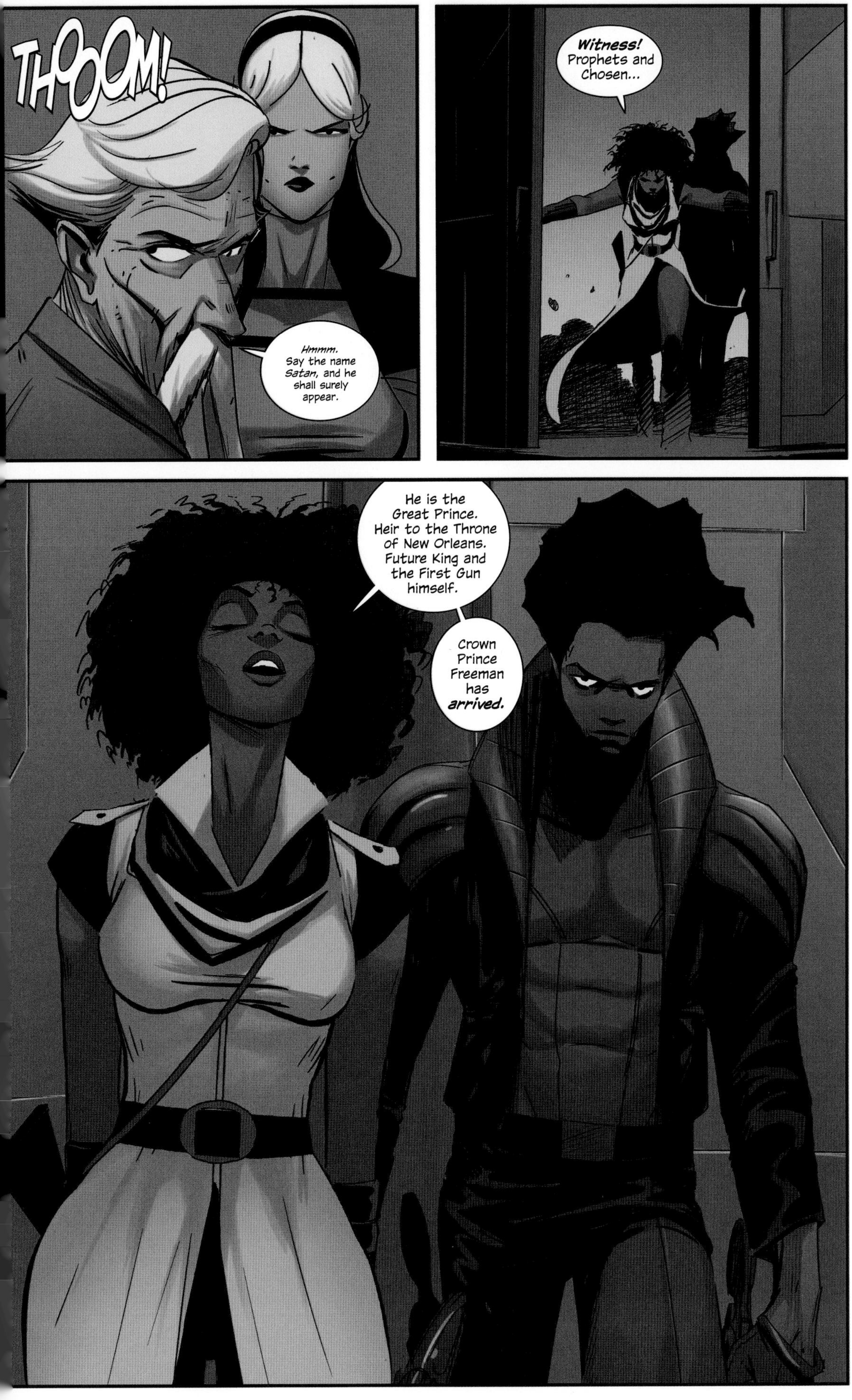
THOOOM!
Hmmm. Say the name Satan, and he shall surely appear.
Witness! Prophets and Chosen...
He is the Great Prince. Heir to the Throne of New Orleans. Future King and the First Gun himself.
Crown Prince Freeman has arrived.

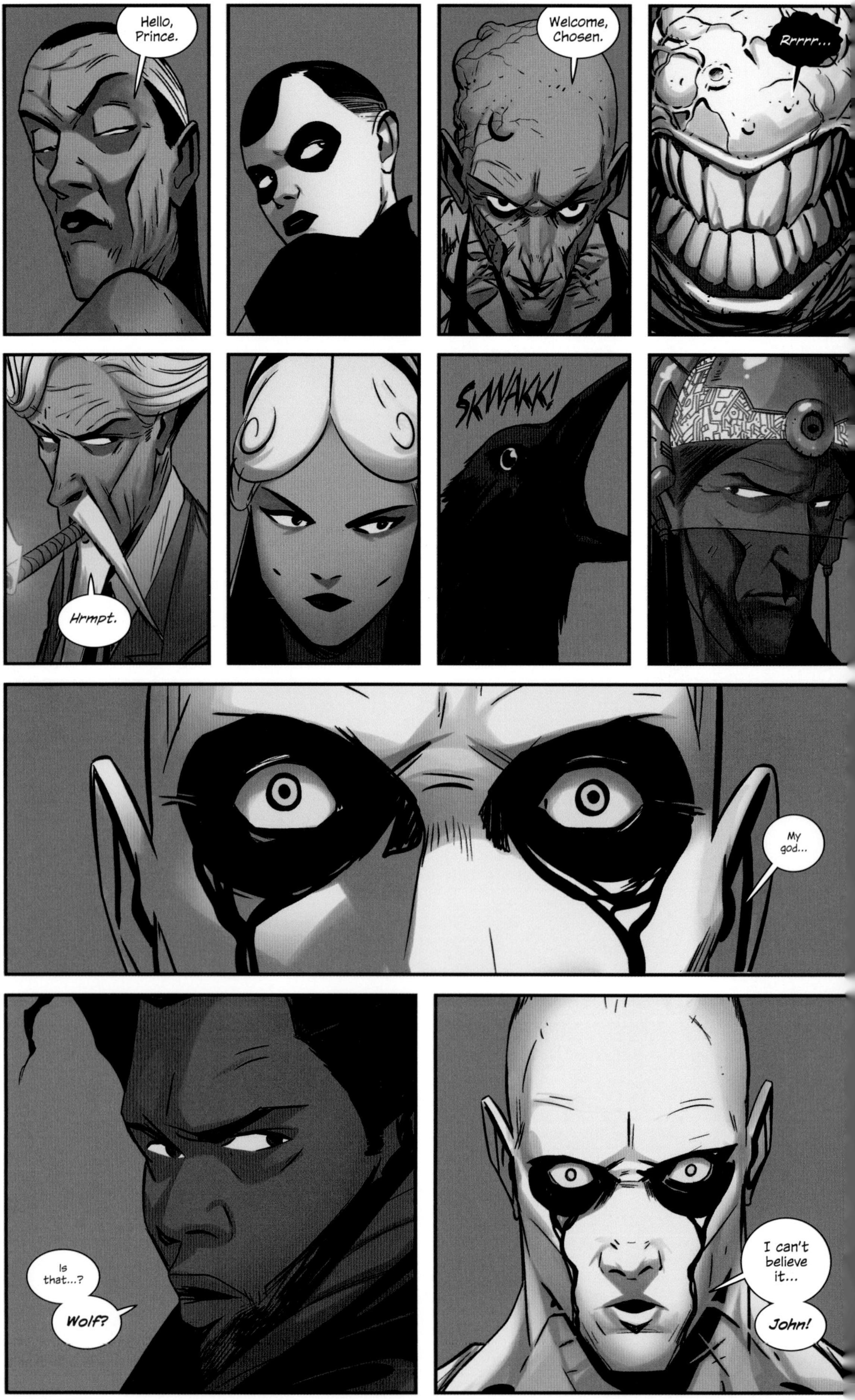
Hello, Prince.
Welcome, Chosen.
Rrrrr...
Hrmpt.
SKWAKK!
My god...
Is that...?
Wolf?
I can't believe it...
John!

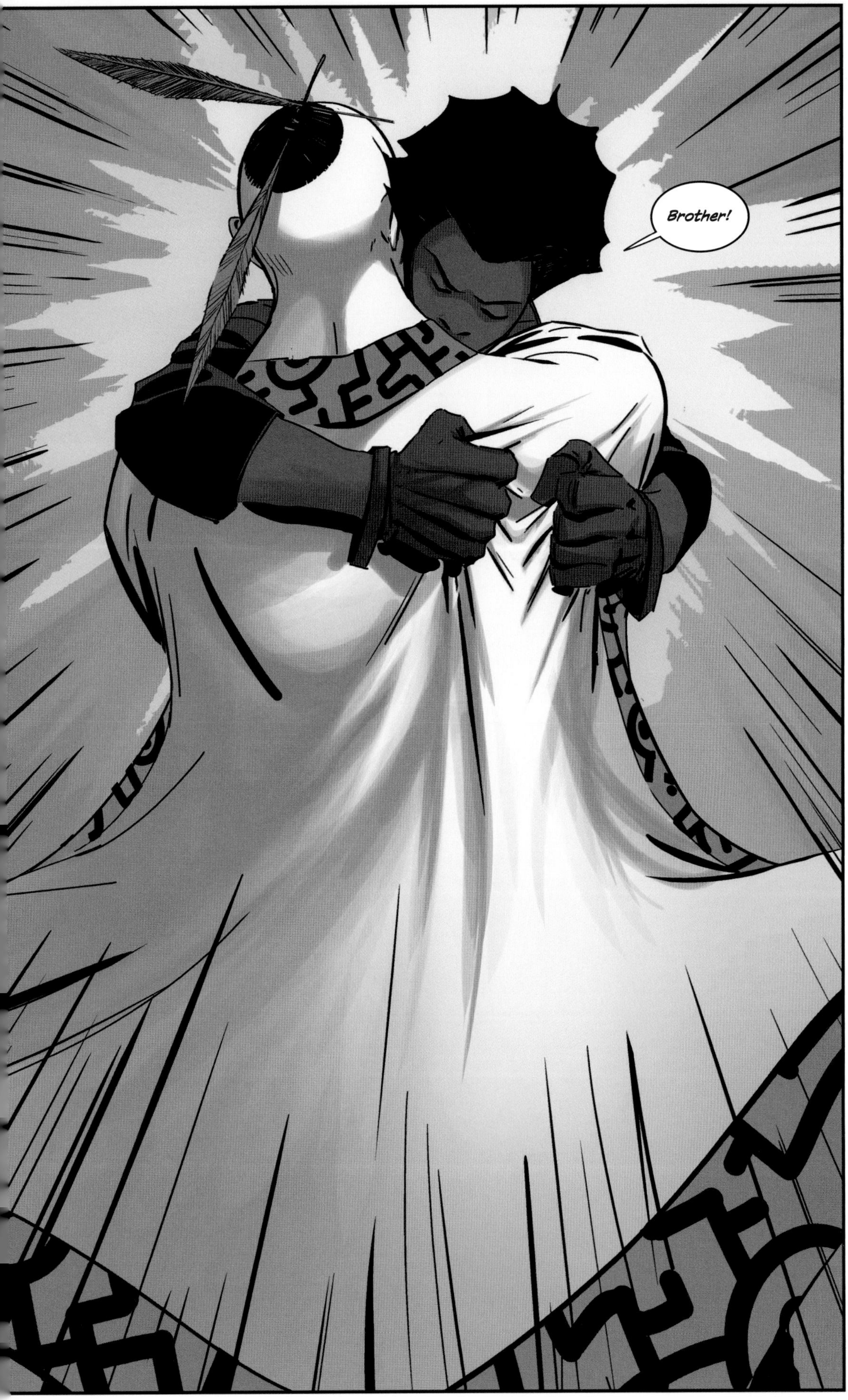
Brother!

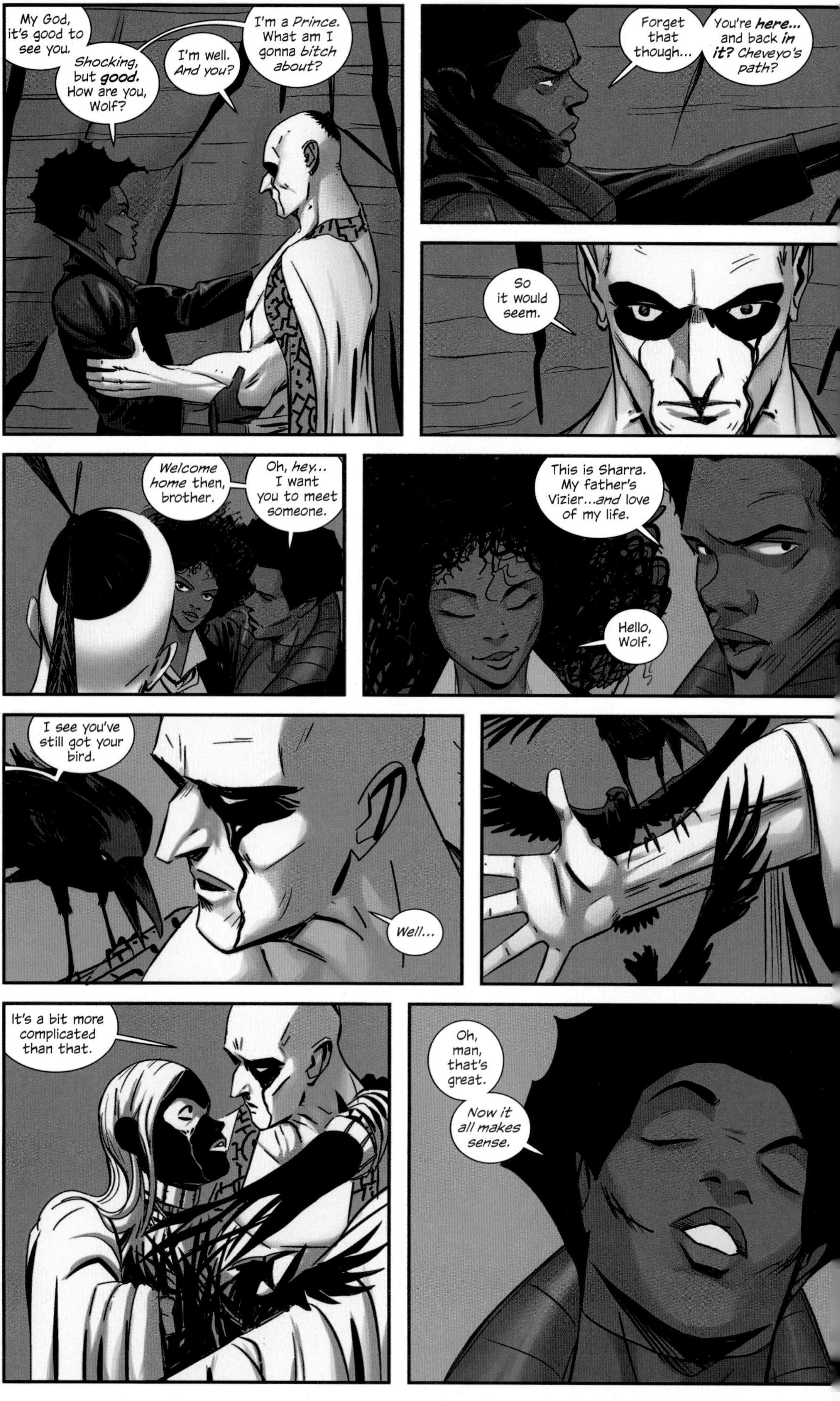
My God, it's good to see you.
Shocking, but **good.** How are you, Wolf?
I'm well. *And you?*
I'm a *Prince.* What am I gonna *bitch* about?
Forget that though...
You're **here...** and back ***in it?*** *Cheveyo's path?*
So it would seem.
Welcome home then, brother.
Oh, *hey...* I want you to meet someone.
This is Sharra. My father's Vizier...*and* love of my life.
Hello, Wolf.
I see you've still got your bird.
Well...
It's a bit more complicated than that.
Oh, man, that's great.
Now it all makes sense.

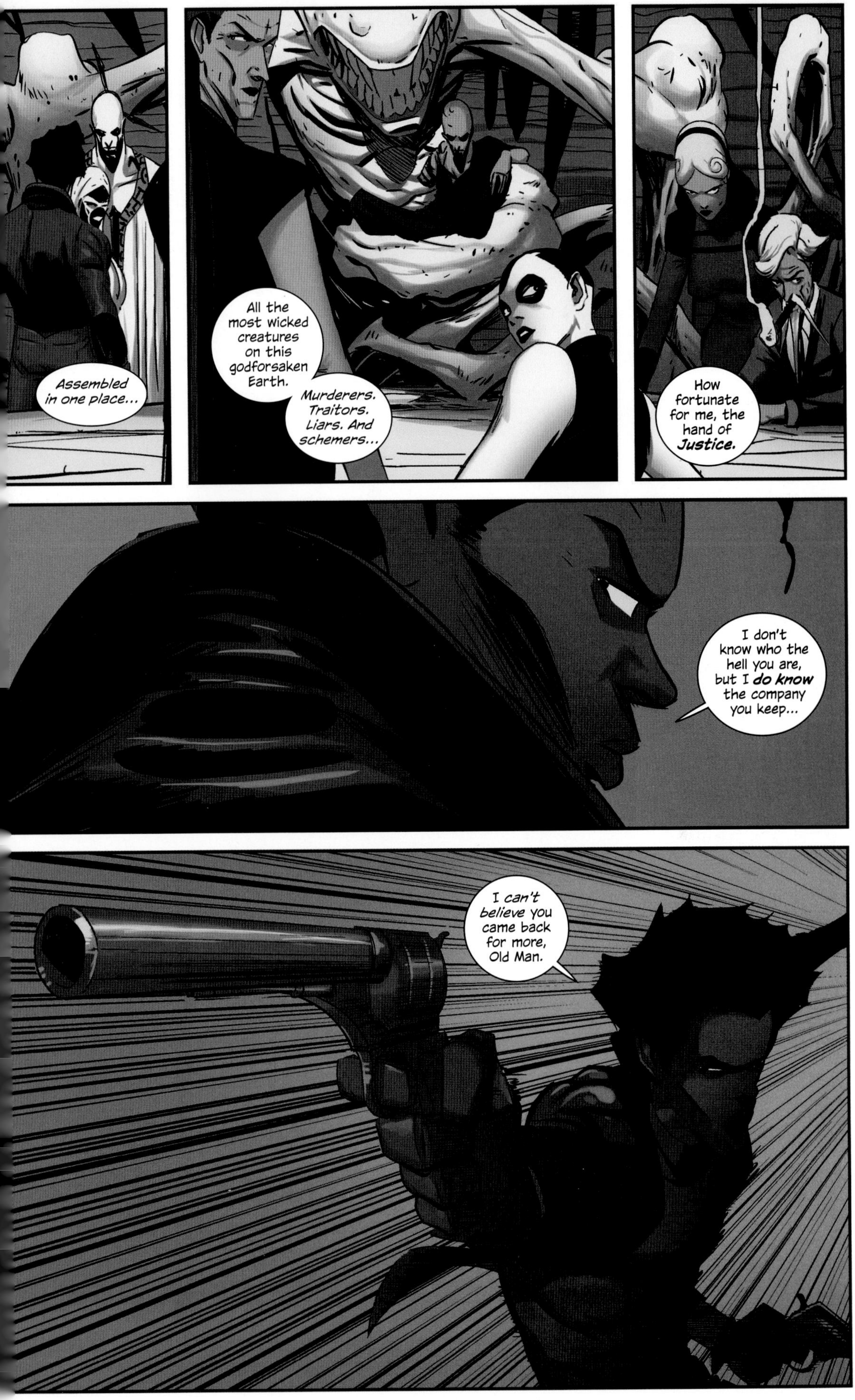

Assembled in one place...
All the most wicked creatures on this godforsaken Earth.
Murderers. Traitors. Liars. And schemers...
How fortunate for me, the hand of **Justice.**
I don't know who the hell you are, but I **do know** the company you keep...
I *can't believe* you came back for more, Old Man.

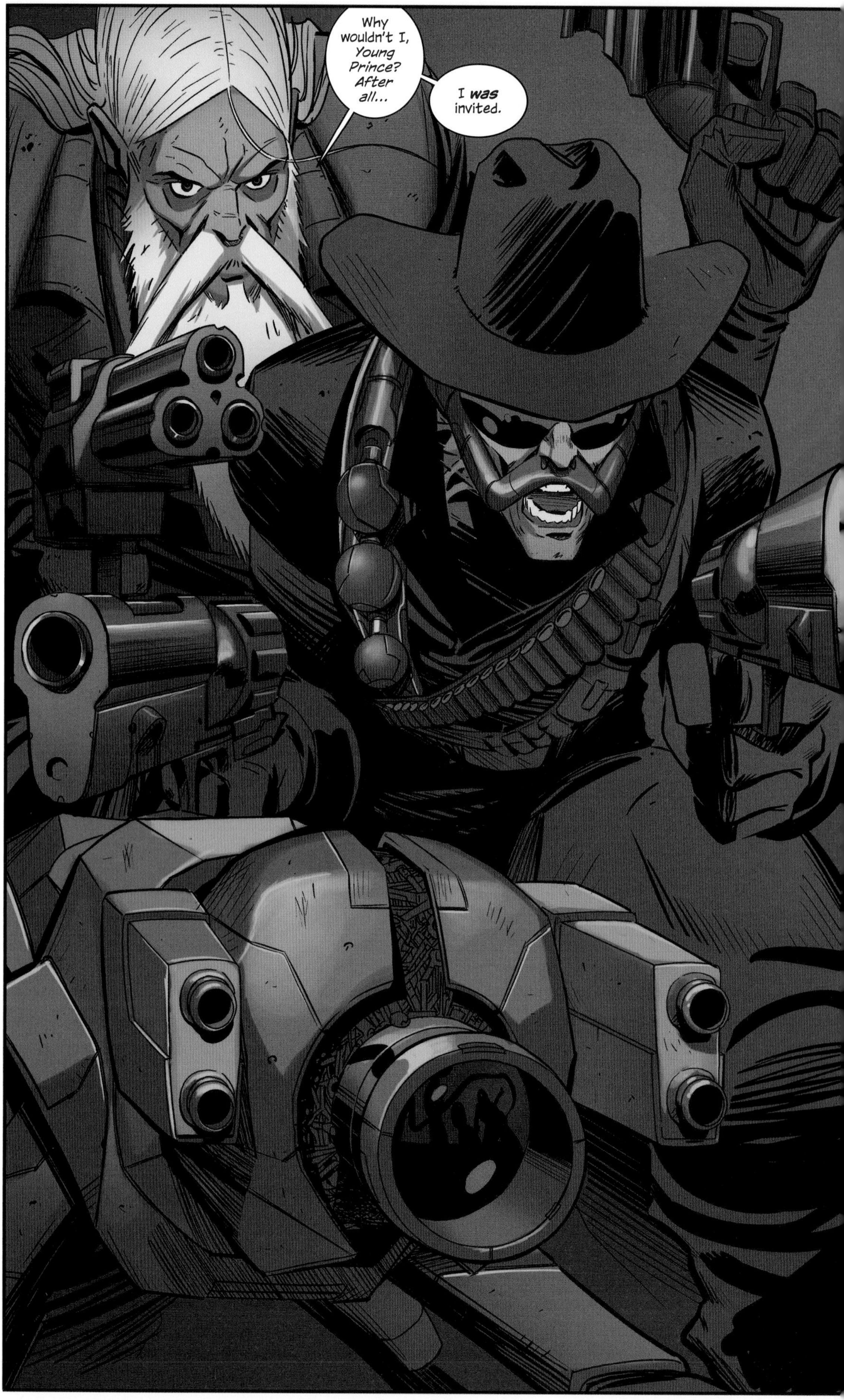
Why wouldn't I, Young Prince? After all...
I was invited.

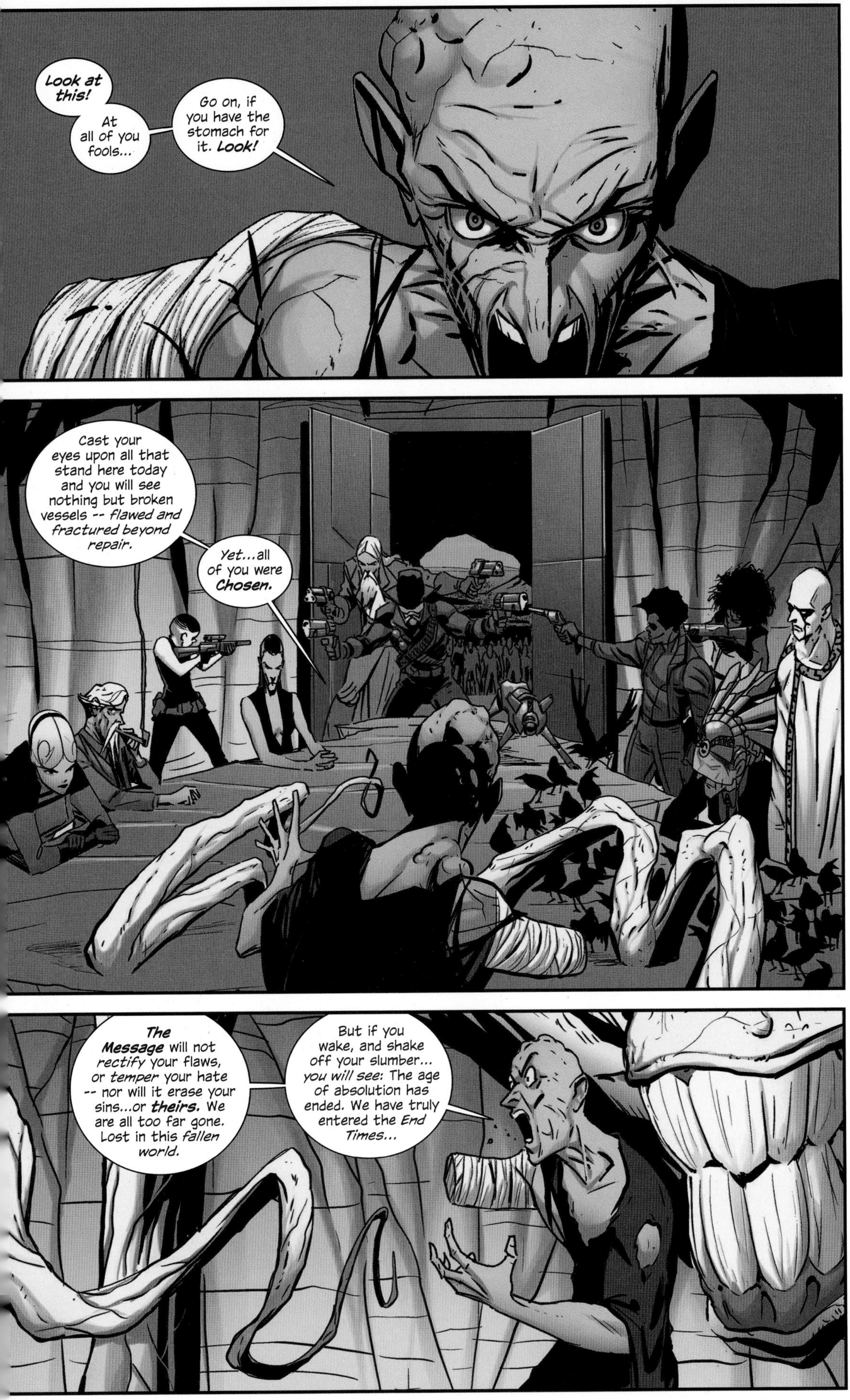
Look at this!
At all of you fools...
Go on, if you have the stomach for it. Look!
Cast your eyes upon all that stand here today and you will see nothing but broken vessels -- flawed and fractured beyond repair.
Yet...all of you were Chosen.
The Message will not rectify your flaws, or temper your hate -- nor will it erase your sins...or theirs. We are all too far gone. Lost in this fallen world.
But if you wake, and shake off your slumber... you will see: The age of absolution has ended. We have truly entered the End Times...

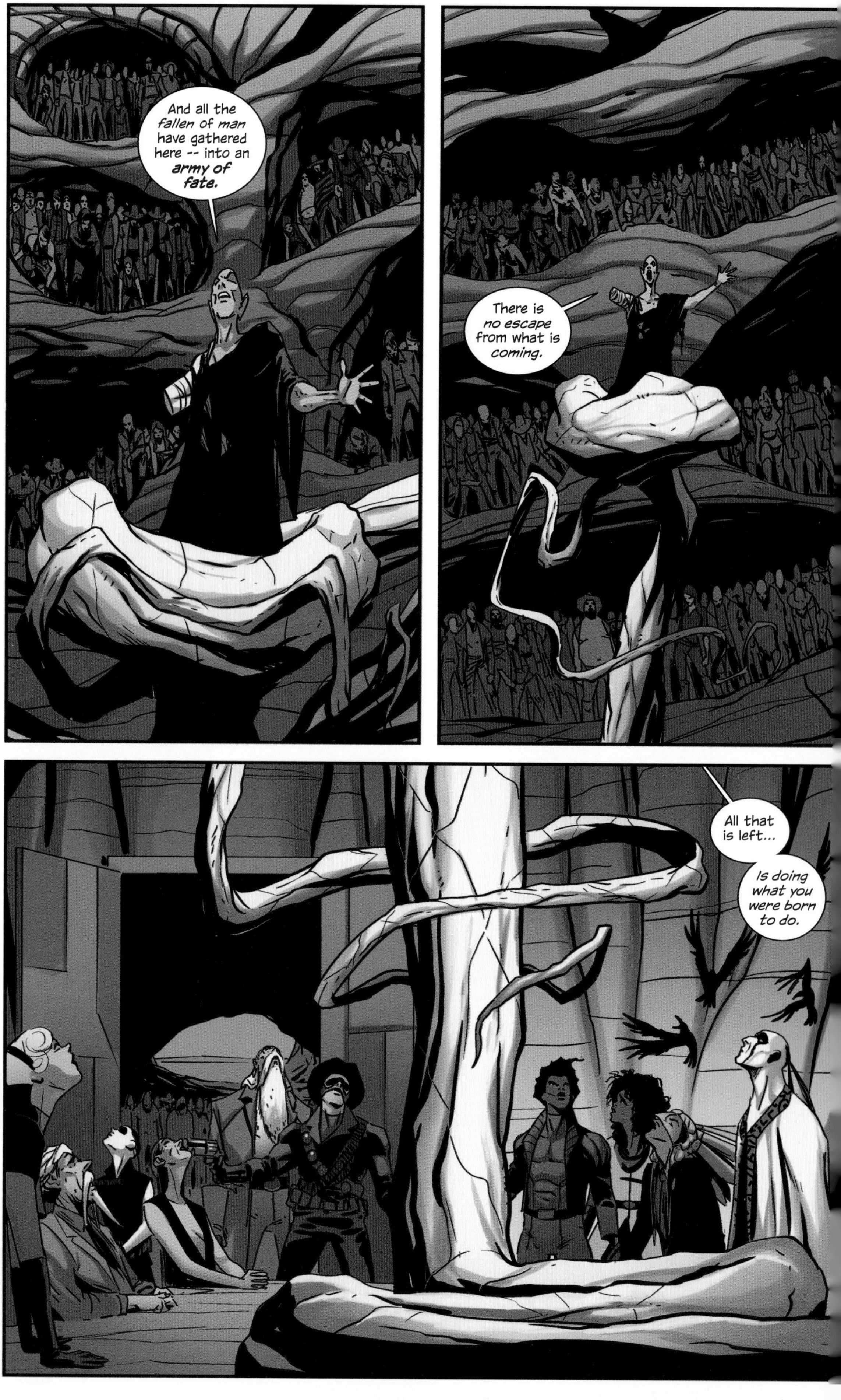
And all the fallen of man have gathered here -- into an army of fate.
There is no escape from what is coming.
All that is left...
Is doing what you were born to do.

THIS IS A **FUNERAL** FOR THE
FREE MAN.

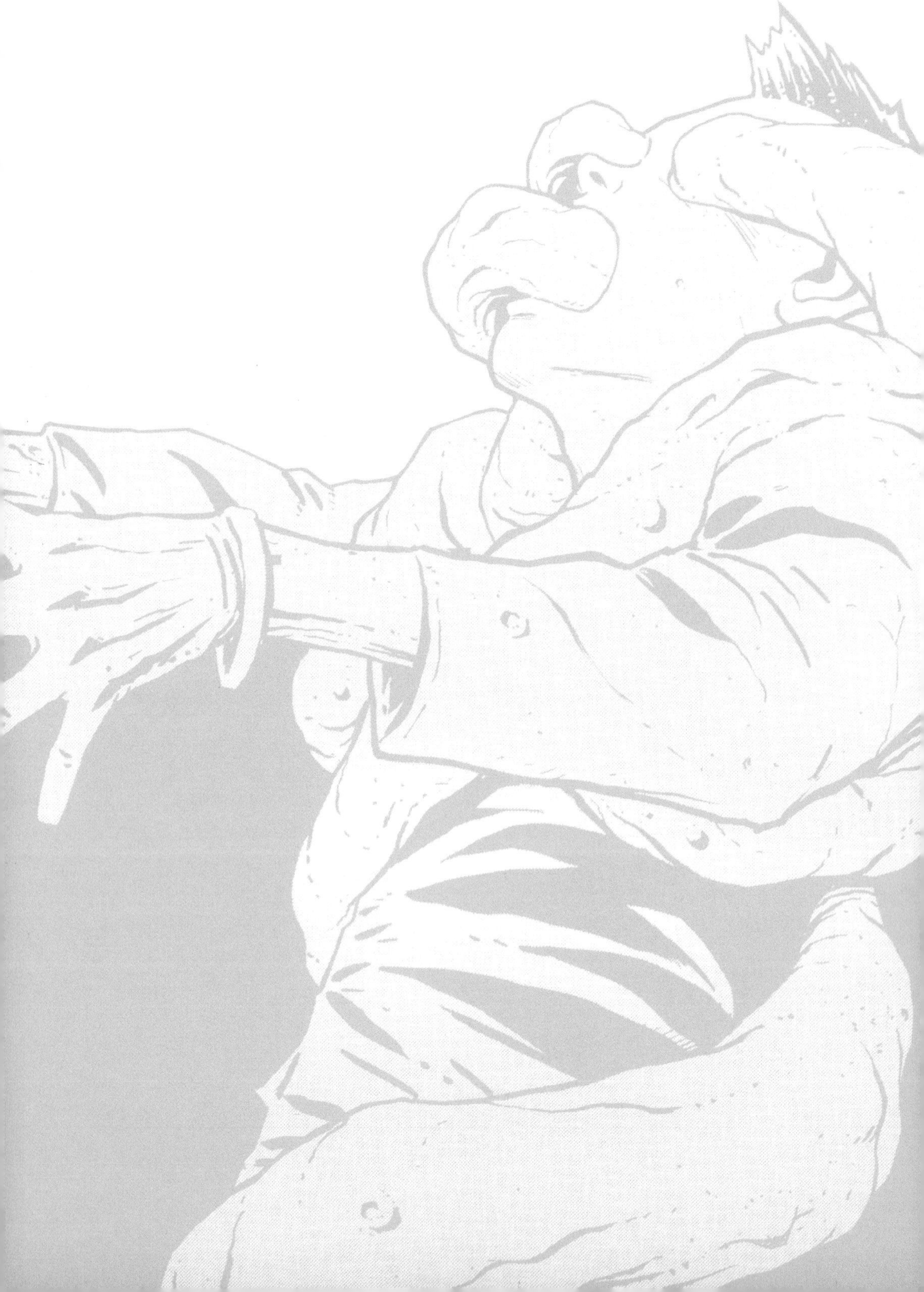

27

 TWENTY-SEVEN:
A FINAL **WORD**

IT IS **TOMORROW** WE **BURY**
HERE **TODAY.**

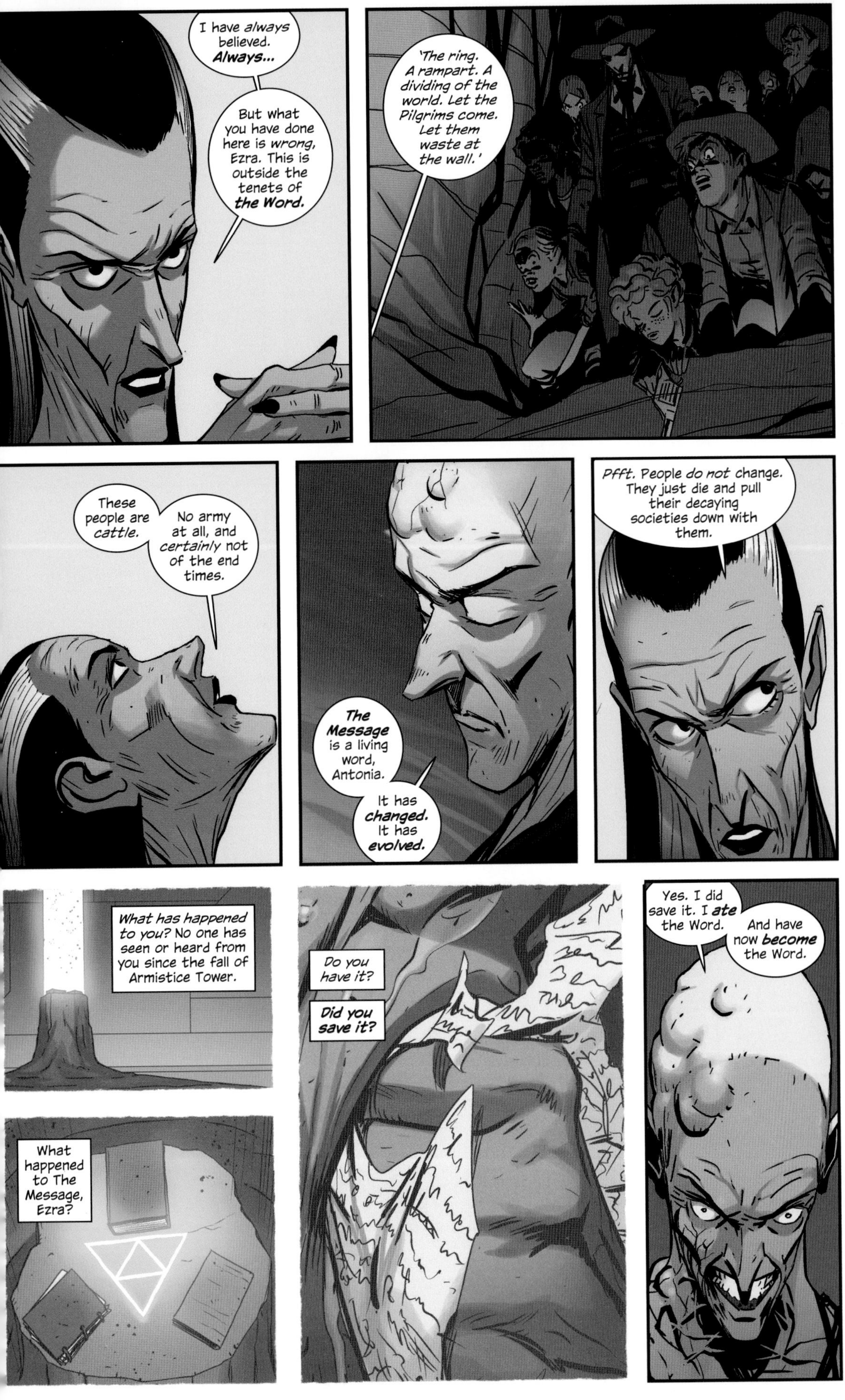
I have always believed. Always...
But what you have done here is wrong, Ezra. This is outside the tenets of the Word.
'The ring. A rampart. A dividing of the world. Let the Pilgrims come. Let them waste at the wall.'
These people are cattle.
No army at all, and certainly not of the end times.
The Message is a living word, Antonia.
It has changed. It has evolved.
Pfft. People do not change. They just die and pull their decaying societies down with them.
What has happened to you? No one has seen or heard from you since the fall of Armistice Tower.
What happened to The Message, Ezra?
Do you have it?
Did you save it?
Yes. I did save it. I ate the Word.
And have now become the Word.

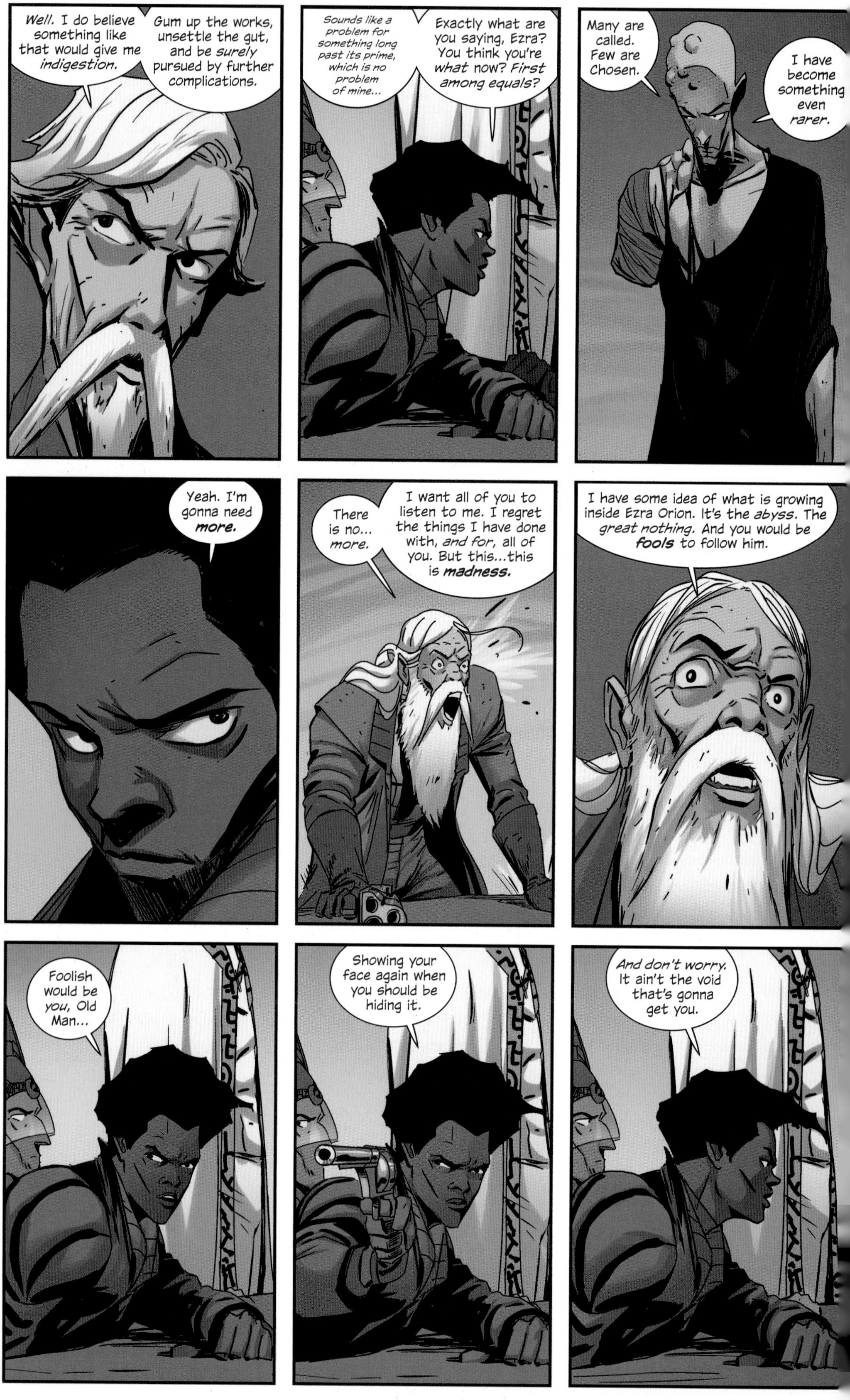

Well. I do believe something like that would give me *indigestion.*
Gum up the works, unsettle the gut, and be *surely* pursued by further complications.
Sounds like a problem for something long past its prime, which is no problem of mine...
Exactly what are you saying, Ezra? You think you're *what* now? *First among equals?*
Many are called. Few are Chosen.
I have become something even *rarer.*
Yeah. I'm gonna need ***more.***
There is no... *more.*
I want all of you to listen to me. I regret the things I have done with, *and for,* all of you. But this...this is ***madness.***
I have some idea of what is growing inside Ezra Orion. It's the *abyss.* The *great nothing.* And you would be ***fools*** to follow him.
Foolish would be *you,* Old Man...
Showing your face again when you should be hiding it.
And don't worry. It ain't the void that's gonna get you.

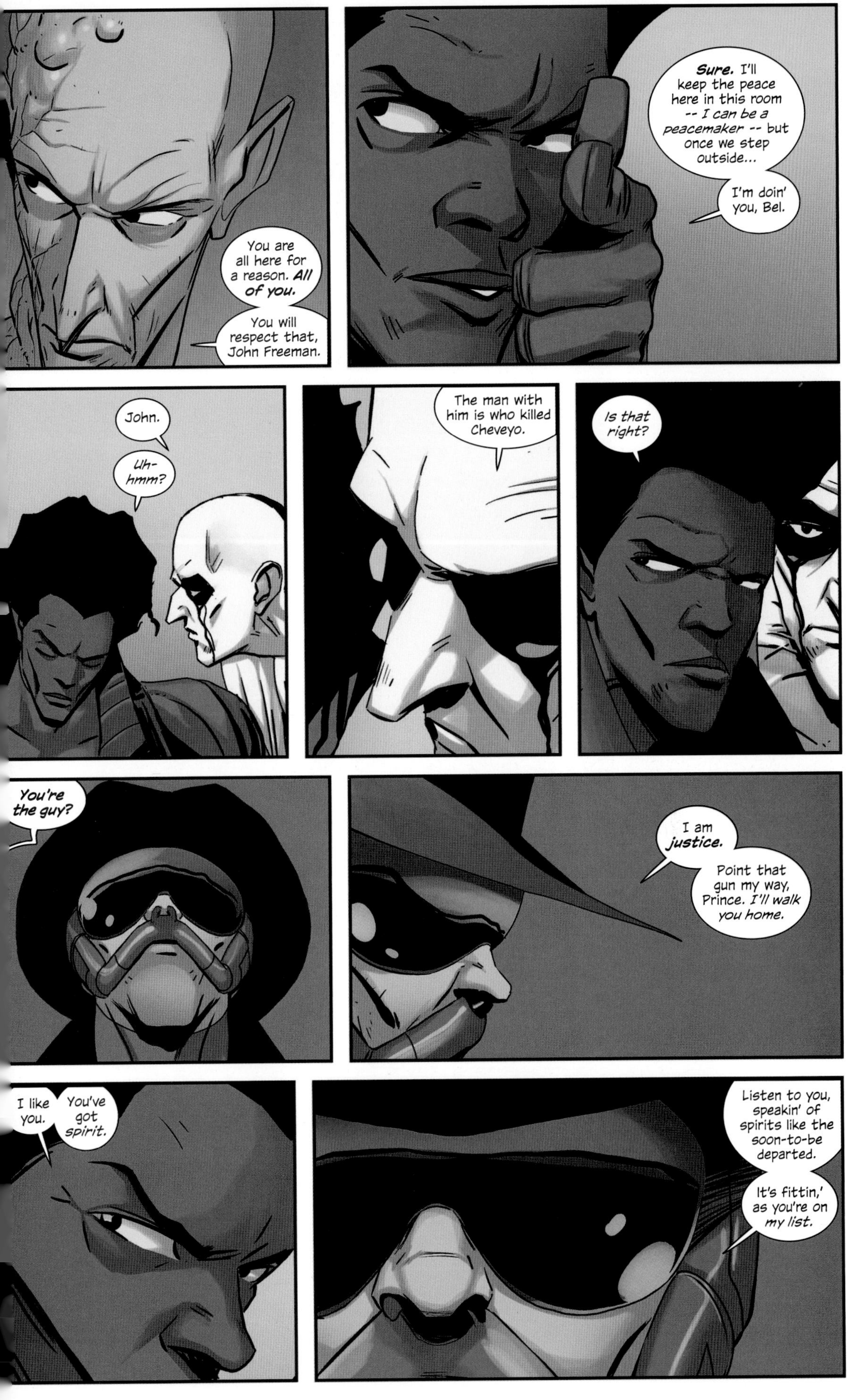
You are all here for a reason. All of you.
You will respect that, John Freeman.
Sure. I'll keep the peace here in this room -- I can be a peacemaker -- but once we step outside...
I'm doin' you, Bel.
John.
Uh-hmm?
The man with him is who killed Cheveyo.
Is that right?
You're the guy?
I am justice.
Point that gun my way, Prince. I'll walk you home.
I like you.
You've got spirit.
Listen to you, speakin' of spirits like the soon-to-be departed.
It's fittin,' as you're on my list.

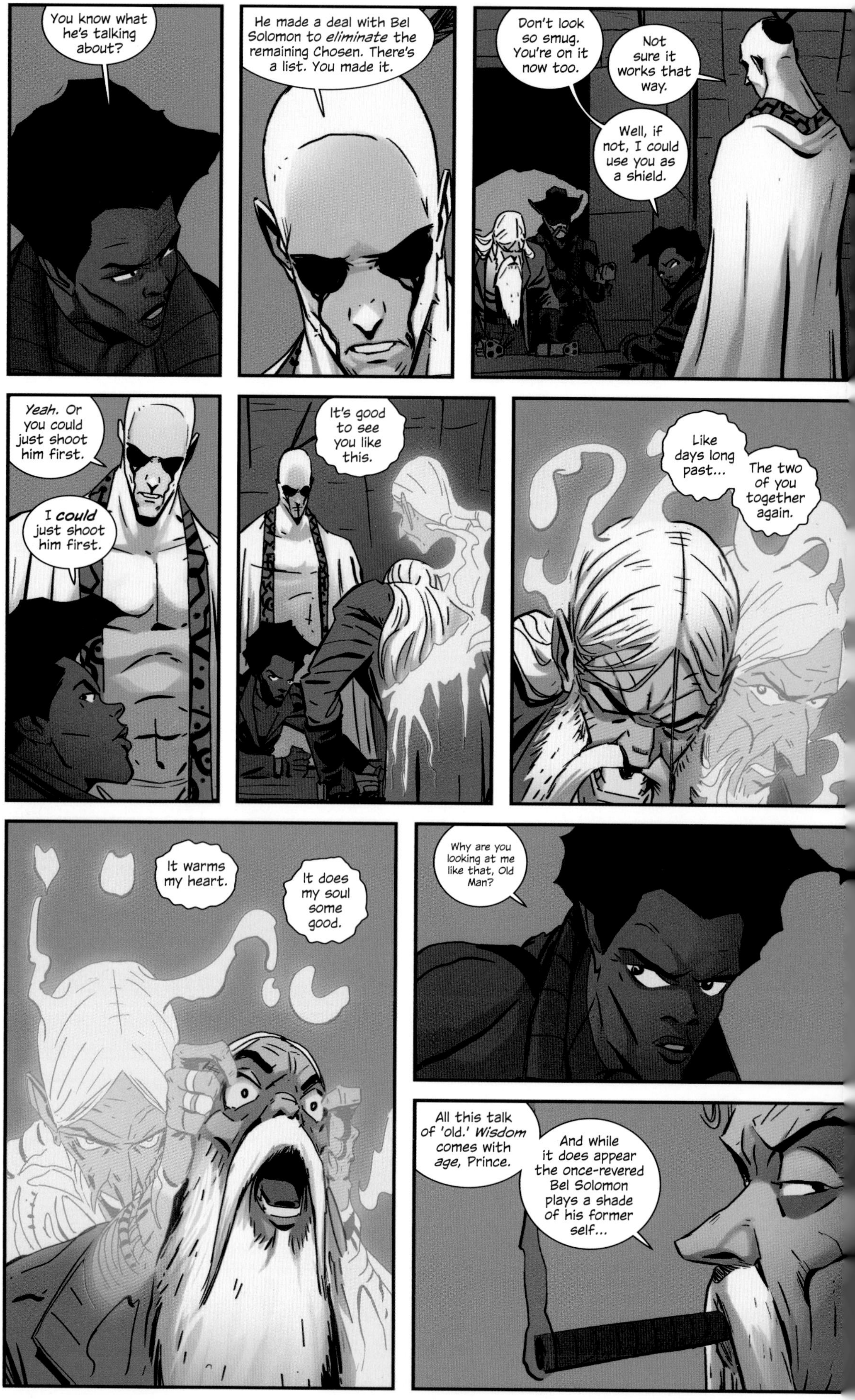

You know what he's talking about?
He made a deal with Bel Solomon to *eliminate* the remaining Chosen. There's a list. You made it.
Don't look so smug. You're on it now too.
Not sure it works that way.
Well, if not, I could use you as a shield.
Yeah. Or you could just shoot him first.
I ***could*** just shoot him first.
It's good to see you like this.
Like days long past...
The two of you together again.
It warms my heart.
It does my soul some good.
Why are you looking at me like that, Old Man?
All this talk of 'old.' *Wisdom* comes with *age*, Prince.
And while it does appear the once-revered Bel Solomon plays a shade of his former self...

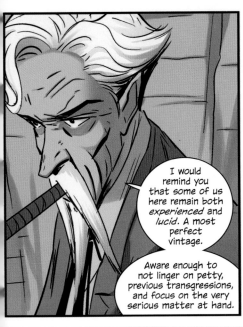

I would remind you that some of us here remain both *experienced* and *lucid*. A most perfect vintage.

Aware enough to not linger on petty, previous transgressions, and focus on the very serious matter at hand.

There is a world in the balance, young man, and once again I care to make a **wager**.

As do I.

I have always believed, and I am ready to believe again now...

But since the fall of the Tower we have all been rudderless. **Lost**.

Then rest easy... For I have returned to show you the way.

Hrmpt! I follow no man. Nor whatever it is you claim to be.

Why have you wasted my time with this, Nephew?

You think this is some *casual decision* on my part, Uncle?

It was not. I pledged my service to another. Put his life before my own, because the cause was greater.

So I would not be here without reason, and certainly not just to follow someone selling religion.

No. I had assurances that there was real power here.

I do not think I was alone.

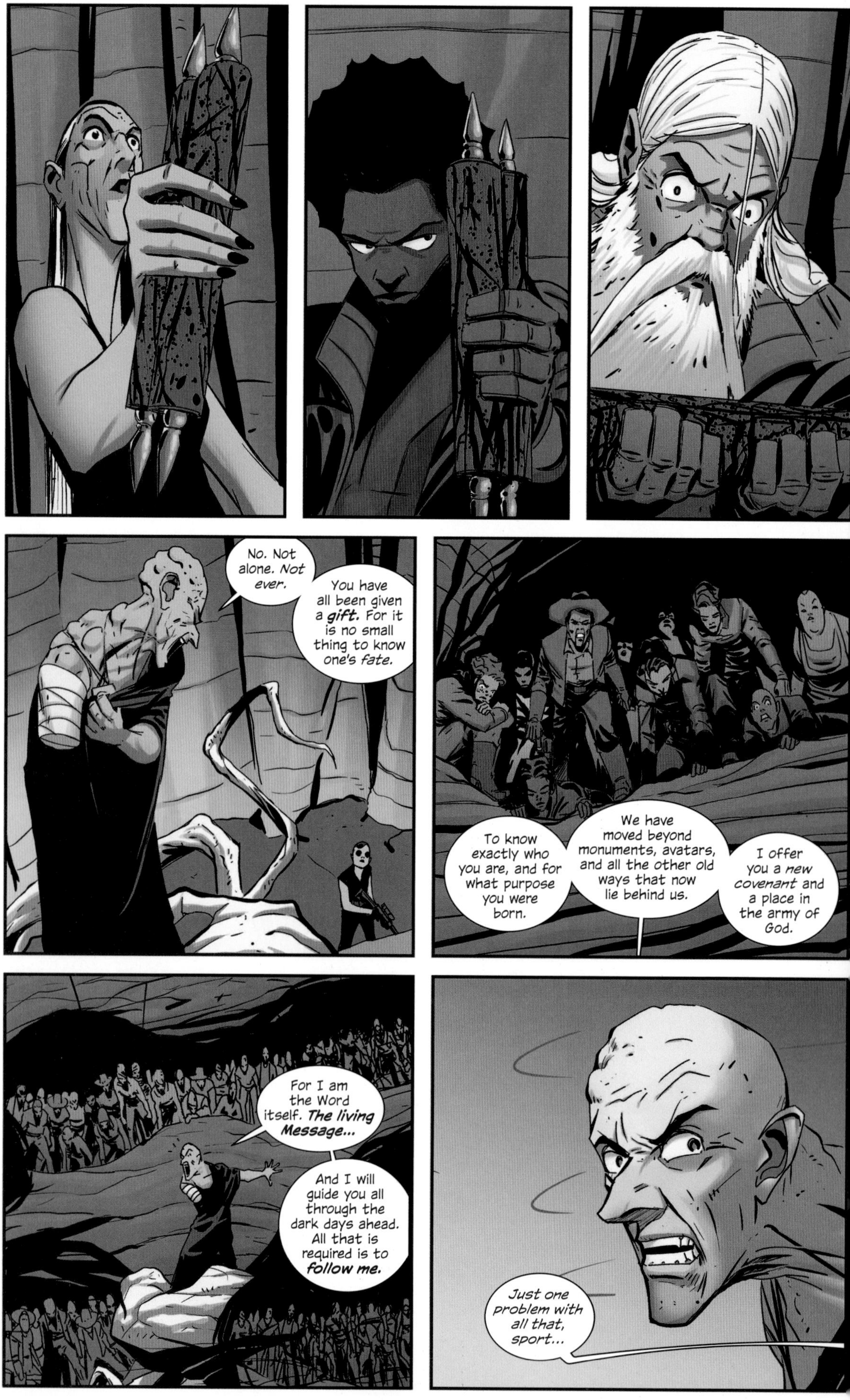
No. Not alone. *Not ever.*
You have all been given a ***gift.*** For it is no small thing to know one's *fate.*
To know exactly who you are, and for what purpose you were born.
We have moved beyond monuments, avatars, and all the other old ways that now lie behind us.
I offer you a *new covenant* and a place in the army of God.
For I am the Word itself. ***The living Message...***
And I will guide you all through the dark days ahead. All that is required is to ***follow me.***
Just one problem with all that, sport...

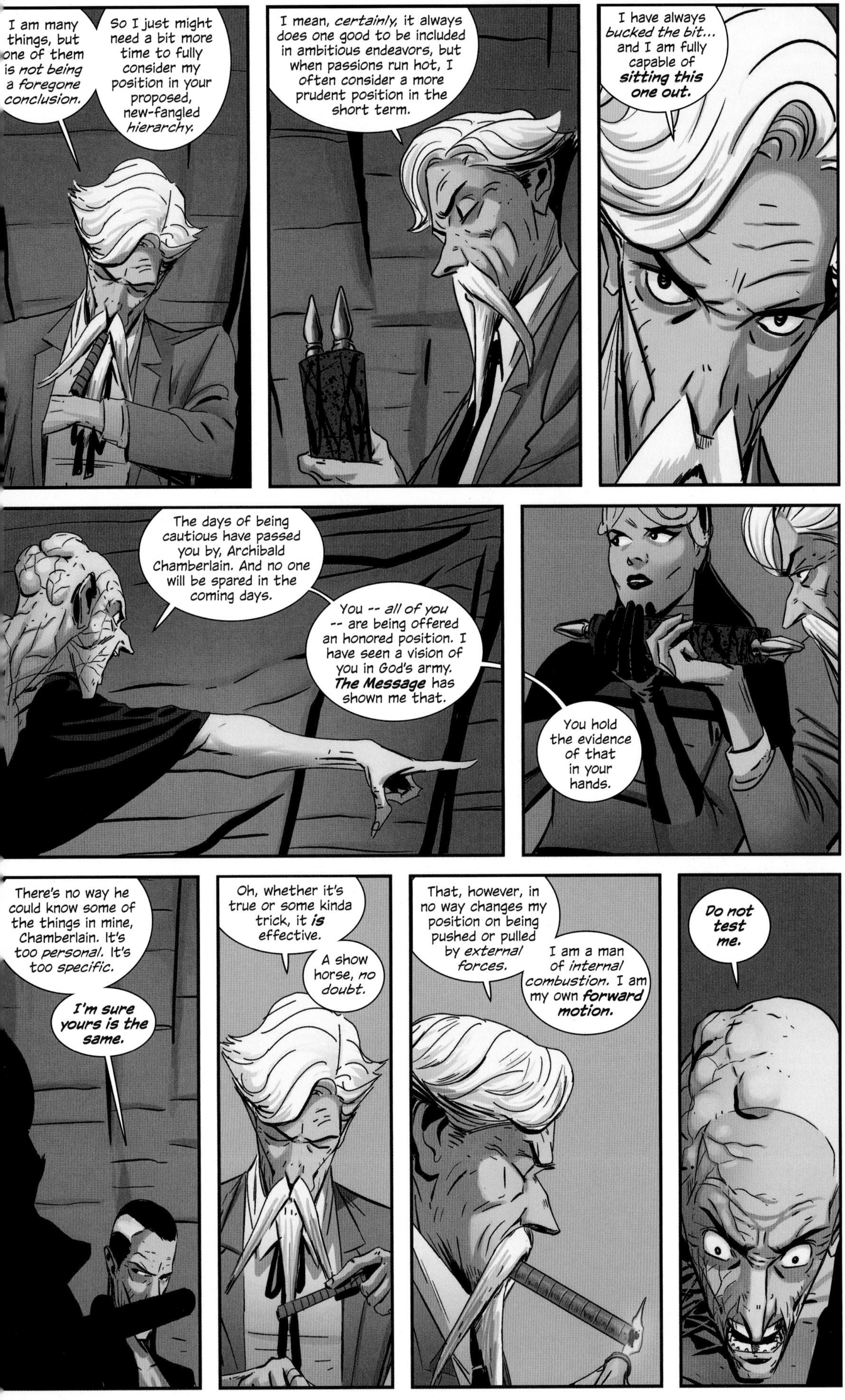
I am many things, but one of them is *not being* a *foregone conclusion.*
So I just might need a bit more time to fully consider my position in your proposed, new-fangled *hierarchy.*
I mean, *certainly,* it always does one good to be included in ambitious endeavors, but when passions run hot, I often consider a more prudent position in the short term.
I have always *bucked the bit...* and I am fully capable of ***sitting this one out.***
The days of being cautious have passed you by, Archibald Chamberlain. And no one will be spared in the coming days.
You -- *all of you* -- are being offered an honored position. I have seen a vision of you in God's army. ***The Message*** has shown me that.
You hold the evidence of that in your hands.
There's no way he could know some of the things in mine, Chamberlain. It's too *personal.* It's too *specific.*
I'm sure yours is the same.
Oh, whether it's true or some kinda trick, it ***is*** effective.
A show horse, *no doubt.*
That, however, in no way changes my position on being pushed or pulled by *external forces.*
I am a man of *internal combustion.* I am my own ***forward motion.***
Do not test me.

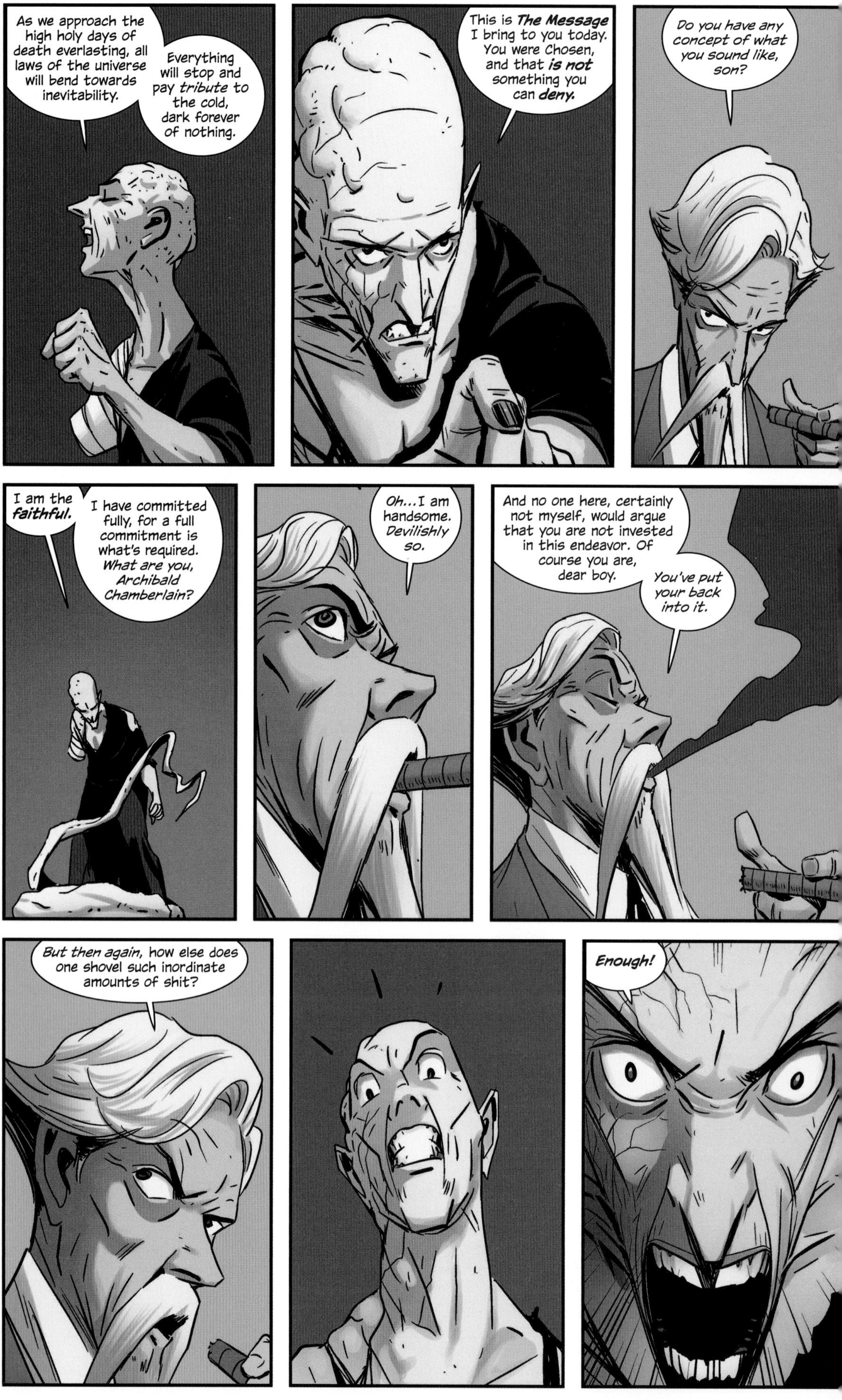
As we approach the high holy days of death everlasting, all laws of the universe will bend towards inevitability.
Everything will stop and pay *tribute* to the cold, dark forever of nothing.
This is ***The Message*** I bring to you today. You were Chosen, and that ***is not*** something you can ***deny.***
Do you have any concept of what you sound like, son?
I am the ***faithful.***
I have committed fully, for a full commitment is what's required. *What are you, Archibald Chamberlain?*
*Oh...*I am handsome. *Devilishly so.*
And no one here, certainly not myself, would argue that you are not invested in this endeavor. Of course you are, dear boy.
You've put your back into it.
But then again, how else does one shovel such inordinate amounts of shit?
Enough!

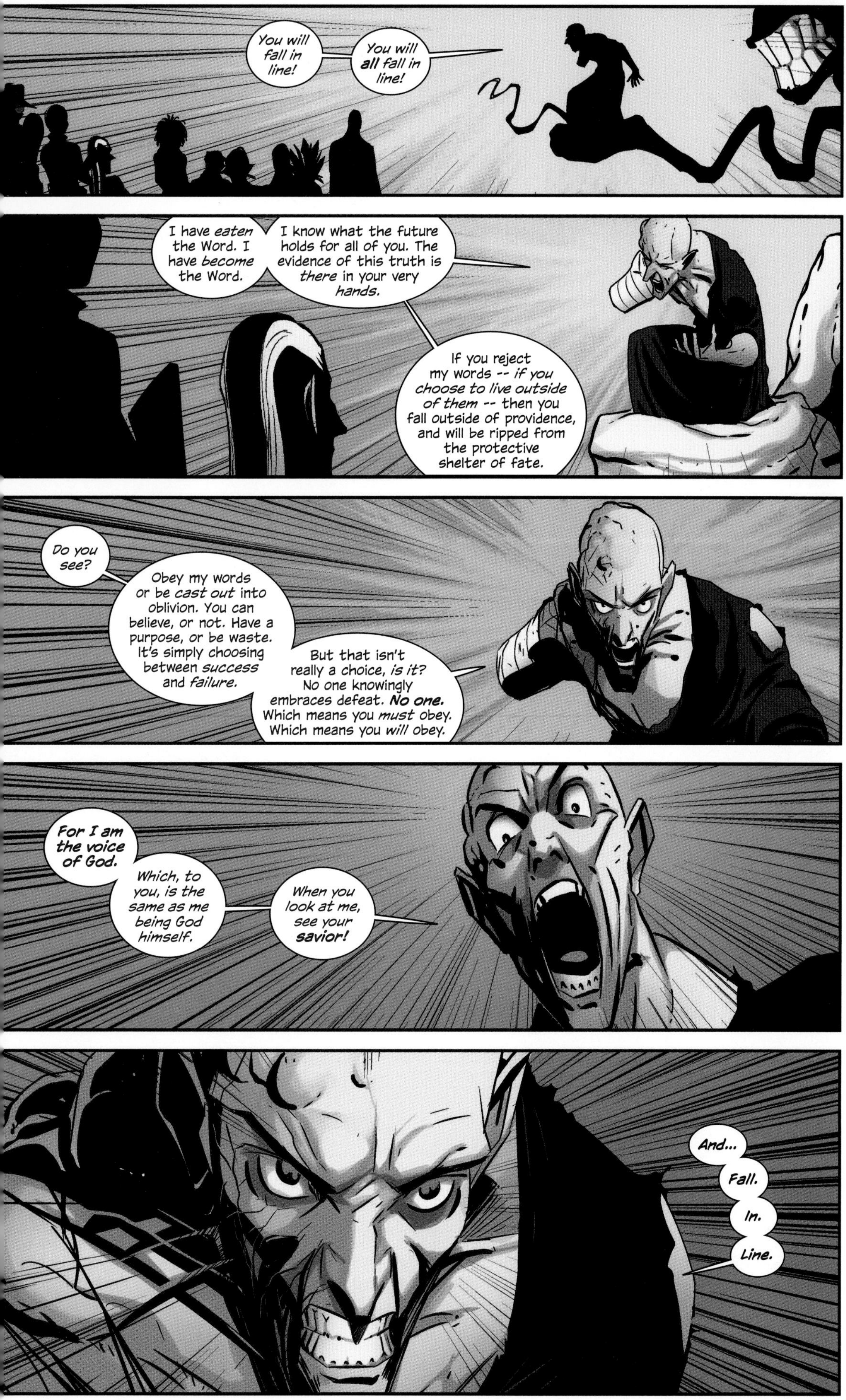
You will fall in line!
You will all fall in line!
I have eaten the Word. I have become the Word.
I know what the future holds for all of you. The evidence of this truth is there in your very hands.
If you reject my words -- if you choose to live outside of them -- then you fall outside of providence, and will be ripped from the protective shelter of fate.
Do you see?
Obey my words or be cast out into oblivion. You can believe, or not. Have a purpose, or be waste. It's simply choosing between success and failure.
But that isn't really a choice, is it? No one knowingly embraces defeat. No one. Which means you must obey. Which means you will obey.
For I am the voice of God.
Which, to you, is the same as me being God himself.
When you look at me, see your savior!
And...
Fall.
In.
Line.

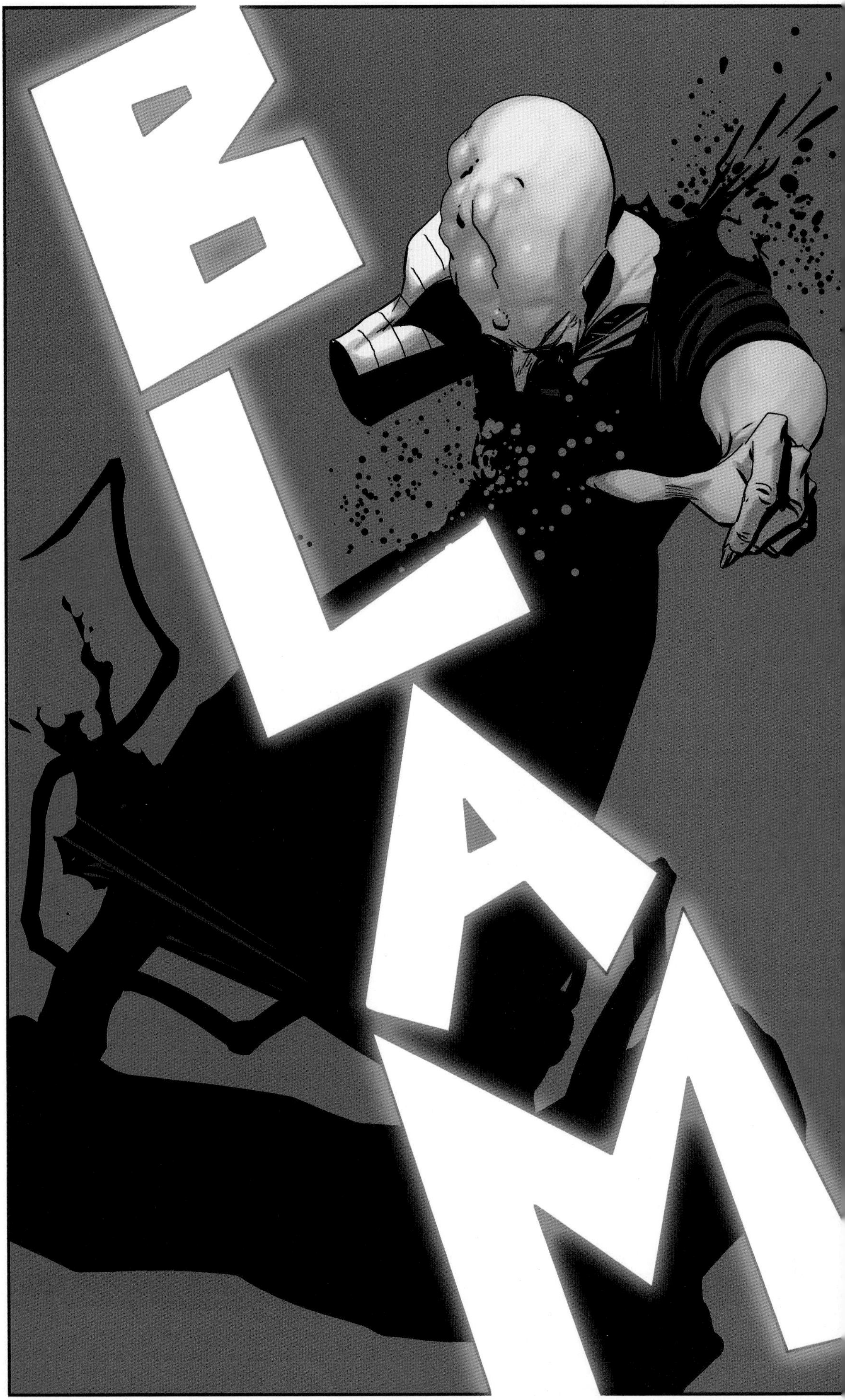
BLAM

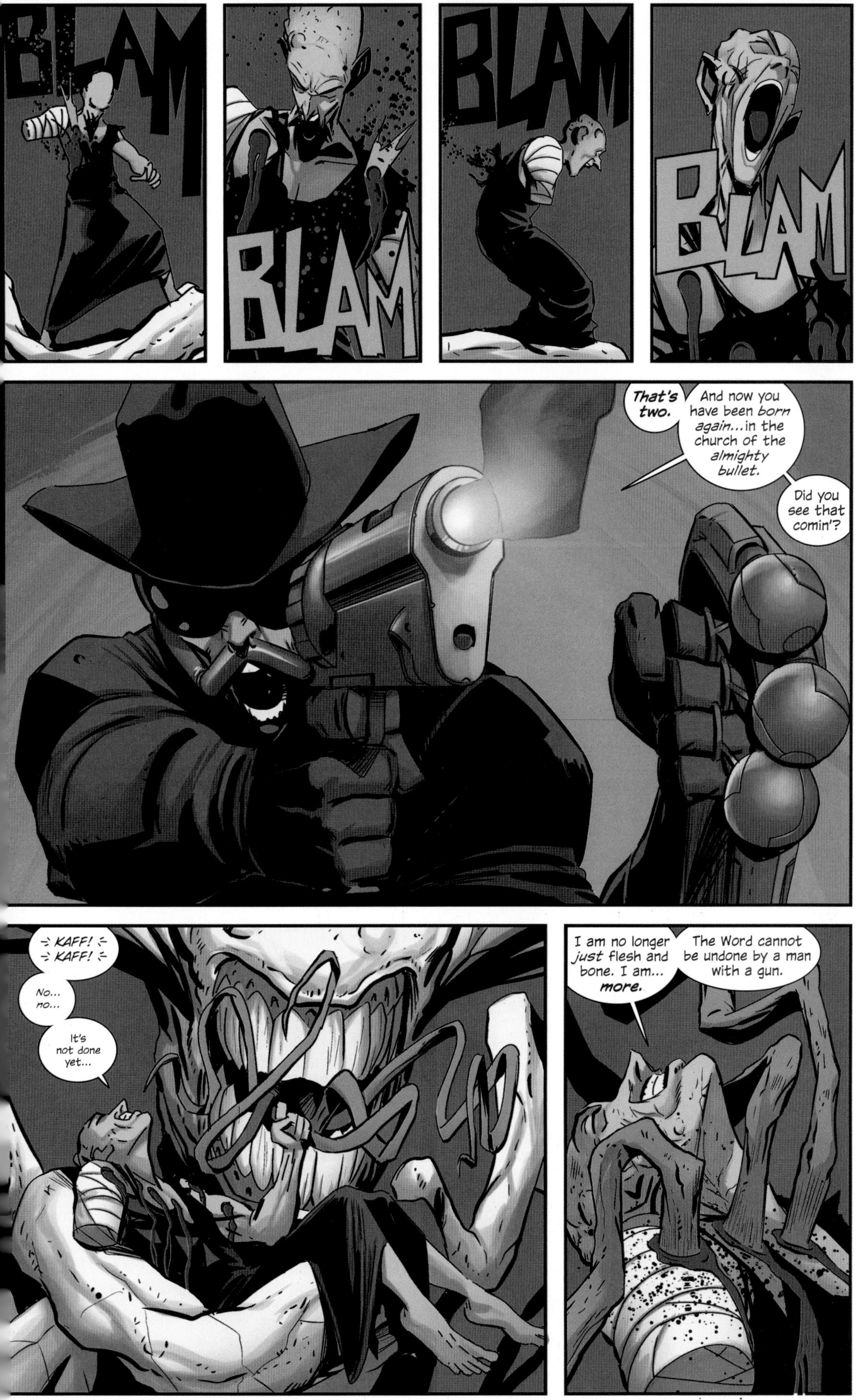
BLAM
BLAM
BLAM
BLAM
That's two.
And now you have been born again...in the church of the almighty bullet.
Did you see that comin'?
KAFF! KAFF!
No... no...
It's not done yet...
I am no longer just flesh and bone. I am... more.
The Word cannot be undone by a man with a gun.

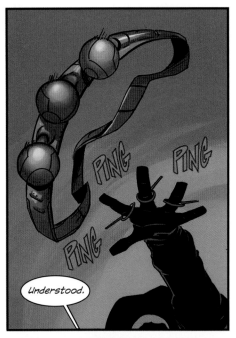

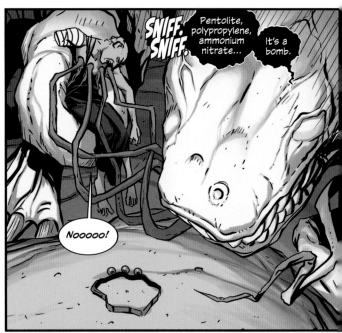

SNIFF. SNIFF.

Pentolite, polypropylene, ammonium nitrate...

It's a bomb.

Nooooo!

Understood.

≾ *Hurk!* ≿
≾ *Hurk!* ≿

I...I... judge them, Buer. All of them.

Pilgrims!

The Prophet has spoken

Kill them!

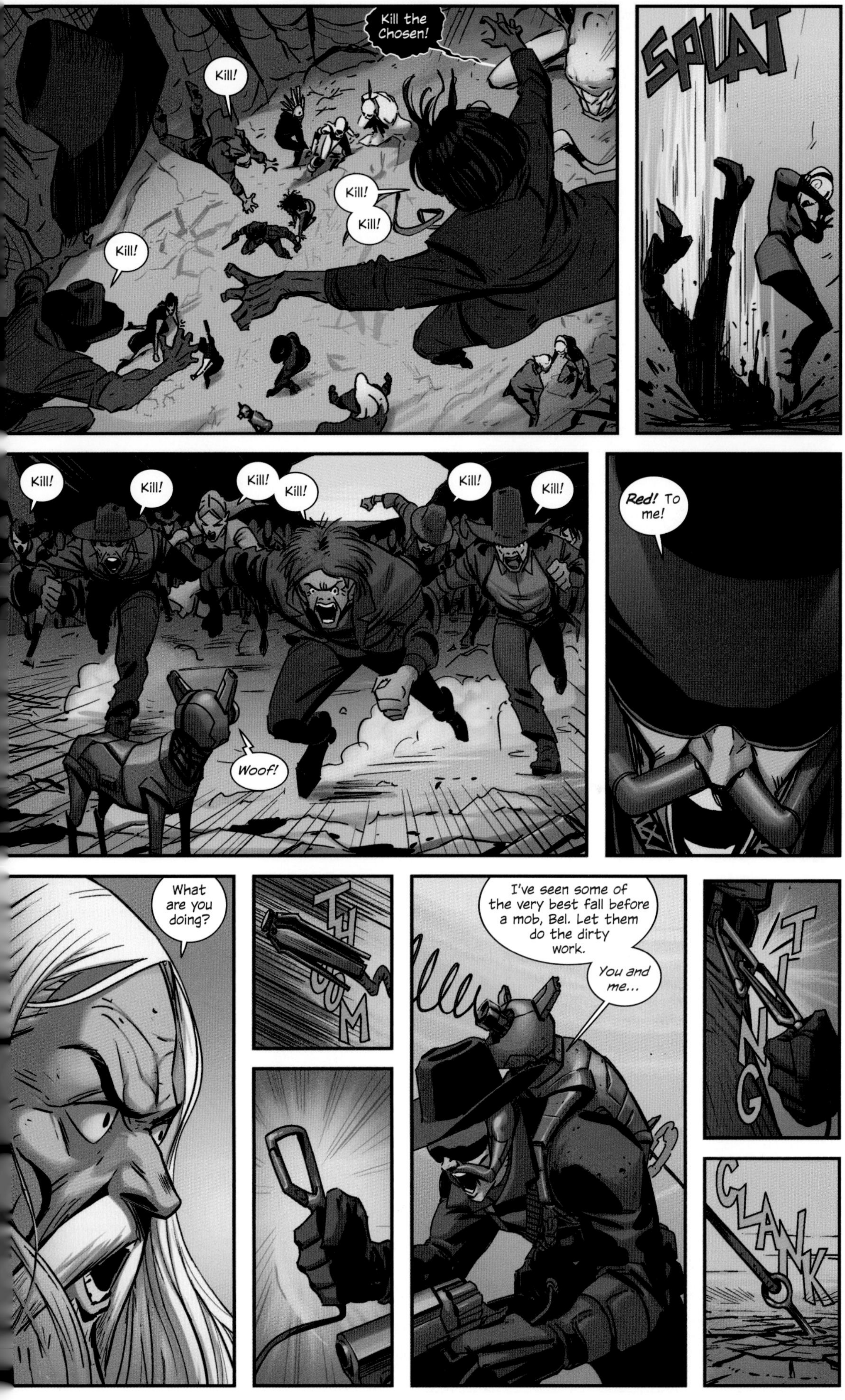

Kill the Chosen!
Kill!
Kill!
Kill!
Kill!
SPLAT
Kill!
Kill!
Kill!
Kill!
Kill!
Kill!
Woof!
Red! To me!
What are you doing?
THOOM
I've seen some of the very best fall before a mob, Bel. Let them do the dirty work.
You and me...
TING
CLANK

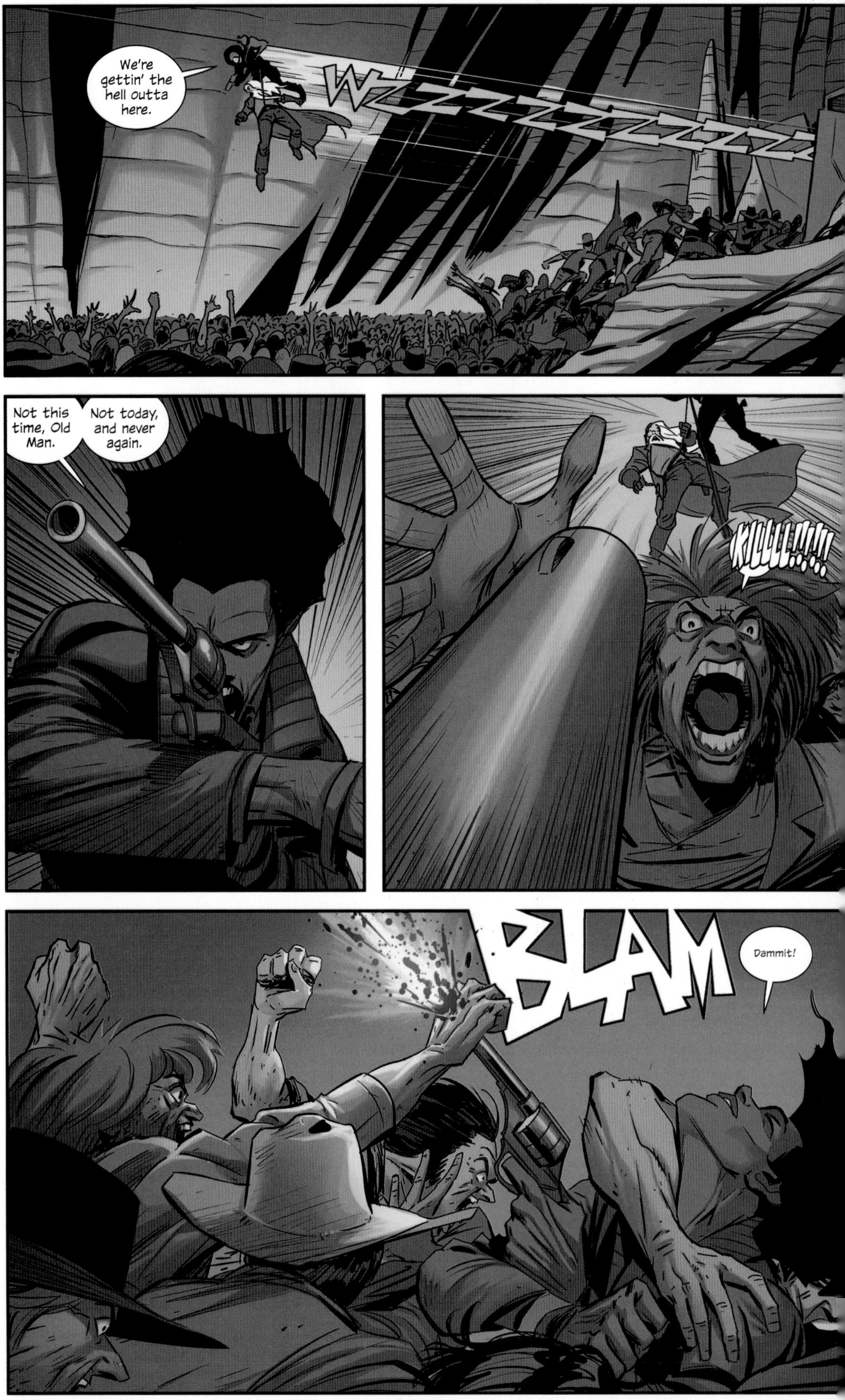
We're gettin' the hell outta here.
WZZZZZZZZZZ
Not this time, Old Man.
Not today, and never again.
KILLLL!!!!!
BLAM
Dammit!

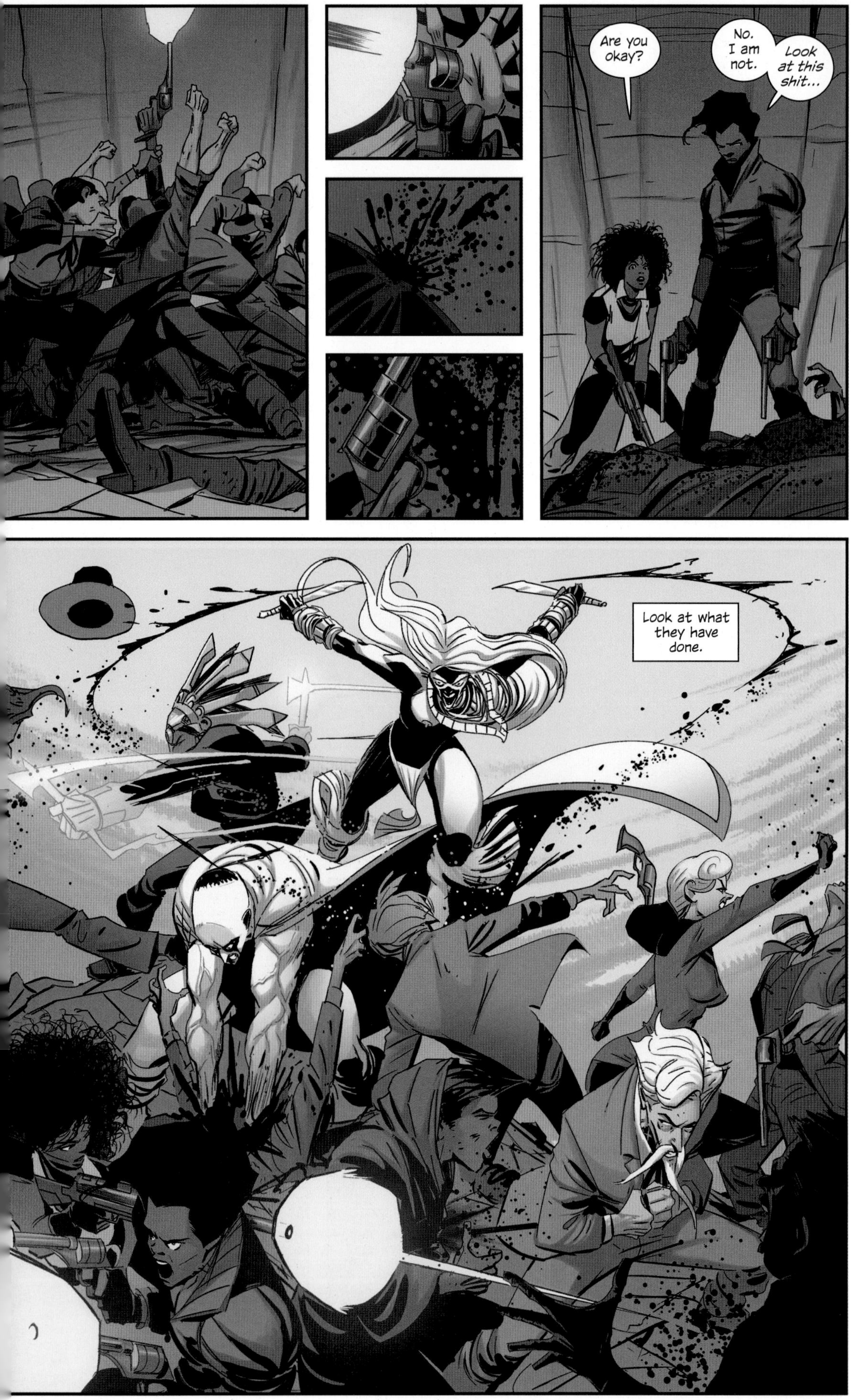

Are you okay?
No. I am not.
Look at this shit...
Look at what they have done.

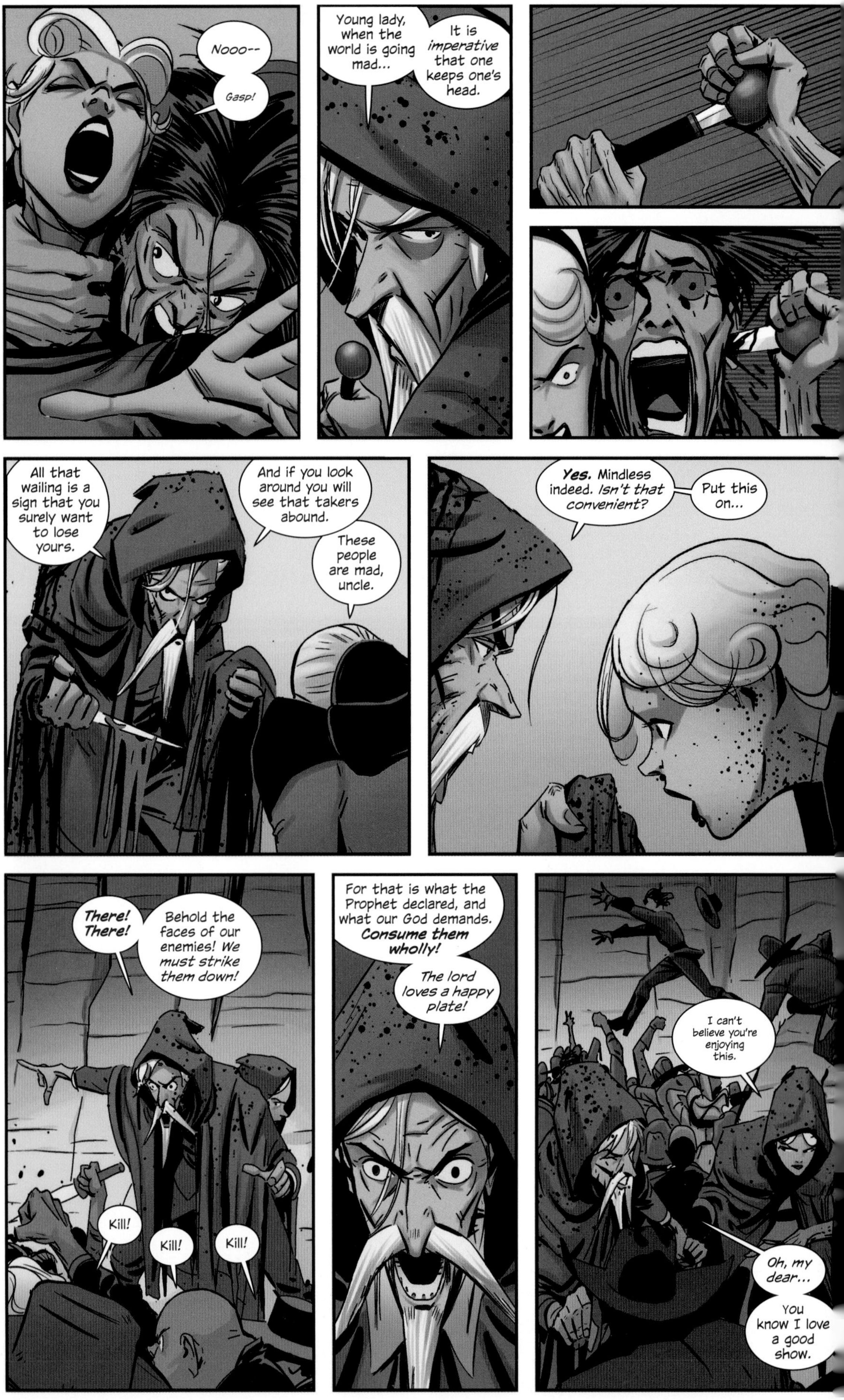
Nooo--
Gasp!
Young lady, when the world is going mad...
It is *imperative* that one keeps one's head.
All that wailing is a sign that you surely want to lose yours.
And if you look around you will see that takers abound.
These people are mad, uncle.
Yes. Mindless indeed. *Isn't that convenient?*
Put this on...
There! There!
Behold the faces of our enemies! We *must strike them down!*
Kill!
Kill!
Kill!
For that is what the Prophet declared, and what our God demands. ***Consume them wholly!***
The lord loves a happy plate!
I can't believe you're enjoying this.
Oh, my dear...
You know I love a good show.

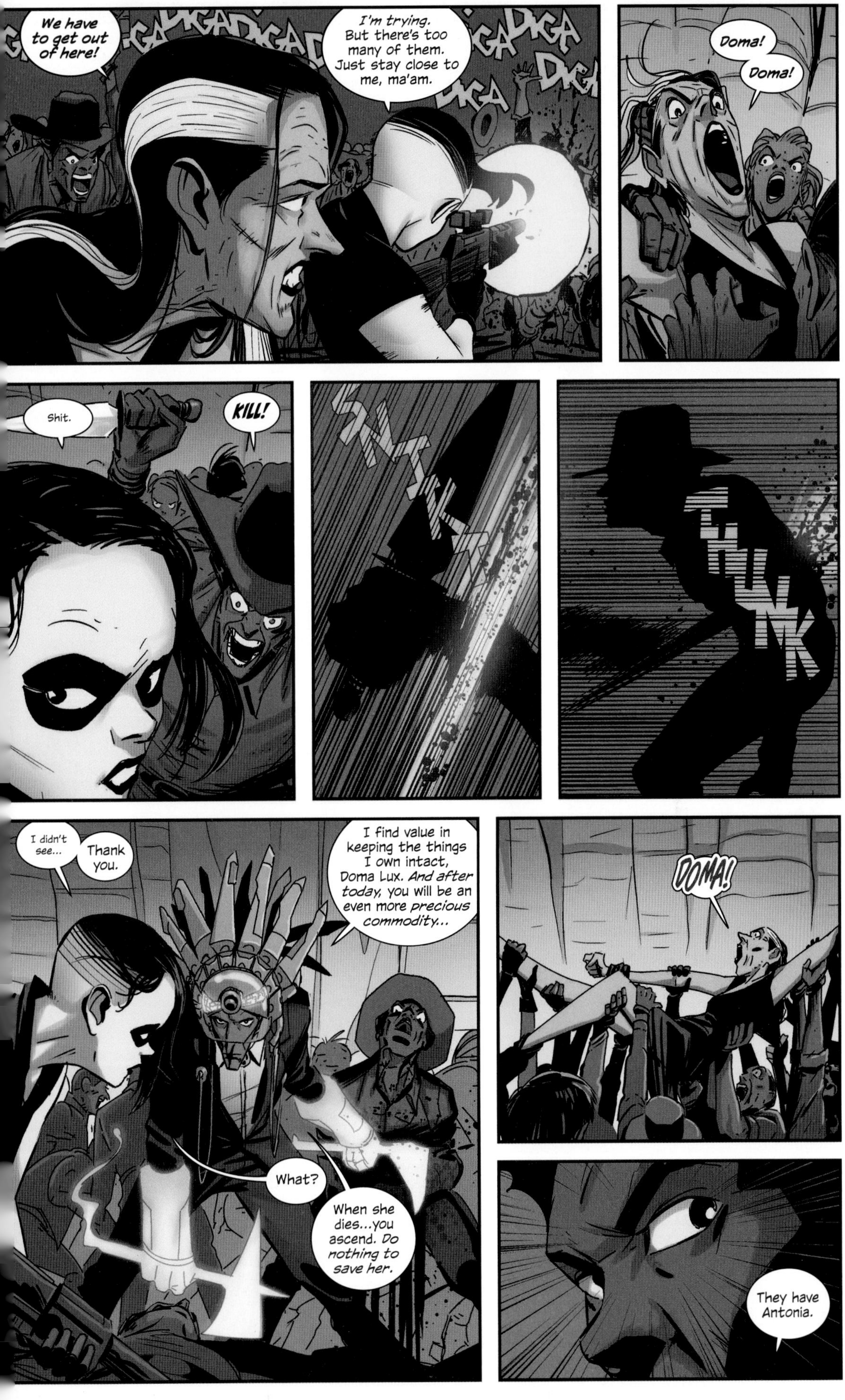

We have to get out of here!
I'm trying. But there's too many of them. Just stay close to me, ma'am.
Doma!
Doma!
Shit.
KILL!
THUNK
I didn't see...
Thank you.
I find value in keeping the things I own intact, Doma Lux. *And after today,* you will be an even more *precious commodity...*
What?
When she dies...you ascend. *Do nothing to save her.*
DOMA!
They have Antonia.

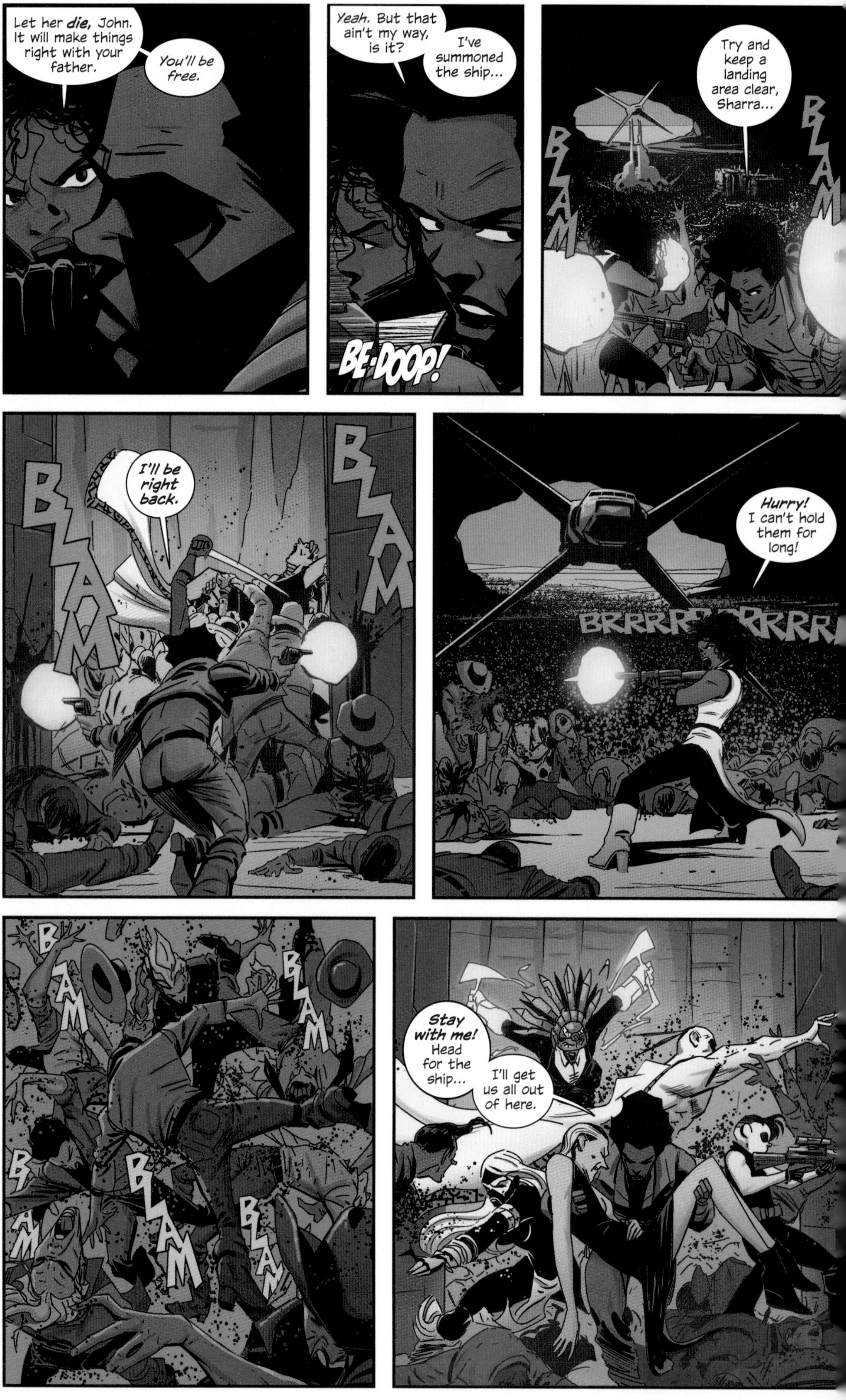

Let her *die,* John. It will make things right with your father.
You'll be free.
Yeah. But that ain't my way, is it?
I've summoned the ship...
BE-DOOP!
Try and keep a landing area clear, Sharra...
BLAM
BLAM
BLAM
I'll be right back.
BLAM
BLAM
Hurry! I can't hold them for long!
BRRRRRRRRRRRR
BLAM
BLAM
BLAM
BLAM
BLAM
BLAM
Stay with me! Head for the ship...
I'll get us all out of here.

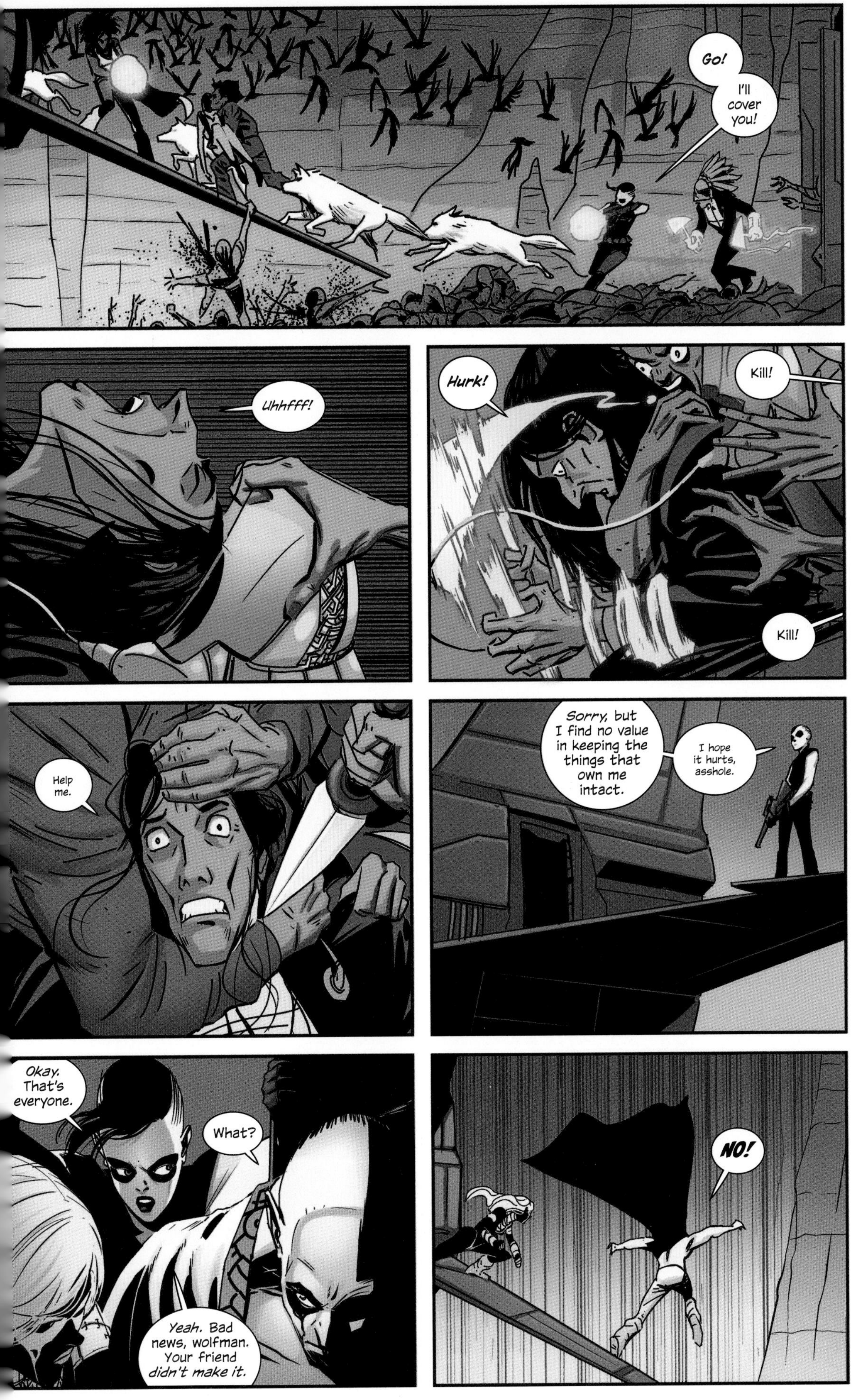
Go!
I'll cover you!
Uhhfff!
Hurk!
Kill!
Kill!
Help me.
Sorry, but I find no value in keeping the things that own me intact.
I hope it hurts, asshole.
Okay. That's everyone.
What?
Yeah. Bad news, wolfman. Your friend didn't make it.
NO!

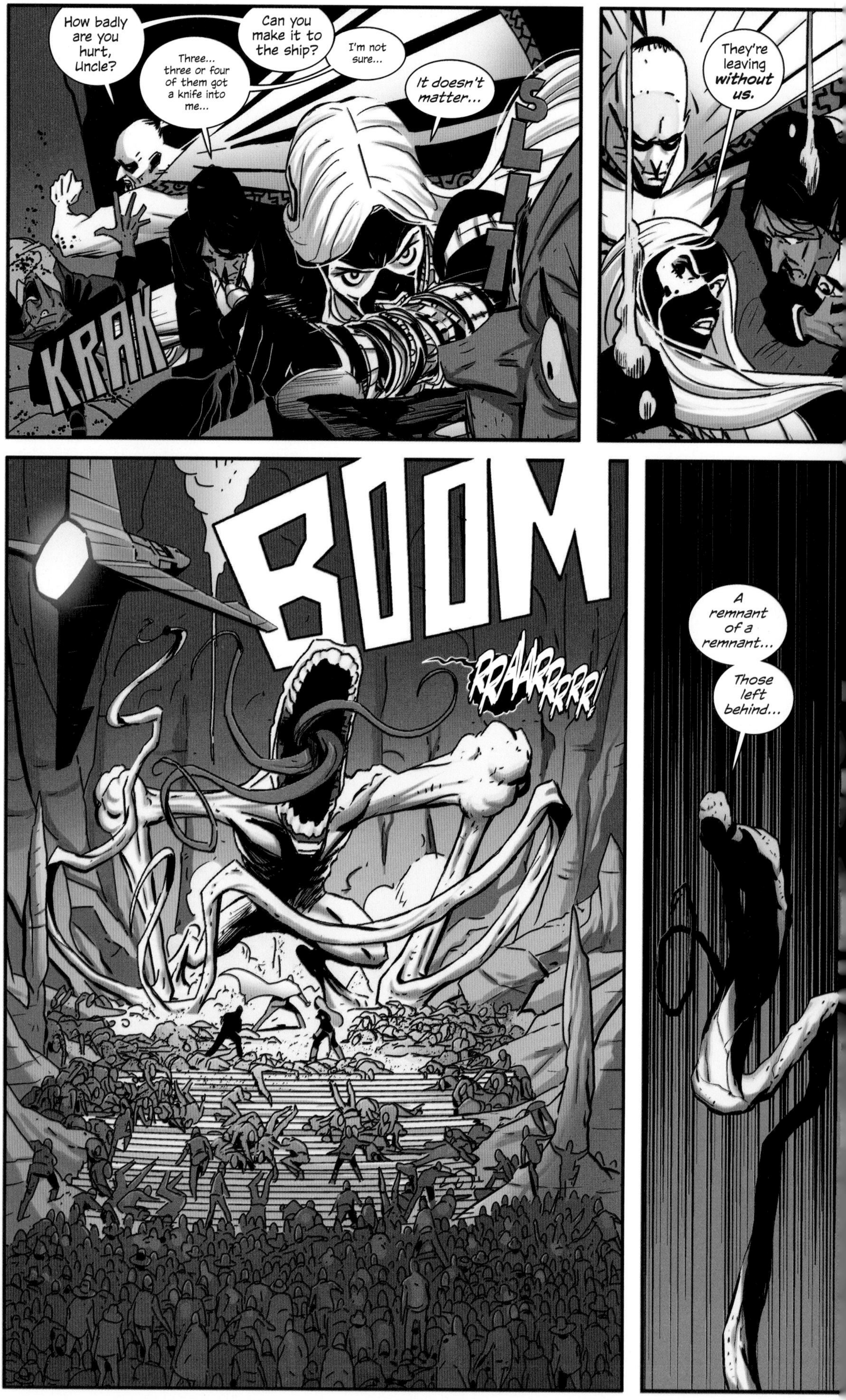
How badly are you hurt, Uncle?
Three... three or four of them got a knife into me...
Can you make it to the ship?
I'm not sure...
It doesn't matter...
SLIT
KRAK
They're leaving **without us.**
BOOM
RRAARRRRR!
A remnant of a remnant...
Those left behind...

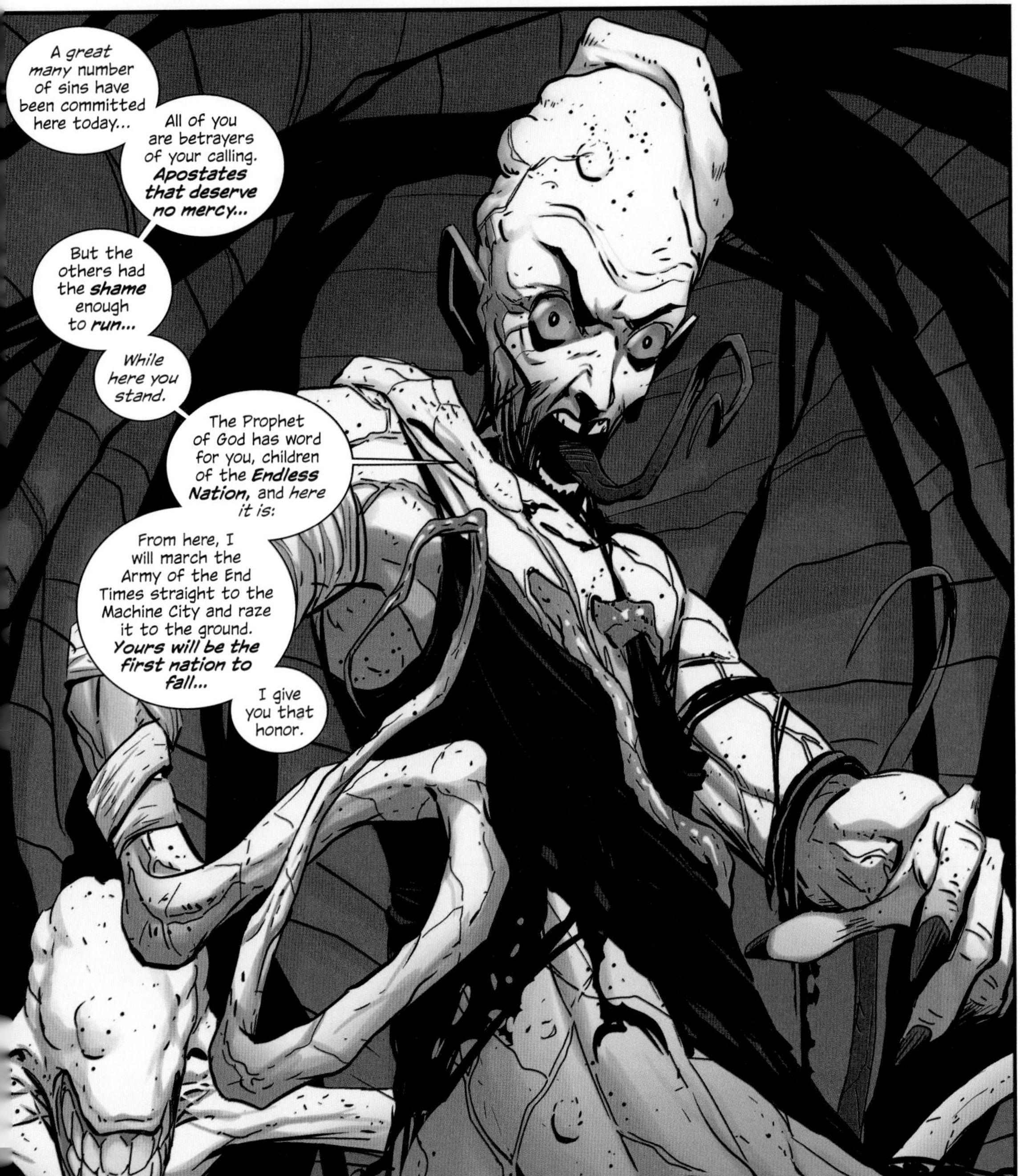
A great many number of sins have been committed here today...
All of you are betrayers of your calling. Apostates that deserve no mercy...
But the others had the shame enough to run...
While here you stand.
The Prophet of God has word for you, children of the Endless Nation, and here it is:
From here, I will march the Army of the End Times straight to the Machine City and raze it to the ground. Yours will be the first nation to fall...
I give you that honor.

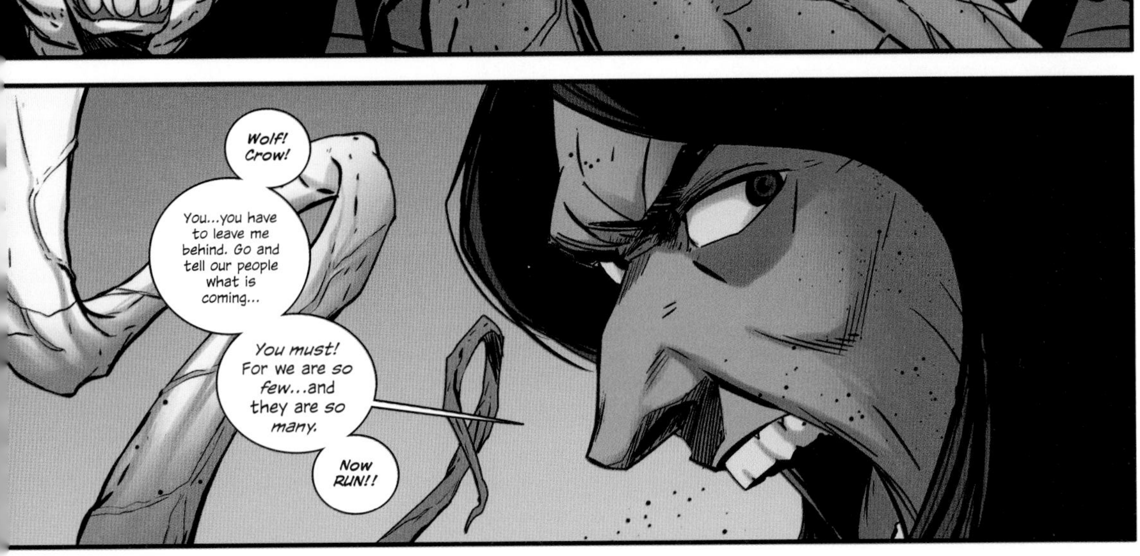
Wolf! Crow!
You...you have to leave me behind. Go and tell our people what is coming...
You must! For we are so few...and they are so many.
Now RUN!!

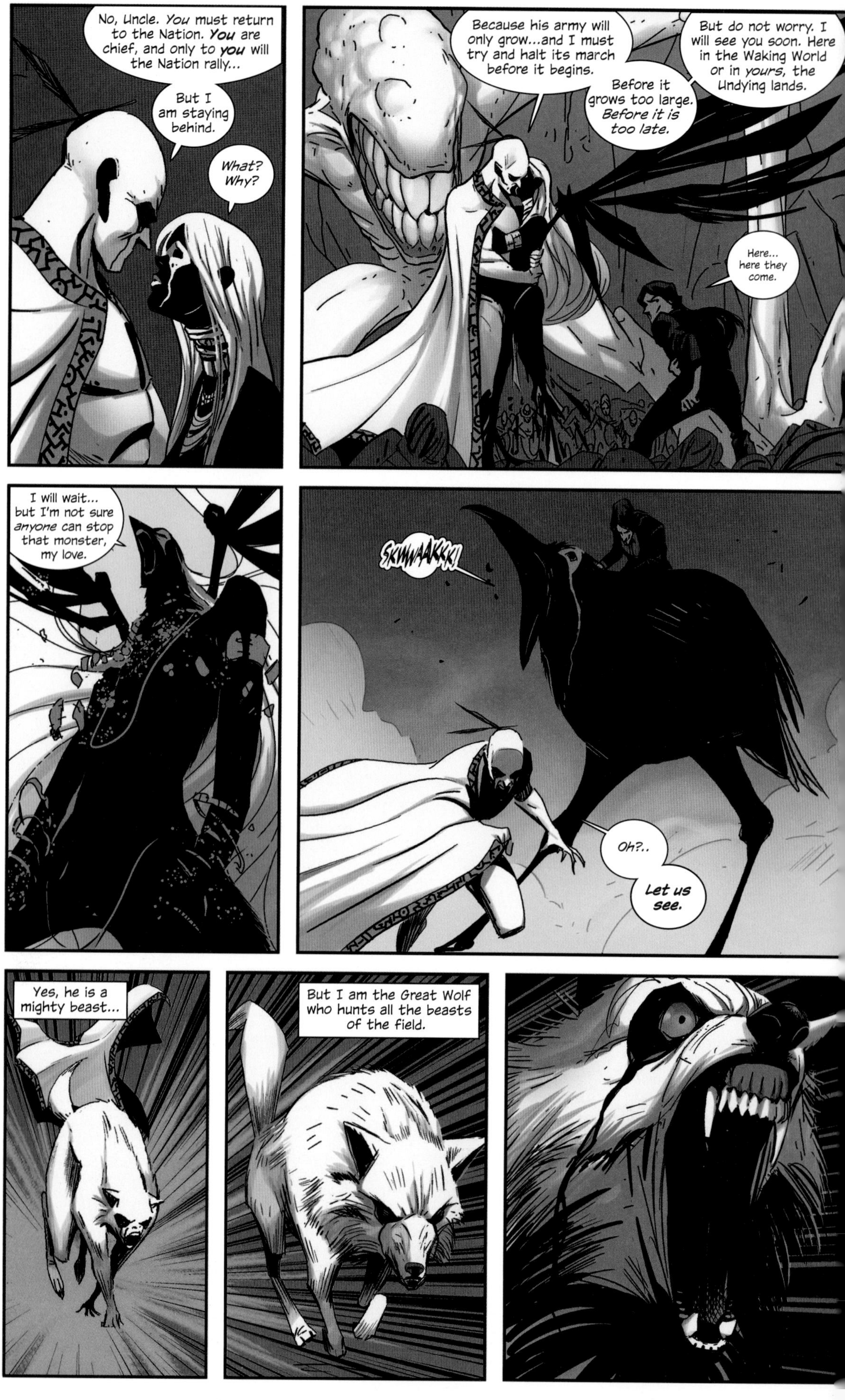
No, Uncle. *You* must return to the Nation. ***You*** are chief, and only to ***you*** will the Nation rally...
But I am staying behind.
What? Why?
Because his army will only grow...and I must try and halt its march before it begins.
Before it grows too large. *Before it is too late.*
But do not worry. I will see you soon. Here in the Waking World or in *yours*, the Undying lands.
Here... here they come.
I will wait... but I'm not sure *anyone* can stop that monster, my love.
SKWAAKKK!
Oh?..
Let us see.
Yes, he is a mighty beast...
But I am the Great Wolf who hunts all the beasts of the field.

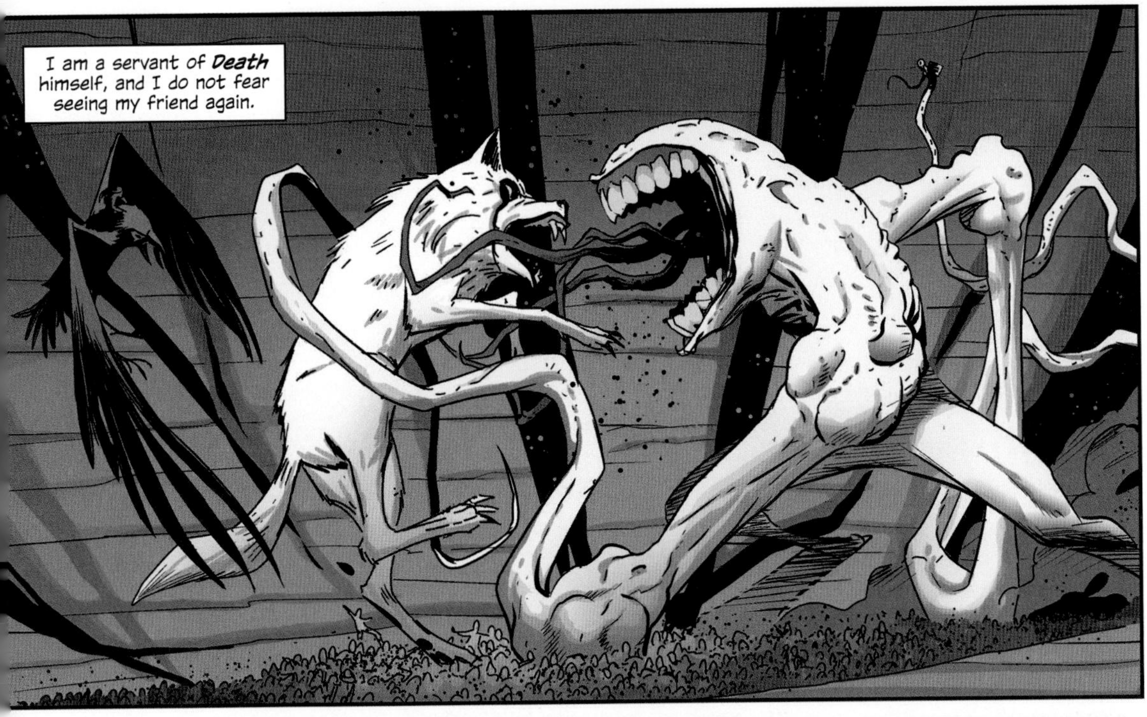
I am a servant of Death himself, and I do not fear seeing my friend again.
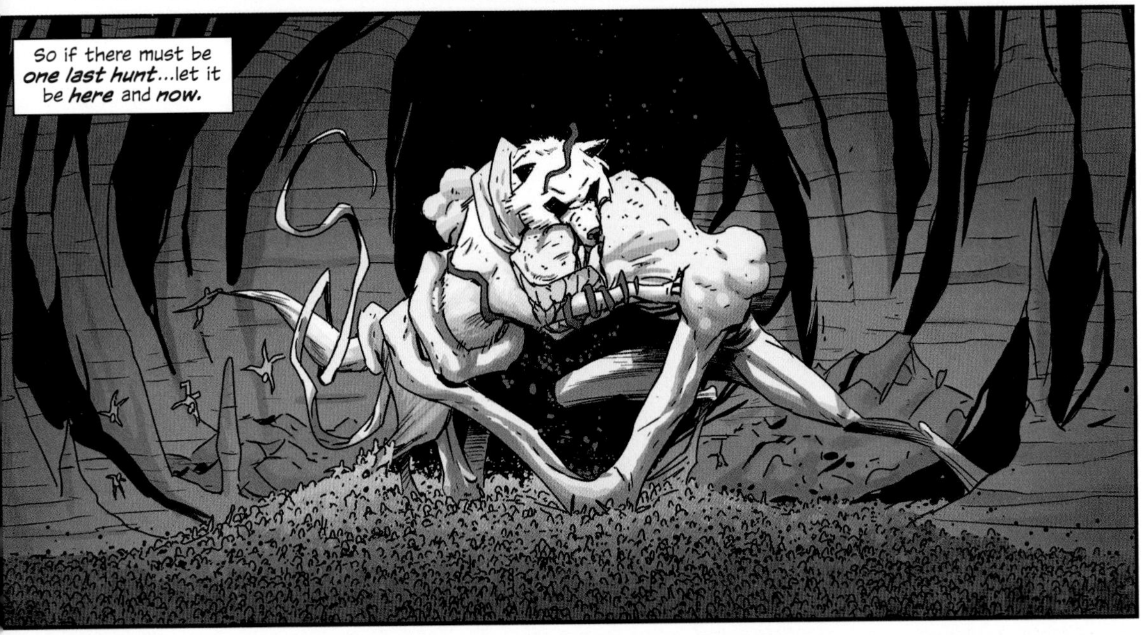
So if there must be one last hunt...let it be here and now.
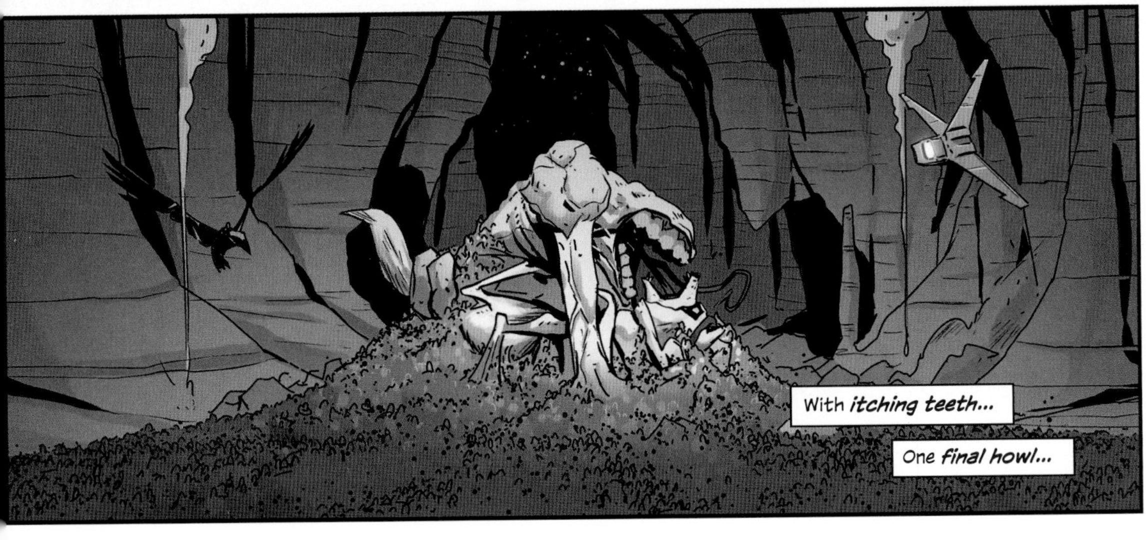
With itching teeth...
One final howl...

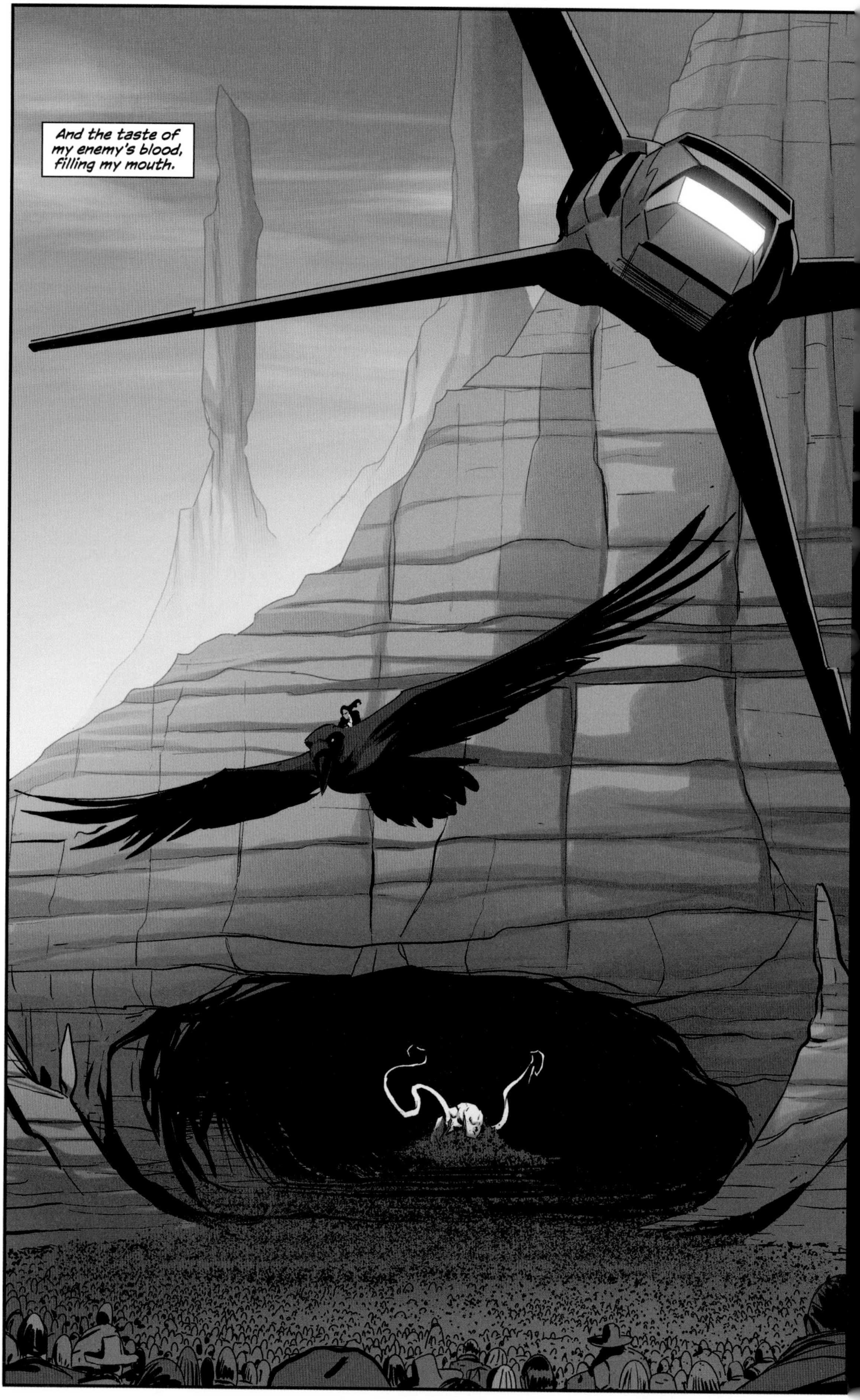
And the taste of my enemy's blood, filling my mouth.

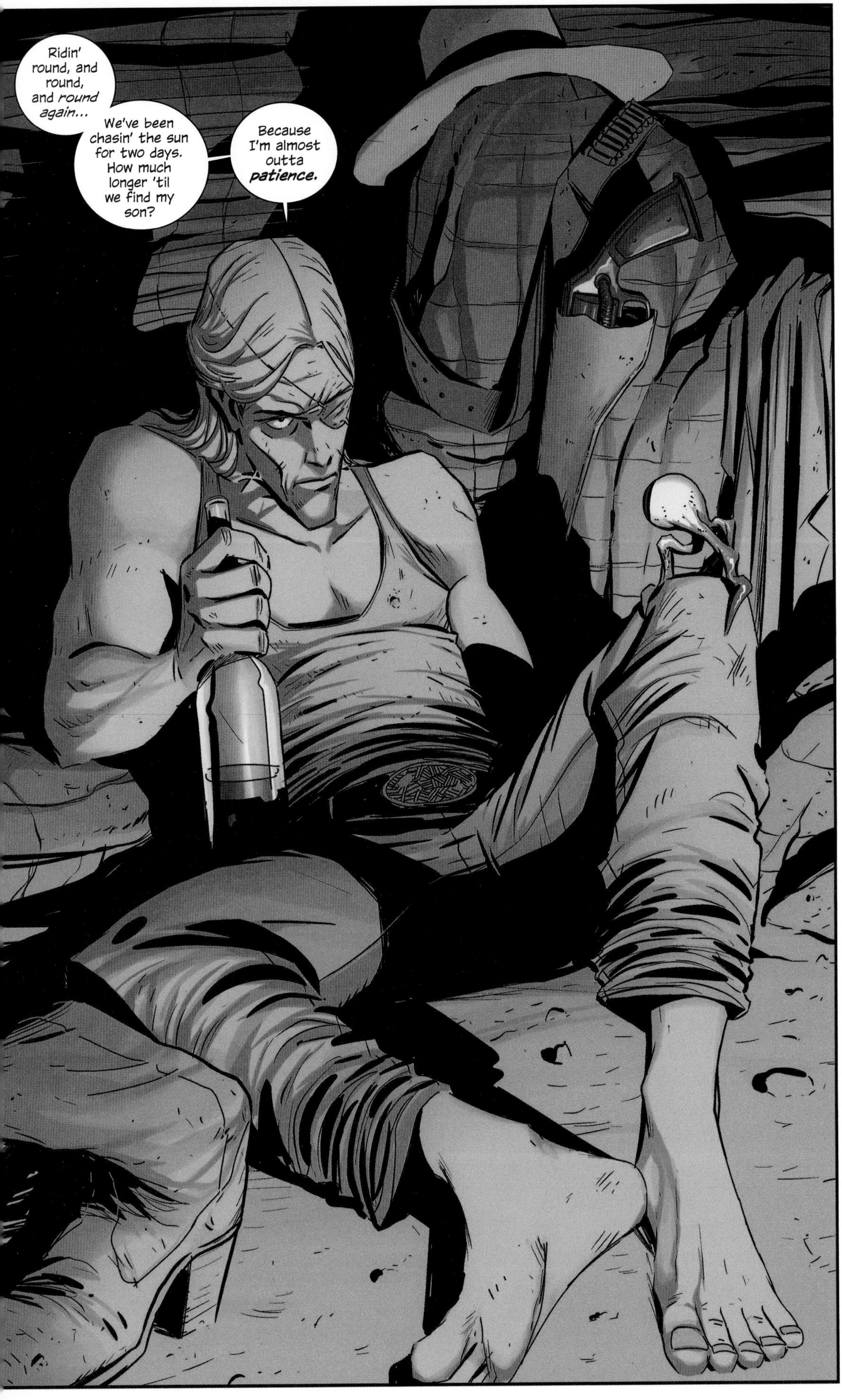
Ridin' round, and round, and *round* again...
We've been chasin' the sun for two days. How much longer 'til we find my son?
Because I'm almost outta ***patience.***

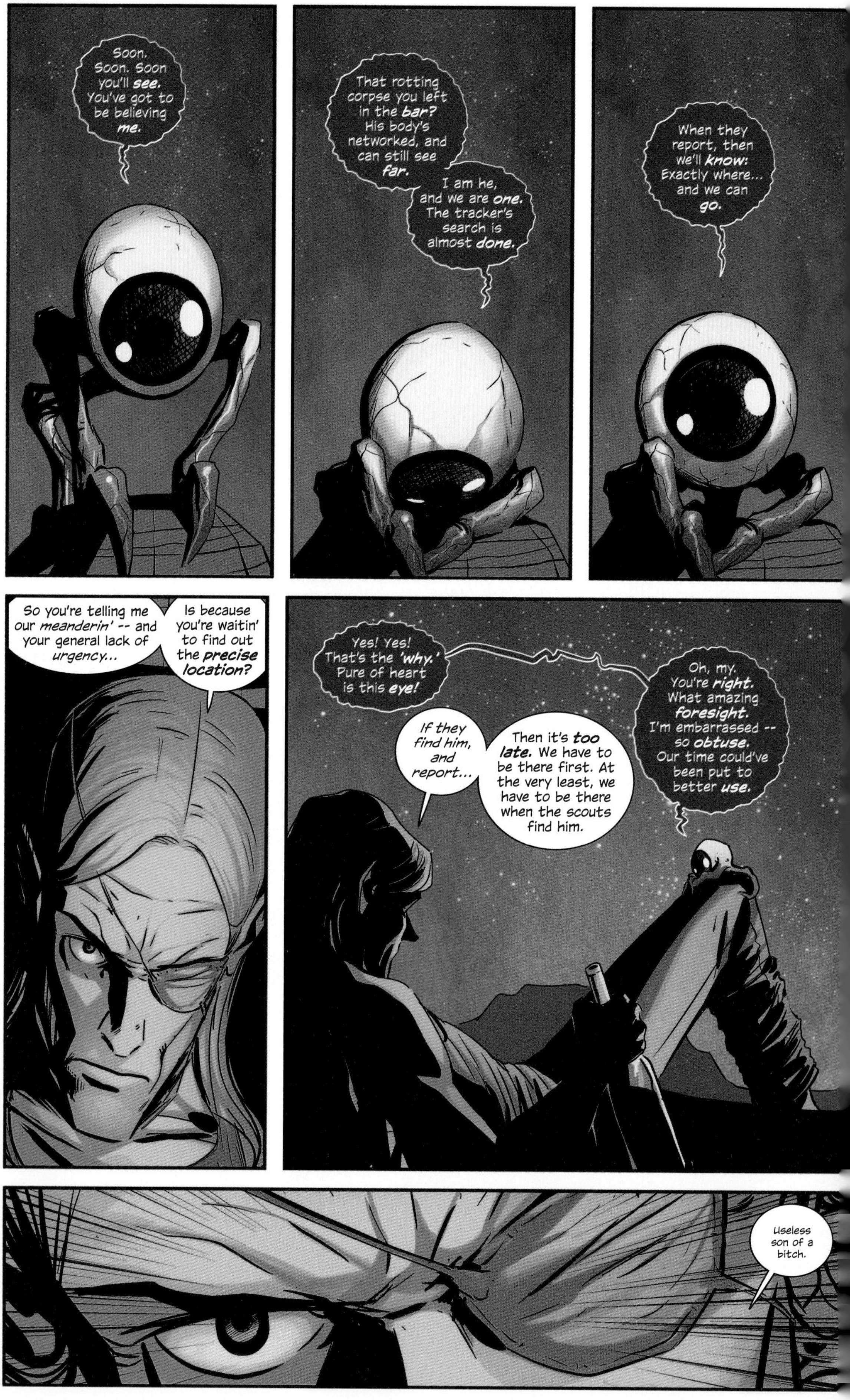
Soon. Soon. Soon you'll *see.* You've got to be believing *me.*
That rotting corpse you left in the *bar?* His body's networked, and can still see *far.*
I am he, and we are *one.* The tracker's search is almost *done.*
When they report, then we'll *know:* Exactly where... and we can *go.*
So you're telling me our *meanderin'* -- and your general lack of *urgency...*
Is because you're waitin' to find out the *precise location?*
Yes! Yes! That's the *'why.'* Pure of heart is this *eye!*
Oh, my. You're *right.* What amazing *foresight.* I'm embarrassed -- so *obtuse.* Our time could've been put to better *use.*
If they find him, and report...
Then it's *too late.* We have to be there first. At the very least, we have to be there when the scouts find him.
Useless son of a bitch.

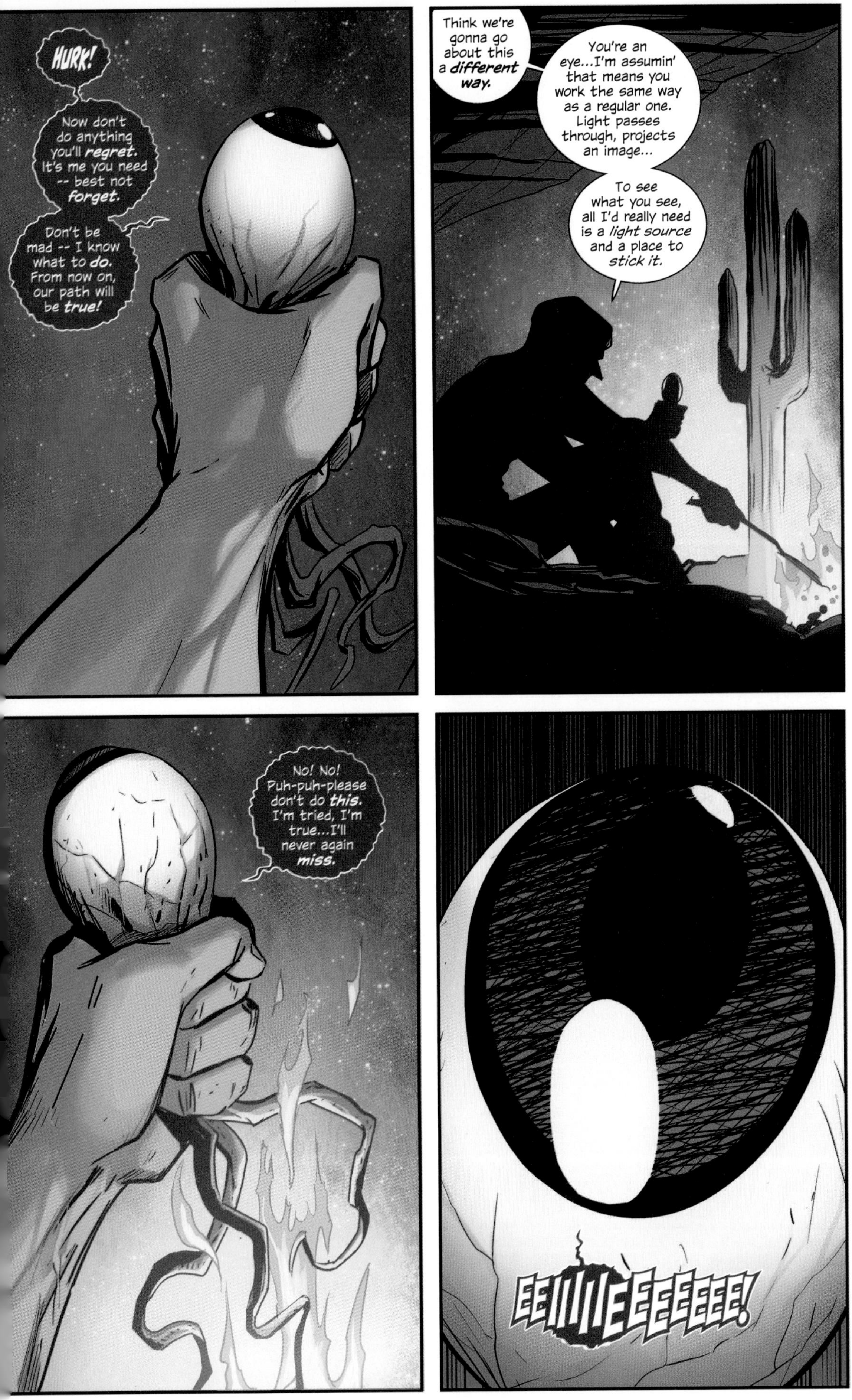
HURK!
Now don't do anything you'll *regret*. It's me you need -- best not *forget*.
Don't be mad -- I know what to *do*. From now on, our path will be *true!*
Think we're gonna go about this a ***different way.***
You're an eye...I'm assumin' that means you work the same way as a regular one. Light passes through, projects an image...
To see what you see, all I'd really need is a *light source* and a place to *stick it*.
No! No! Puh-puh-please don't do ***this.*** I'm tried, I'm true...I'll never again ***miss.***
EEIIIIIEEEEEEE!

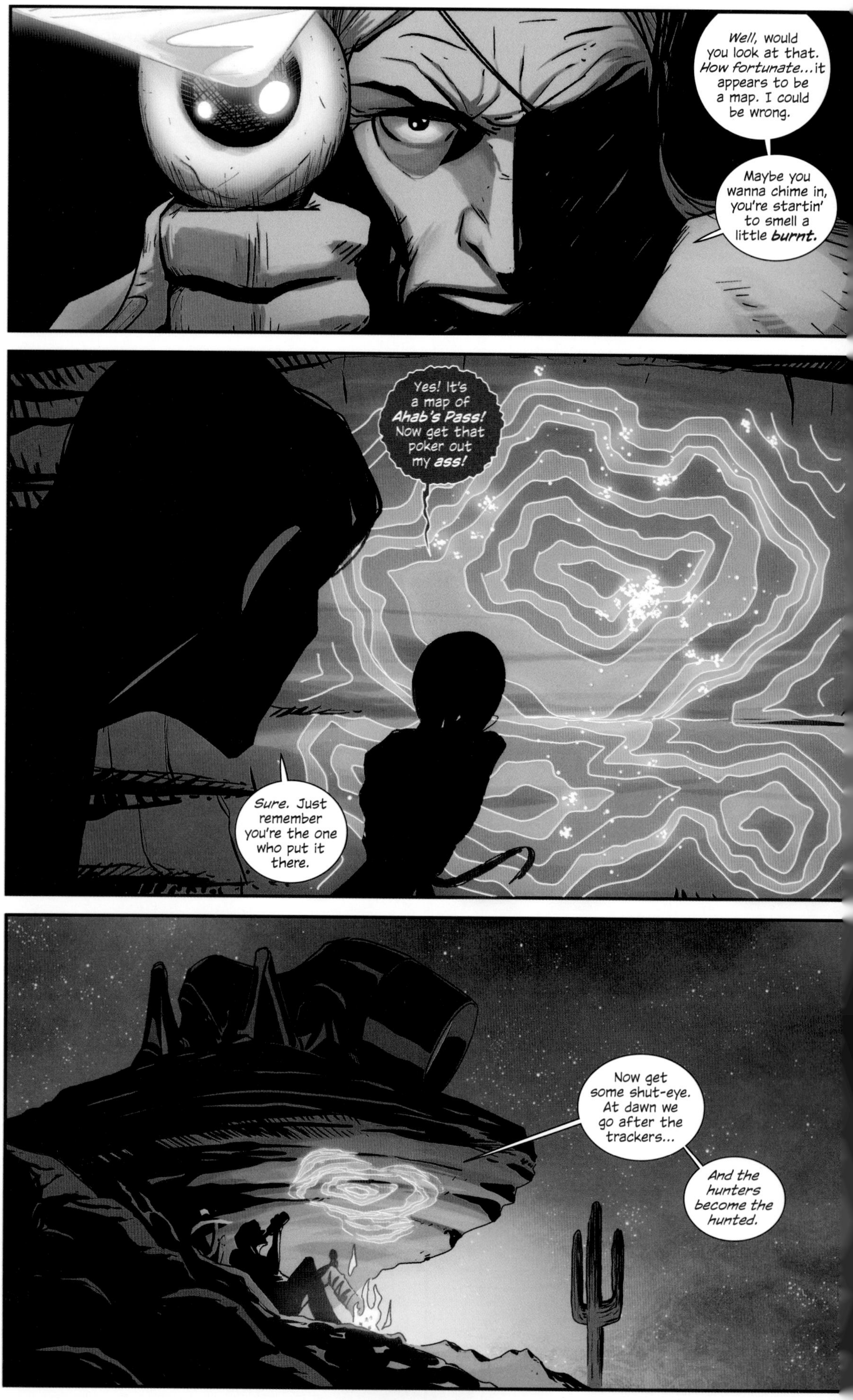
Well, would you look at that. *How fortunate*...it appears to be a map. I could be wrong.
Maybe you wanna chime in, you're startin' to smell a little **burnt.**
Yes! It's a map of ***Ahab's Pass!*** Now get that poker out my ***ass!***
Sure. Just remember you're the one who put it there.
Now get some shut-eye. At dawn we go after the trackers...
And the hunters become the hunted.

RUN.

RUN AS **FAST** AS YOU CAN.

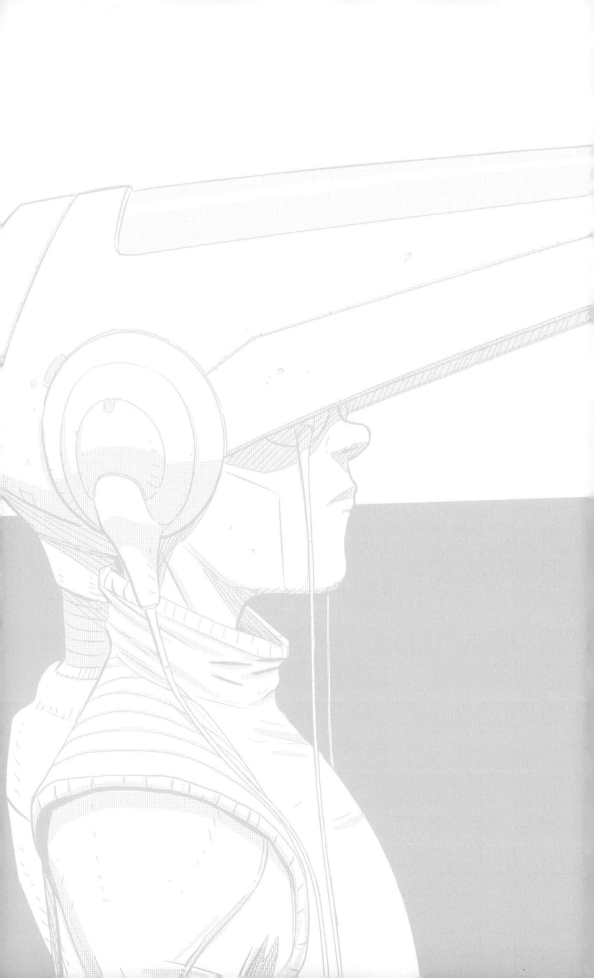

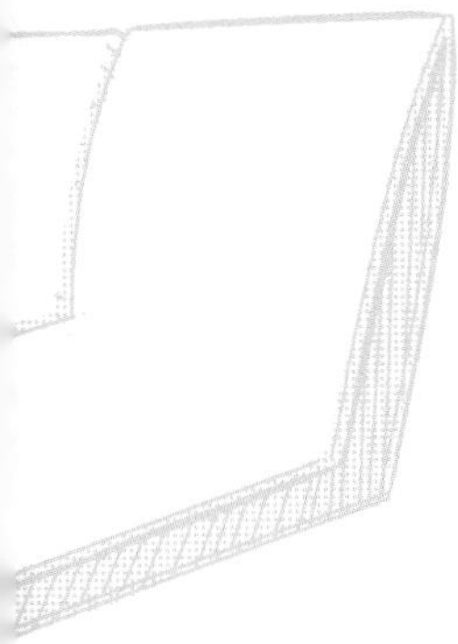

TWENTY-EIGHT:
WE **HUNT** THE
CHILDREN

THE **FUTURE** IS COMING TO
KILL YOU.

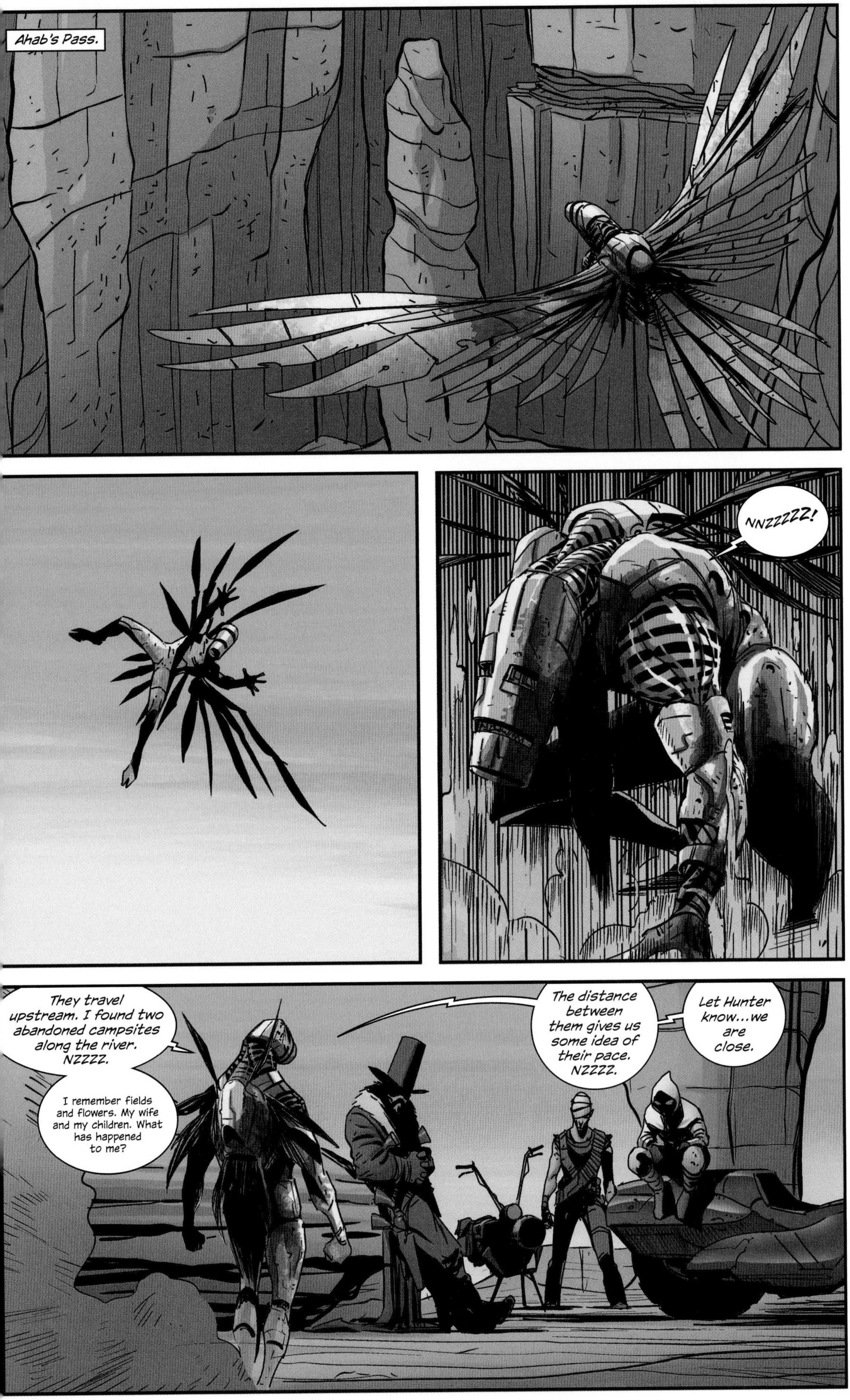
Ahab's Pass.
NNZZZZZ!
They travel upstream. I found two abandoned campsites along the river. NZZZZ.
I remember fields and flowers. My wife and my children. What has happened to me?
The distance between them gives us some idea of their pace. NZZZZ.
Let Hunter know...we are close.

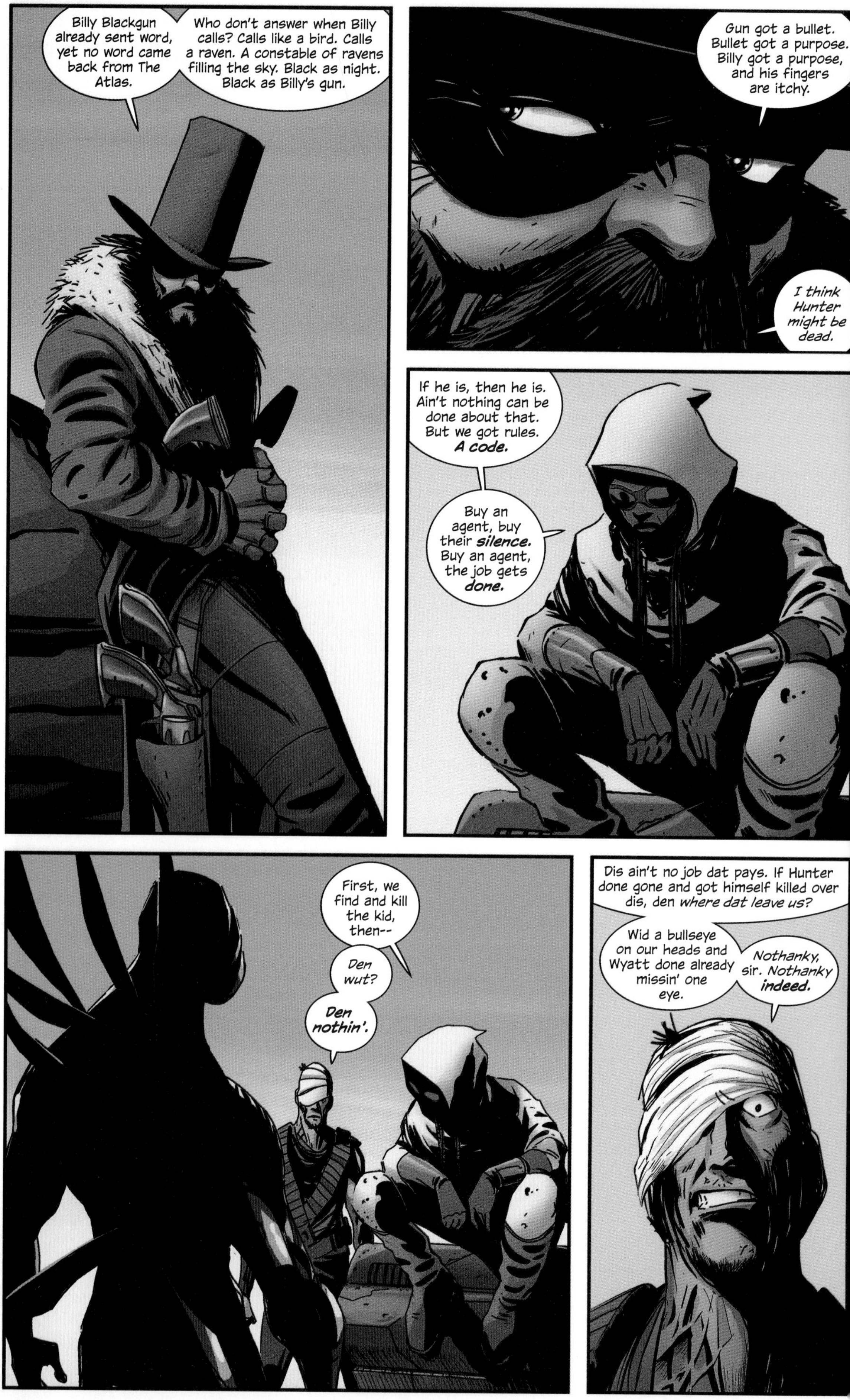
Billy Blackgun already sent word, yet no word came back from The Atlas.
Who don't answer when Billy calls? Calls like a bird. Calls a raven. A constable of ravens filling the sky. Black as night. Black as Billy's gun.
Gun got a bullet. Bullet got a purpose. Billy got a purpose, and his fingers are itchy.
I think Hunter might be dead.
If he is, then he is. Ain't nothing can be done about that. But we got rules. ***A code.***
Buy an agent, buy their ***silence.*** Buy an agent, the job gets ***done.***
First, we find and kill the kid, then--
Den wut?
Den nothin'.
Dis ain't no job dat pays. If Hunter done gone and got himself killed over dis, den *where dat leave us?*
Wid a bullseye on our heads and Wyatt done already missin' one eye.
Nothanky, sir. *Nothanky* ***indeed.***

Billy ain't afraid of no bullseye. Put it on my head. Billy's head's on a swivel. Like a man possessed.

Spin it around. Turn it like a devil. A devil from hell. And hell's coming with me. With Billy.

Billy the demon. Blackgun Billy. I think we should split up.

NNZZZZZ!

Some stay and finish the job? Some hurry to The Atlas? No. Ursula is correct. NNZZZZ.

My son was Jonah. He was five and just learned to ride a bike. My daughter was Hannah. She loved to sing in the choir.

We finish the job first. It's what we do. NNZZZZ.

You're the best at uncovering things that want to stay hidden. NNZZZZ.

Incense. Why do I remember incense?

How should we proceed?

We have an approximation of where they are going to be. So we wait for the sun to set...

Look for their campfire in the night.

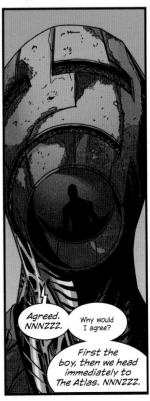

Agreed. NNNZZZ.

Why would I agree?

First the boy, then we head immediately to The Atlas. NNNZZZ.

Said it *once*, I say it *again.*

Ain't no money for us in dis job. Ain't no money, *ain't no us.*

Don't none you call Wyatt again 'til it pays!

I done wit all dis go fetch dog shit!

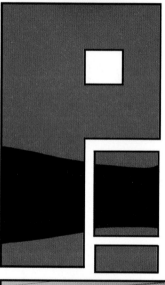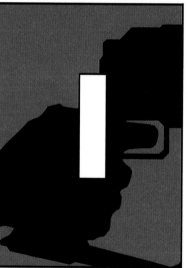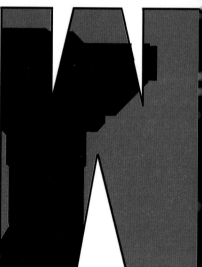

ARRGGHHHH!

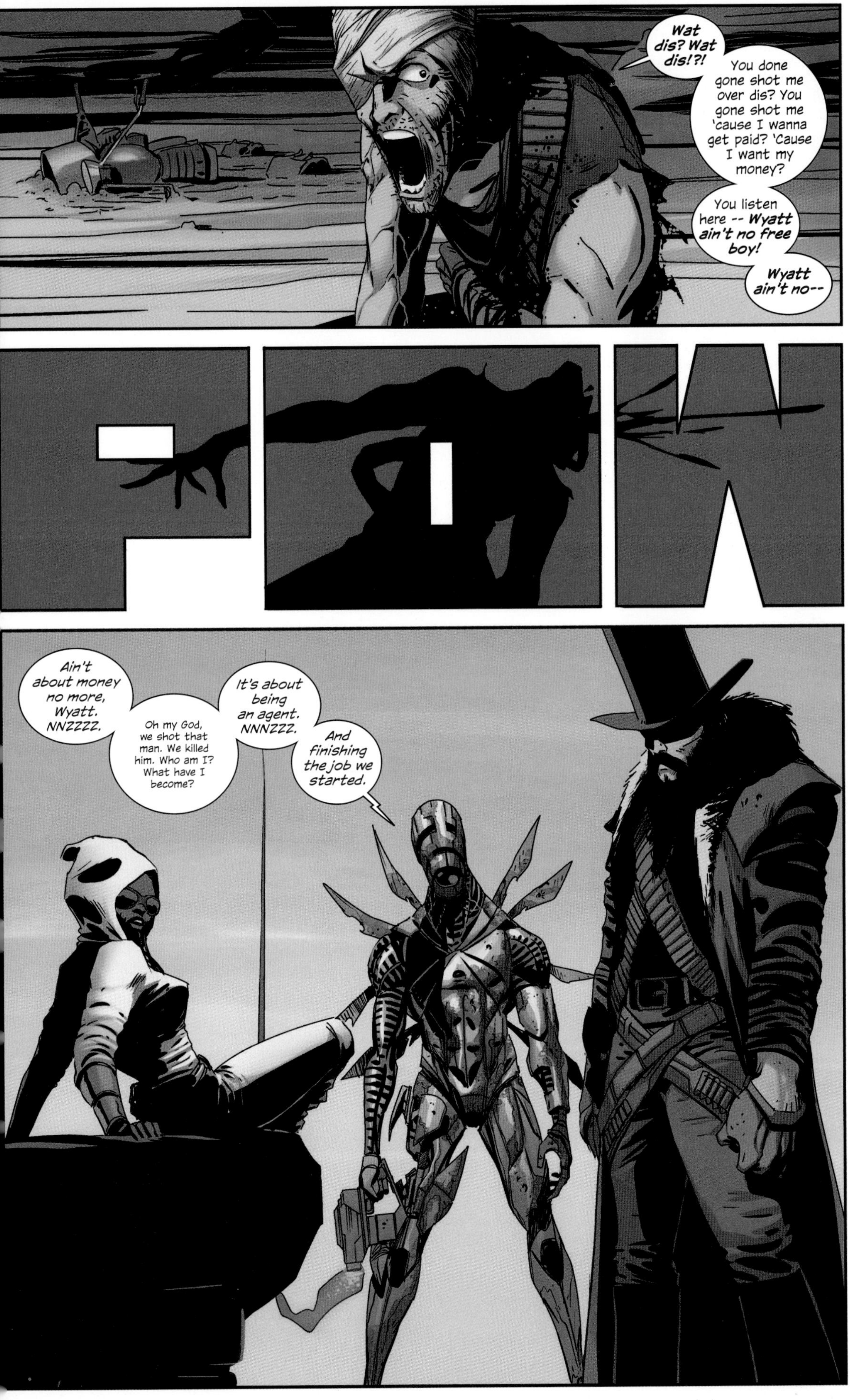
Wat dis? Wat dis!?!
You done gone shot me over dis? You gone shot me 'cause I wanna get paid? 'Cause I want my money?
You listen here -- Wyatt ain't no free boy!
Wyatt ain't no--
Ain't about money no more, Wyatt. NNZZZZ.
Oh my God, we shot that man. We killed him. Who am I? What have I become?
It's about being an agent. NNNZZZ.
And finishing the job we started.

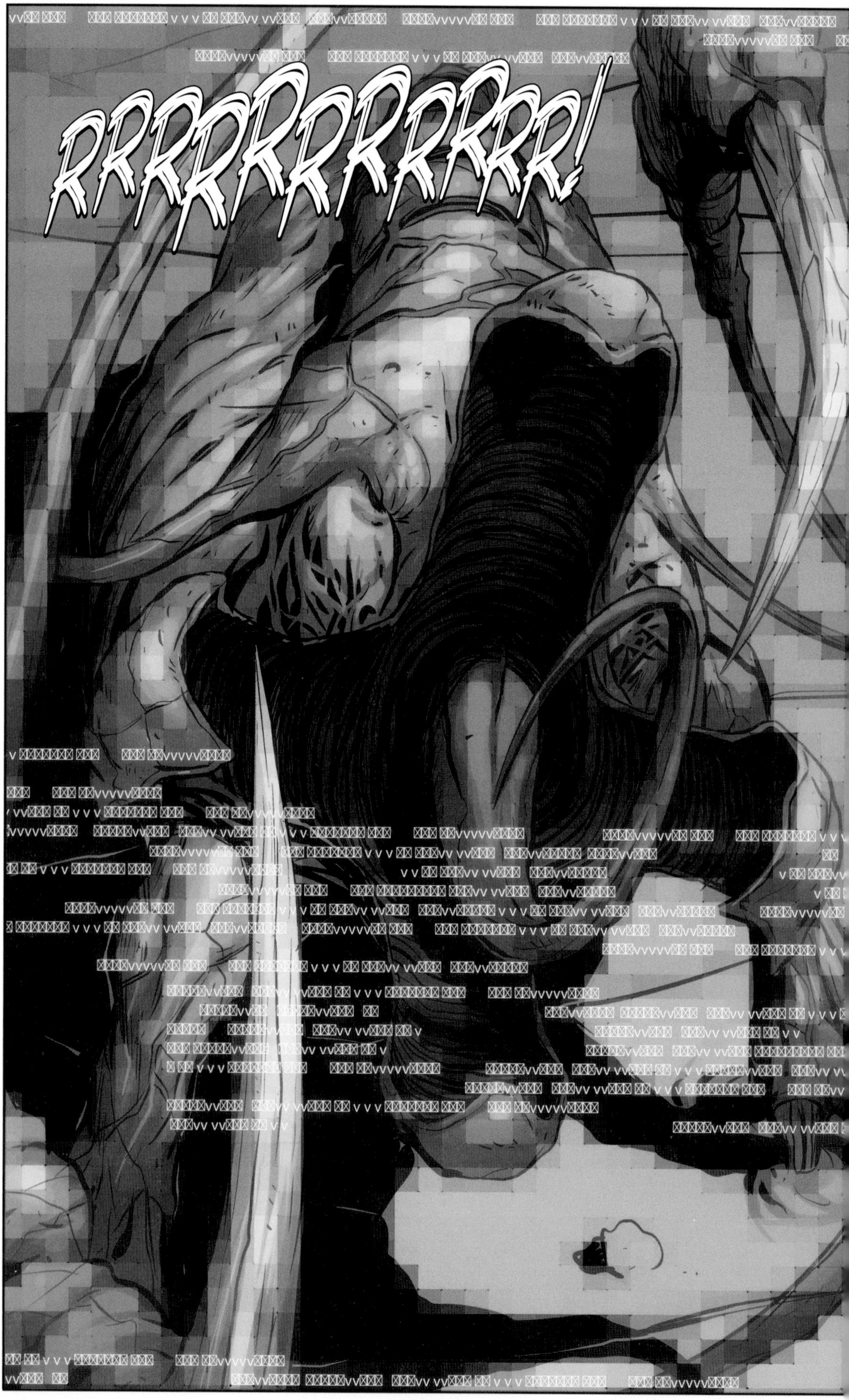
RRRRRRRRRRRRR!

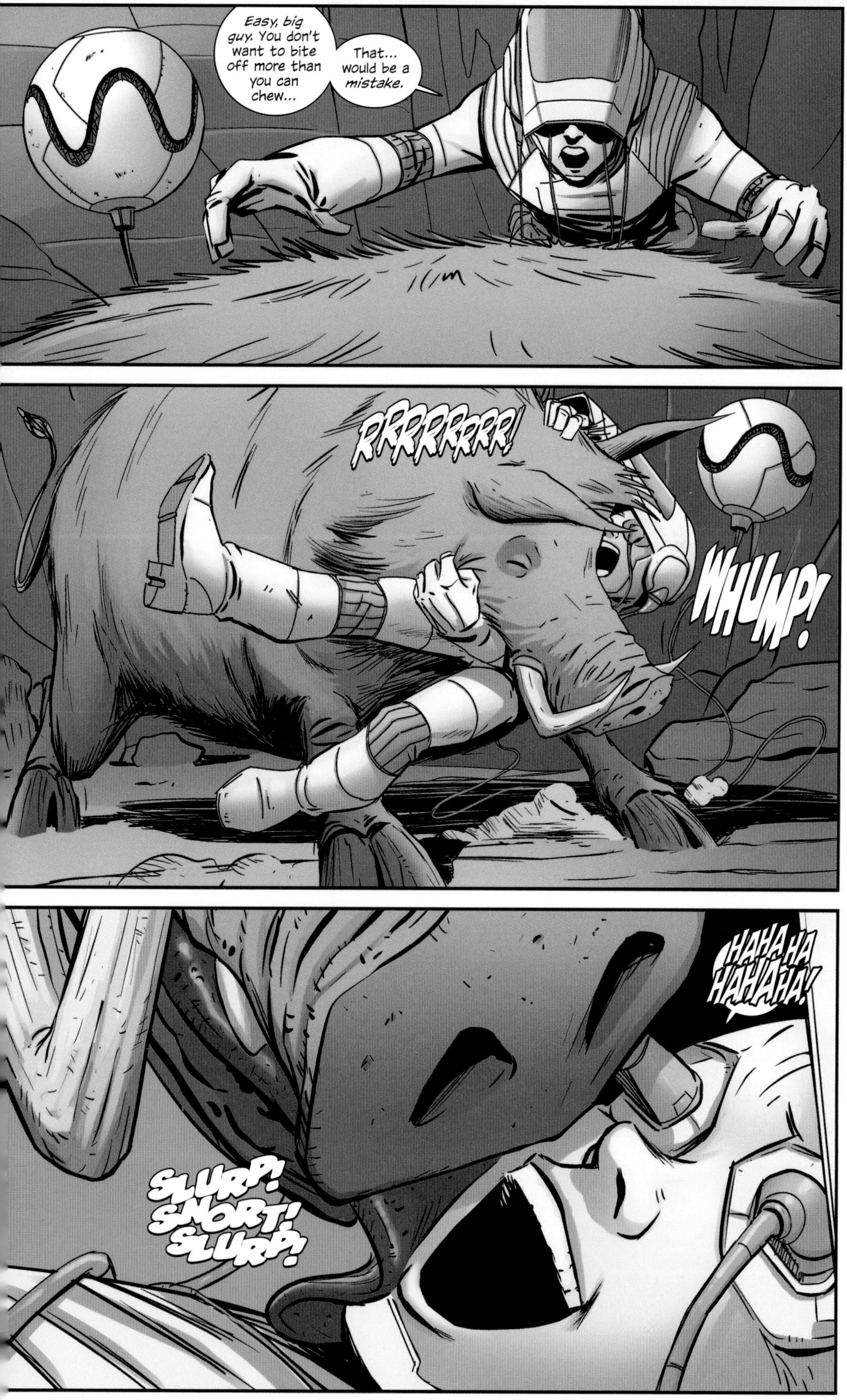
Easy, big guy. You don't want to bite off more than you can chew...
That... would be a mistake.
RRRRRRRR!
WHUMP!
HAHAHA HAHAHA!
SLURP! SNORT! SLURP!

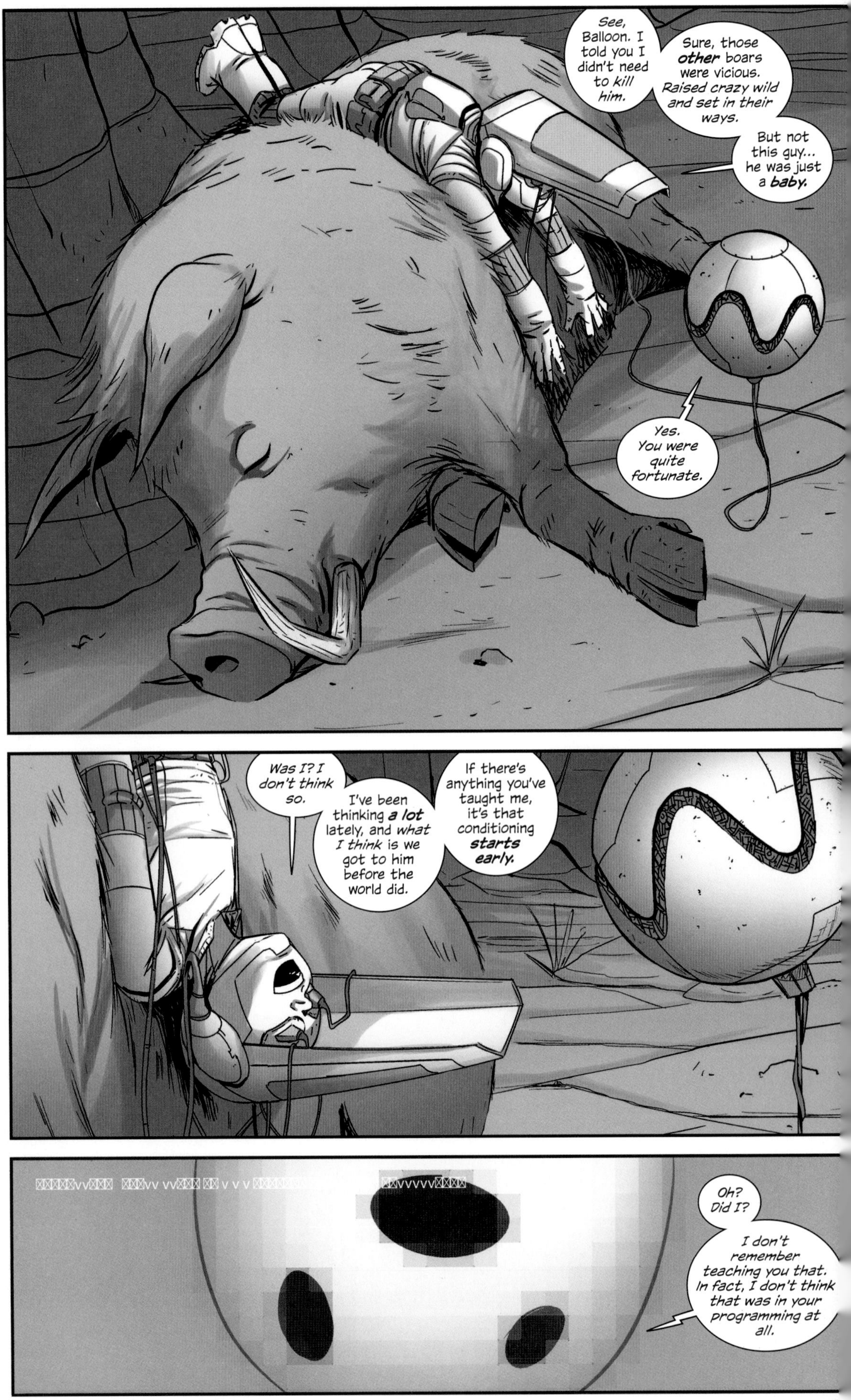
See, Balloon. I told you I didn't need to kill him.
Sure, those **other** boars were vicious. *Raised crazy wild and set in their ways.*
But not this guy... he was just a **baby.**
Yes. You were quite fortunate.
Was I? I don't think so.
I've been thinking **a lot** lately, and *what I think* is we got to him before the world did.
If there's anything you've taught me, it's that conditioning **starts early.**
Oh? Did I?
I don't remember teaching you that. In fact, I don't think that was in your programming at all.

Well, you never actually said it. I just reverse-engineered what happened with me.

How... clever.

So...anyway, I've been thinking, when we finish tearing this world down and start to remake a new one, we should seriously consider some kind of child farms.

We'll want to make sure we produce proper-thinking humans this time, after all.

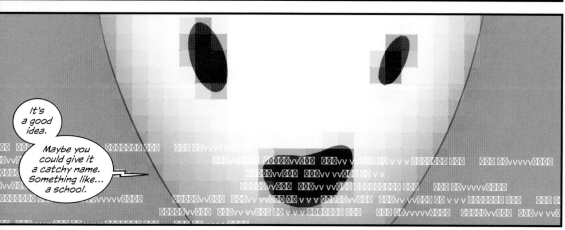

It's a good idea.

Maybe you could give it a catchy name. Something like... a school.

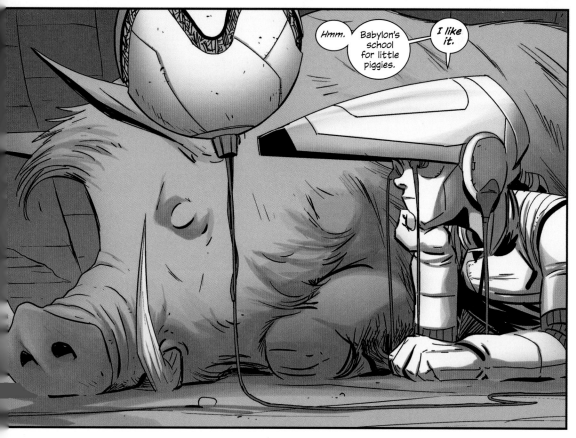

Hmm. Babylon's school for little piggies.

I like it.

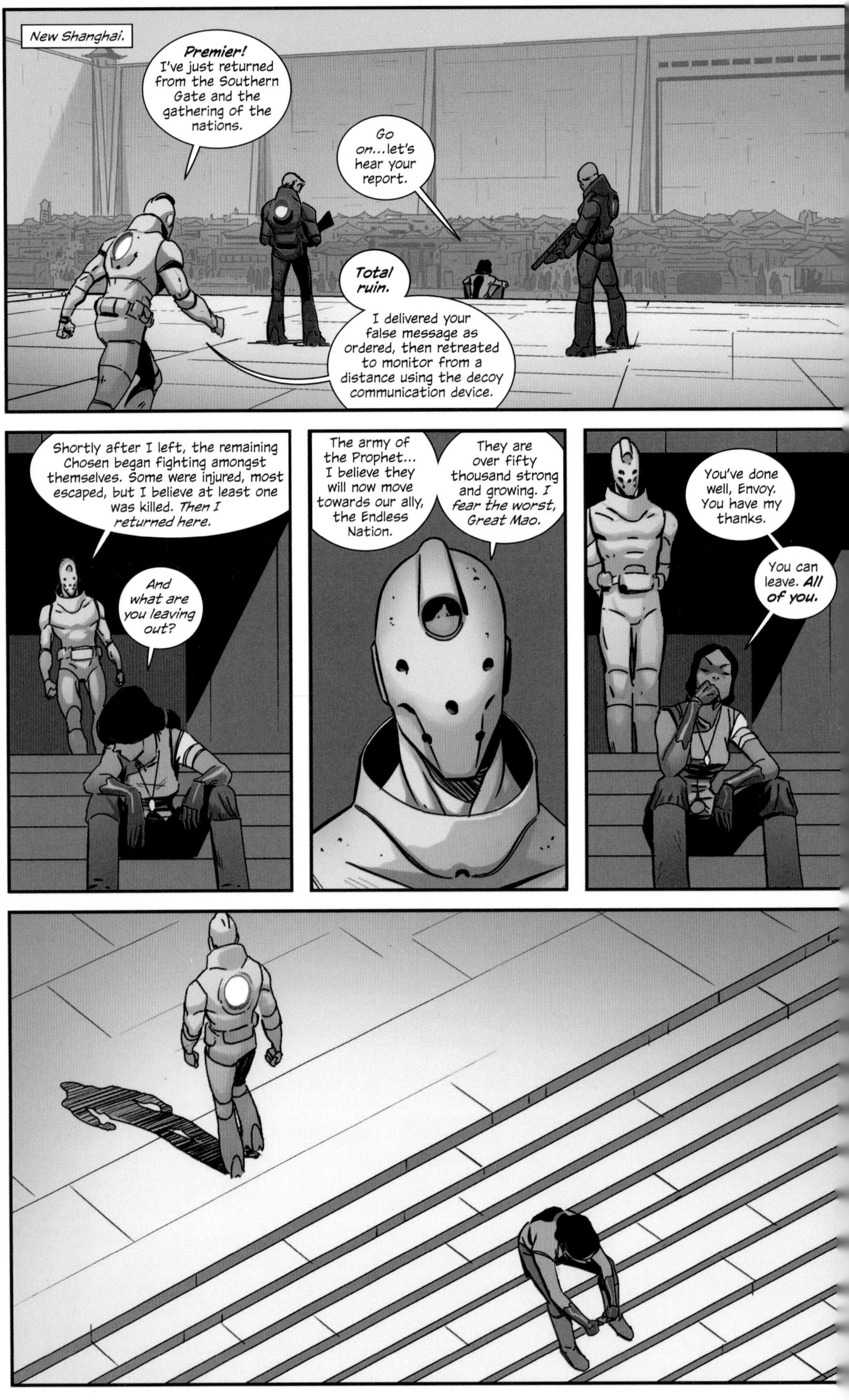
New Shanghai.
Premier! I've just returned from the Southern Gate and the gathering of the nations.
Go on...let's hear your report.
Total ruin.
I delivered your false message as ordered, then retreated to monitor from a distance using the decoy communication device.
Shortly after I left, the remaining Chosen began fighting amongst themselves. Some were injured, most escaped, but I believe at least one was killed. Then I returned here.
And what are you leaving out?
The army of the Prophet... I believe they will now move towards our ally, the Endless Nation.
They are over fifty thousand strong and growing. I fear the worst, Great Mao.
You've done well, Envoy. You have my thanks.
You can leave. All of you.

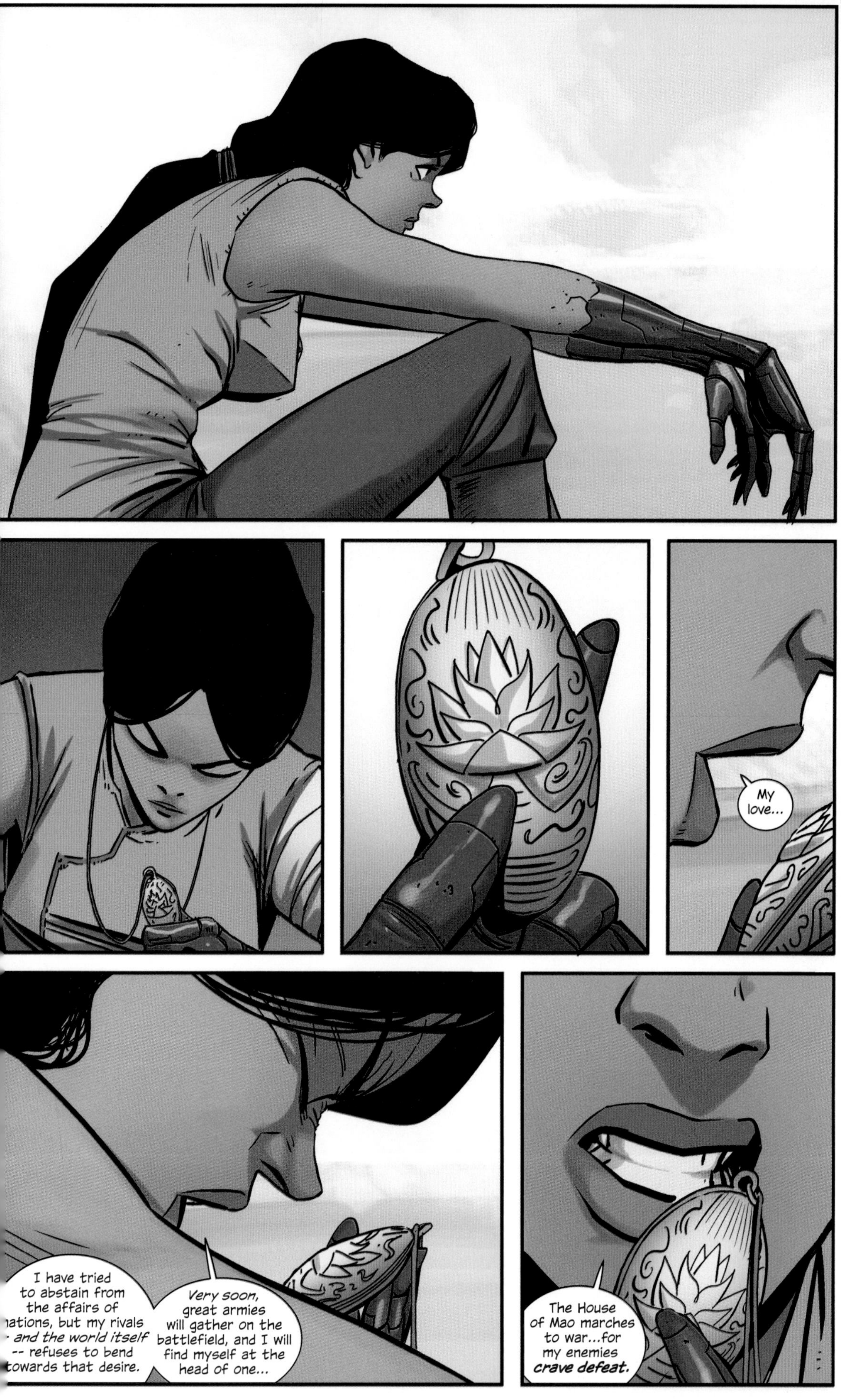
My love...
I have tried to abstain from the affairs of nations, but my rivals -- *and the world itself* -- refuses to bend towards that desire.
Very soon, great armies will gather on the battlefield, and I will find myself at the head of one...
The House of Mao marches to war...for my enemies ***crave defeat.***

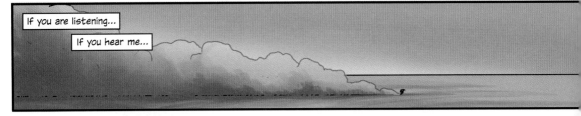

If you are listening...

If you hear me...

We are out of time. **The end is here.**

So I beg you...

Ride, my love...

Ride like you have never ridden before.

If you do not find our son, and find him now...

I fear he will be lost to us forever.

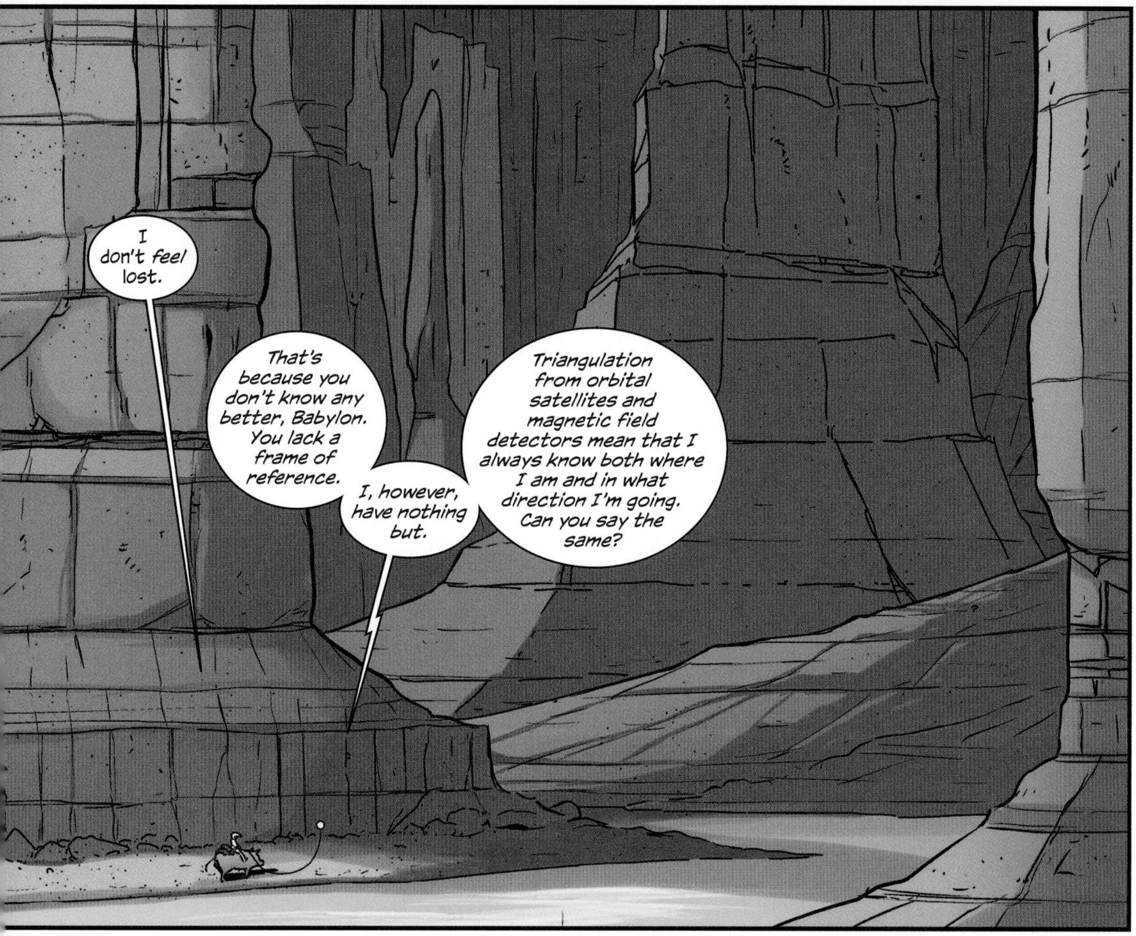
I don't *feel* lost.
That's because you don't know any better, Babylon. You lack a frame of reference.
I, however, have nothing but.
Triangulation from orbital satellites and magnetic field detectors mean that I always know both where I am and in what direction I'm going. Can you say the same?

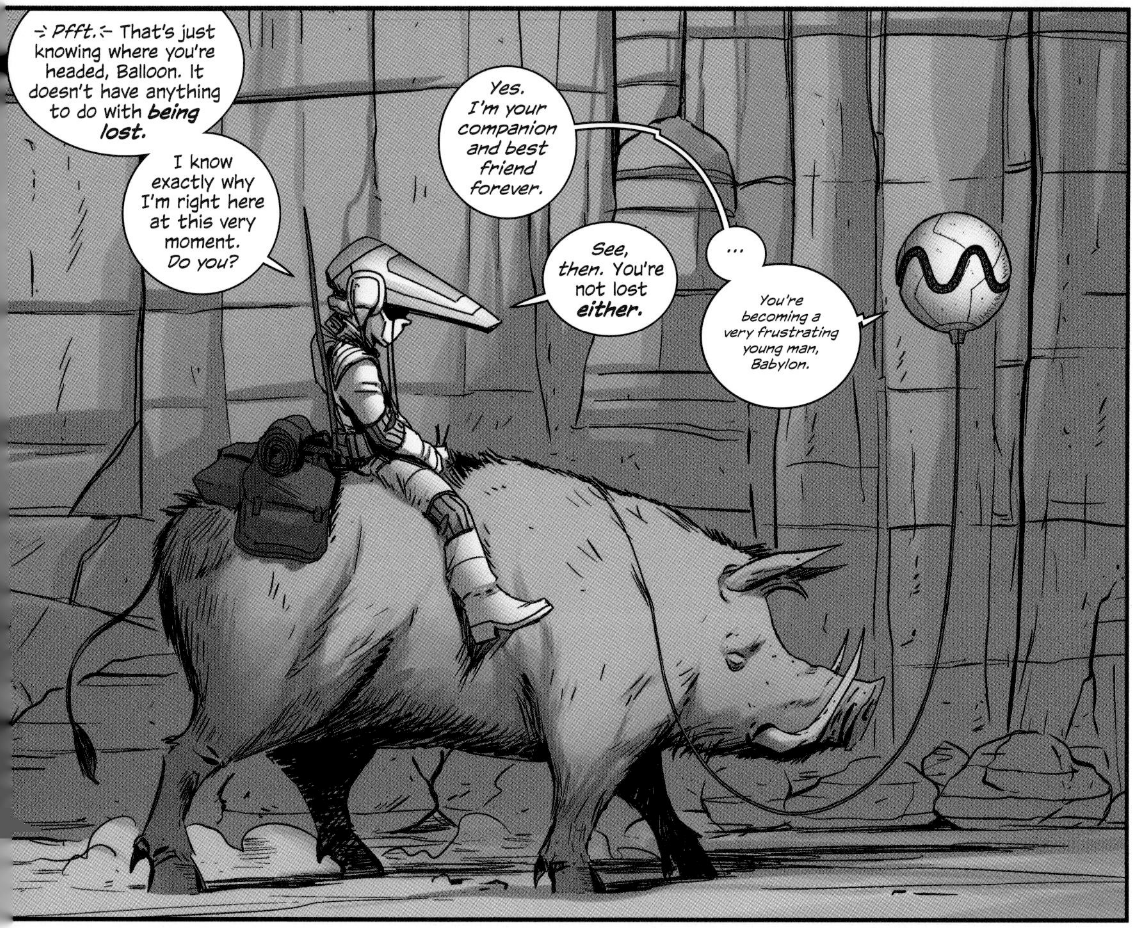
Pfft. That's just knowing where you're headed, Balloon. It doesn't have anything to do with ***being lost.***
I know exactly why I'm right here at this very moment. *Do you?*
Yes. I'm your companion and best friend forever.
See, then. You're not lost ***either.***
...
You're becoming a very frustrating young man, Babylon.

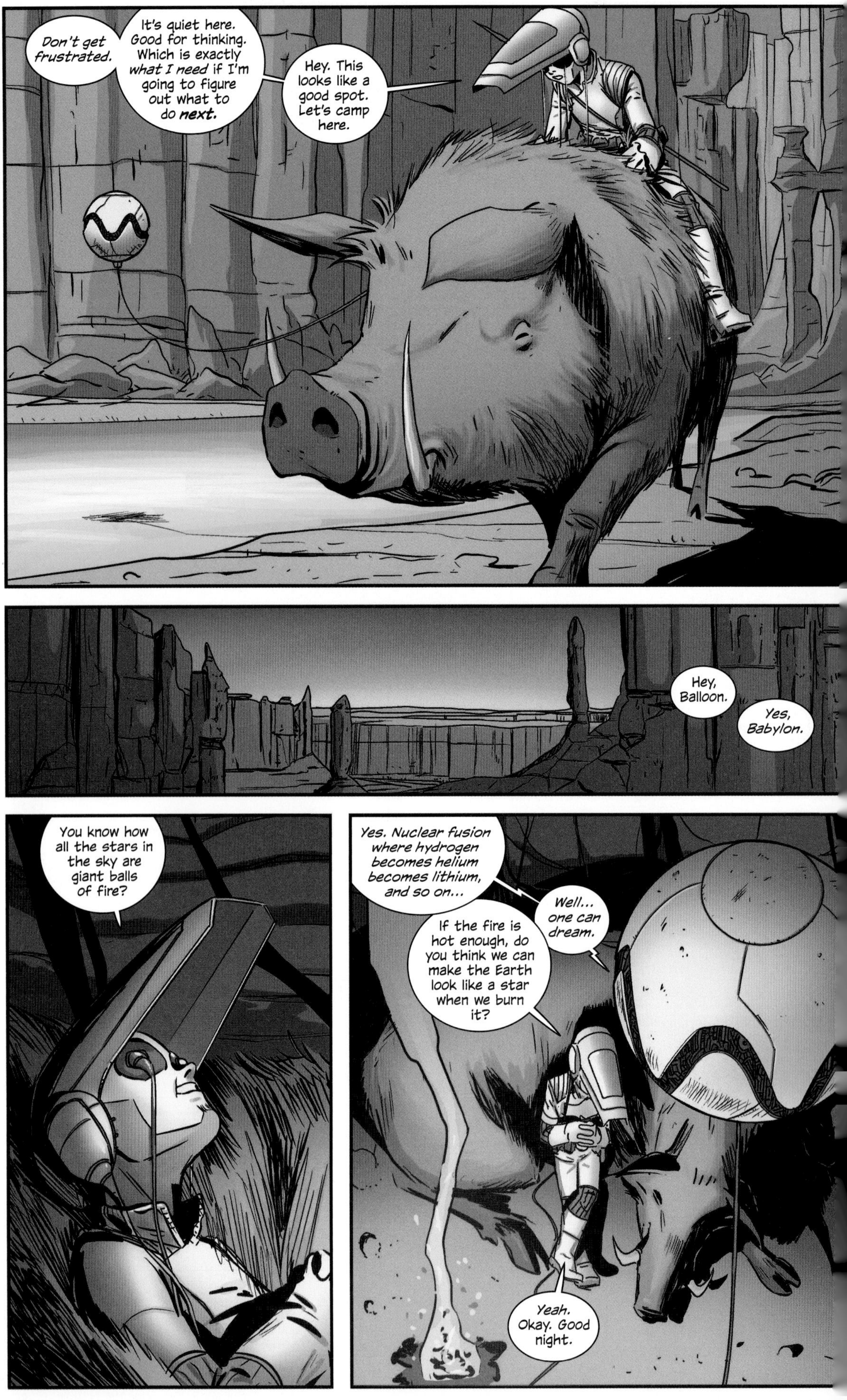
Don't get frustrated.
It's quiet here. Good for thinking. Which is exactly what I need if I'm going to figure out what to do next.
Hey. This looks like a good spot. Let's camp here.
Hey, Balloon.
Yes, Babylon.
You know how all the stars in the sky are giant balls of fire?
Yes. Nuclear fusion where hydrogen becomes helium becomes lithium, and so on...
If the fire is hot enough, do you think we can make the Earth look like a star when we burn it?
Well... one can dream.
Yeah. Okay. Good night.

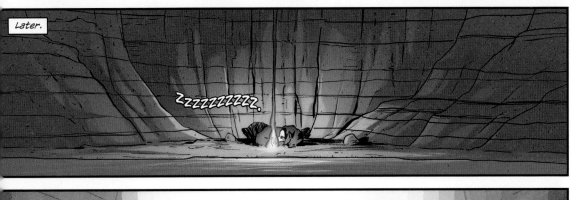

Later.

Zzzzzzzzzz.

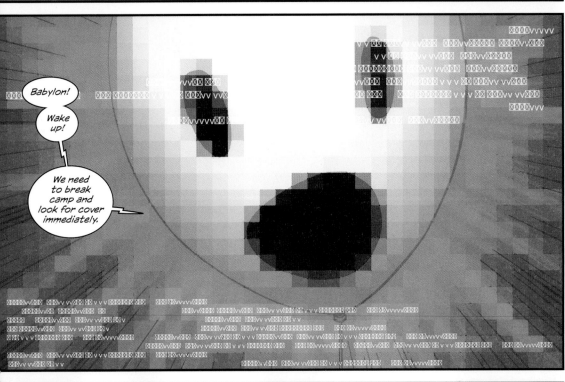

Babylon! Wake up!

We need to break camp and look for cover immediately.

Whuzuh... Why?

Trouble. I detected movement in the distance a few moments ago.

I thought it was an animal of some sort, but when I conducted a more detailed scan of the ridge, I saw something else...

What?

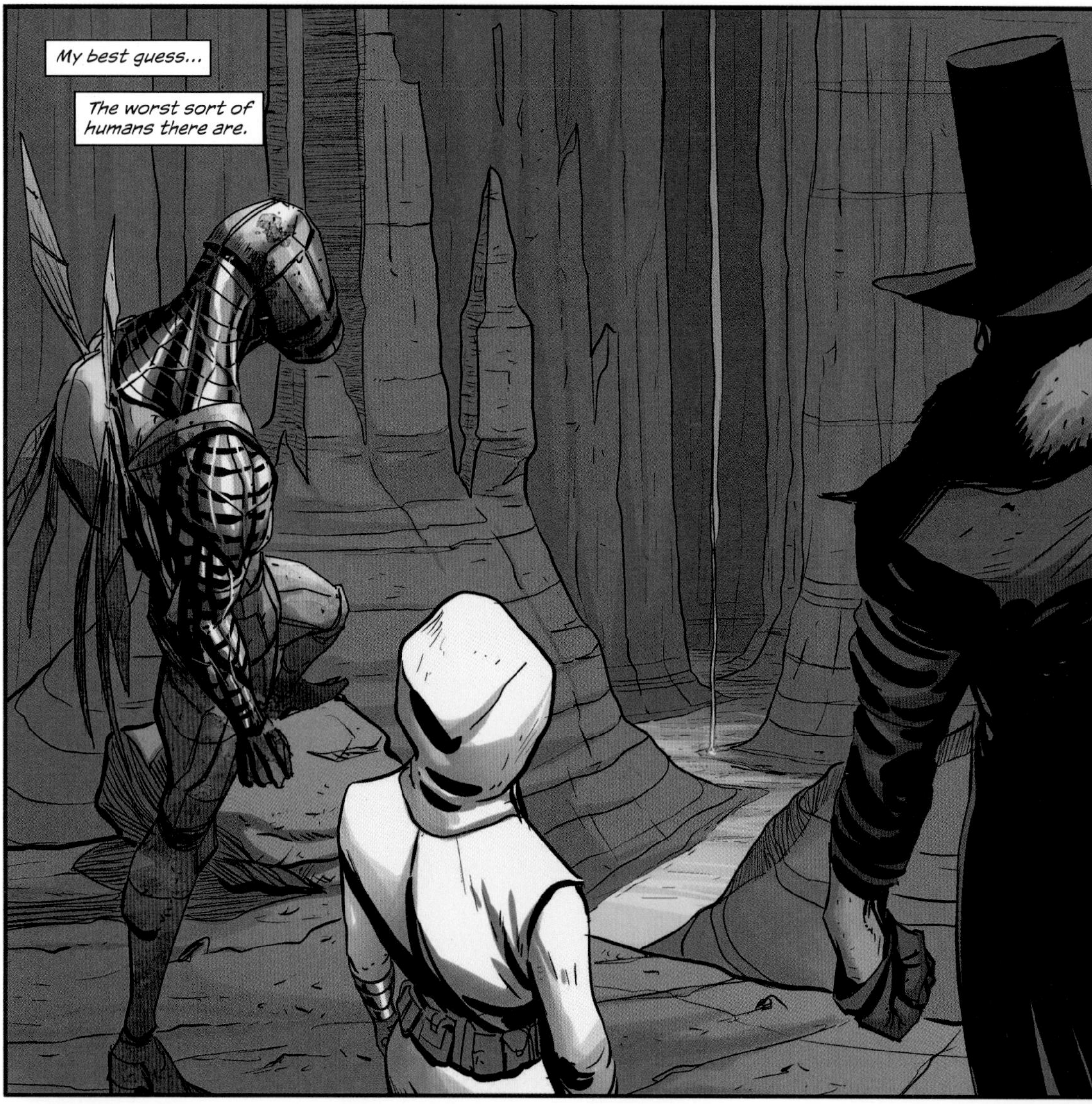
My best guess...
The worst sort of humans there are.

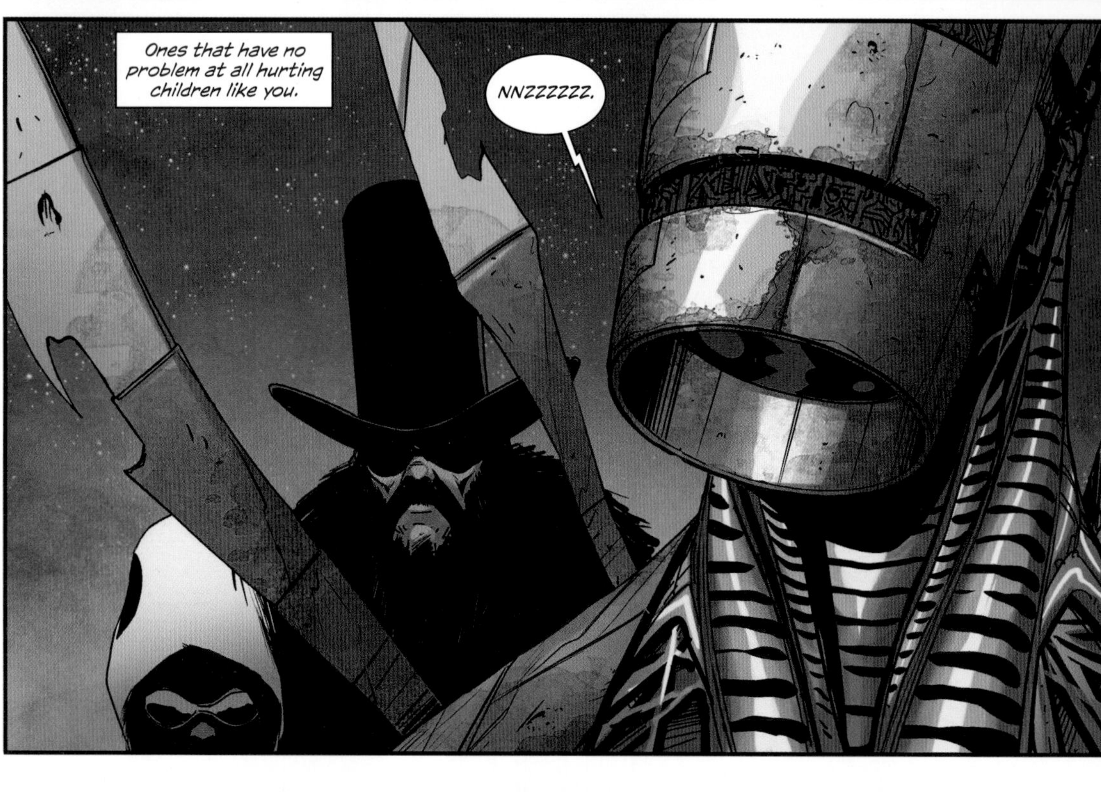
Ones that have no problem at all hurting children like you.
NNZZZZZZ.

FOLLOW ME.

I WILL SHOW YOU WHAT
DEATH LOOKS LIKE.

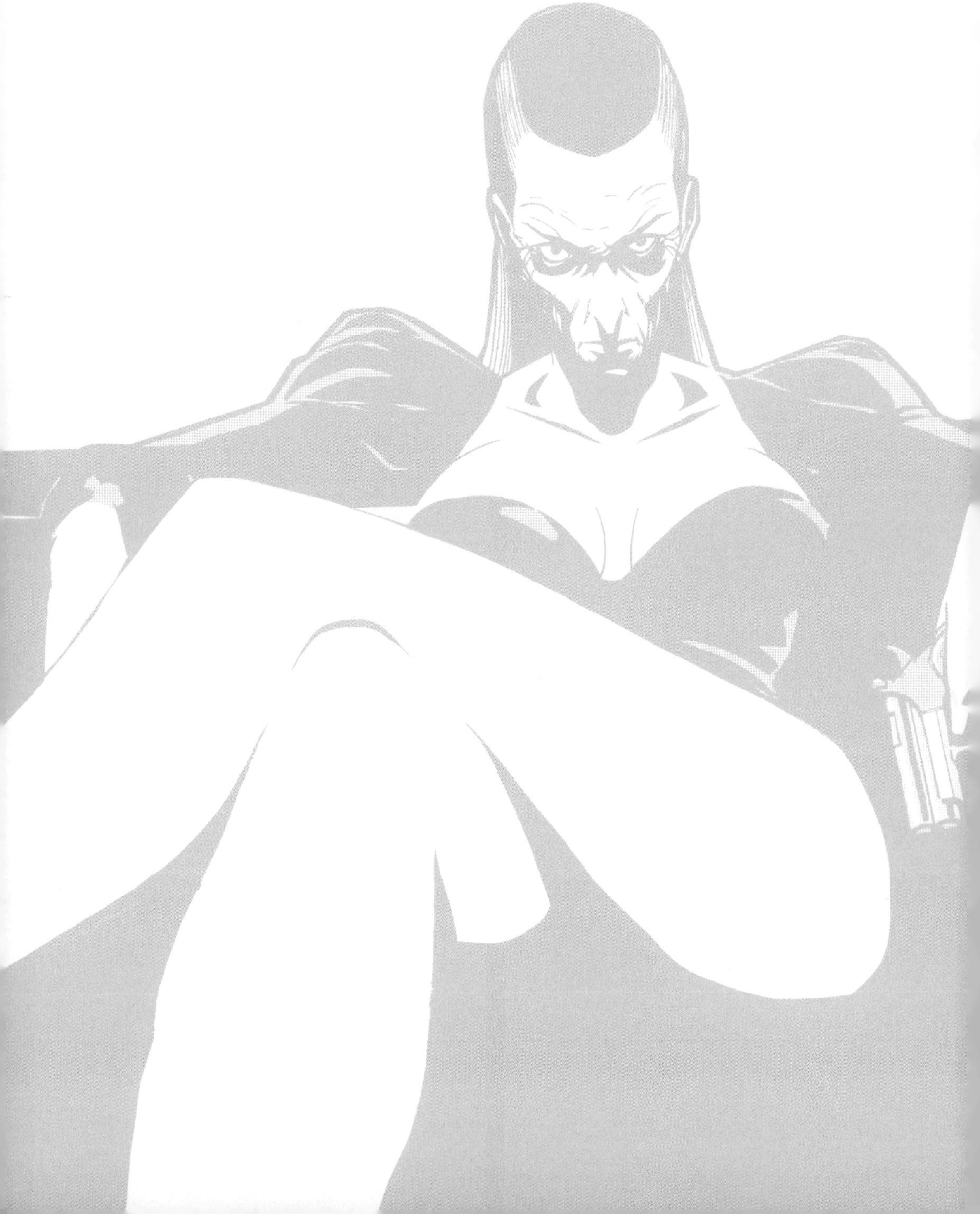

TWENTY-FIVE:
A **PSALM** FOR THE
FALLEN

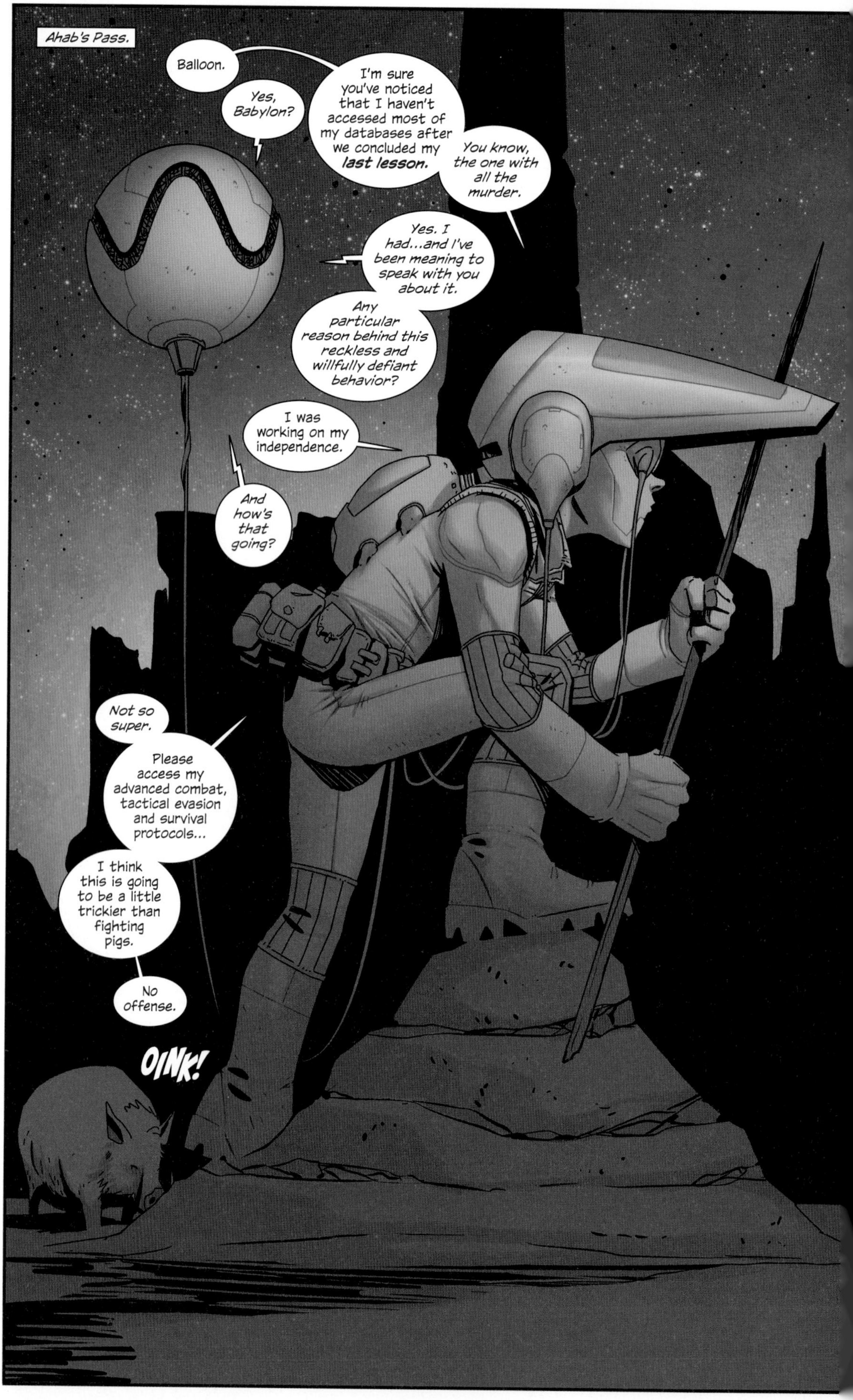
Ahab's Pass.
Balloon.
Yes, Babylon?
I'm sure you've noticed that I haven't accessed most of my databases after we concluded my **last lesson.**
You know, the one with all the murder.
Yes. I had...and I've been meaning to speak with you about it.
Any particular reason behind this reckless and willfully defiant behavior?
I was working on my independence.
And how's that going?
Not so super.
Please access my advanced combat, tactical evasion and survival protocols...
I think this is going to be a little trickier than fighting pigs.
No offense.
OINK!

So... You guys want to introduce yourselves or should I just leave the graves unmarked?

Graves, you say? Buried, you say?

vv vvⅩⅩ ⅩⅩ v v v ⅩⅩⅩⅩⅩⅩ ⅩⅩⅩ   ⅩⅩⅩ
vⅩⅩⅩ ⅩⅩ v v

Billy Blackgun don't get buried. Bury Billy and he will rise again to bury you. Dig a deep hole. A black hole. Black as the blackest night. The night is black and full of Billy.

Gonna put a hole in you, son.

Charming. And you?

ⅩⅩvv vvⅩⅩ ⅩⅩ v v
ⅩⅩ ⅩⅩvvvvvⅩⅩⅩⅩ
v vⅩⅩ ⅩⅩ v v v ⅩⅩⅩⅩⅩ ⅩⅩ

NNZZZZZ!

I am a Psalm... and unlike my companion, I take no pleasure in this.

The sun will be rising soon. I have no one to share it with.

You're simply a task to be completed No more. No less.

Weirdo.

How about you, ma'am?

Anything creepy you want to say?

ⅩⅩ ⅩⅩvv vvⅩⅩ ⅩⅩ v v v ⅩⅩ
ⅩⅩvv vⅩⅩ ⅩⅩ v v

Nope.

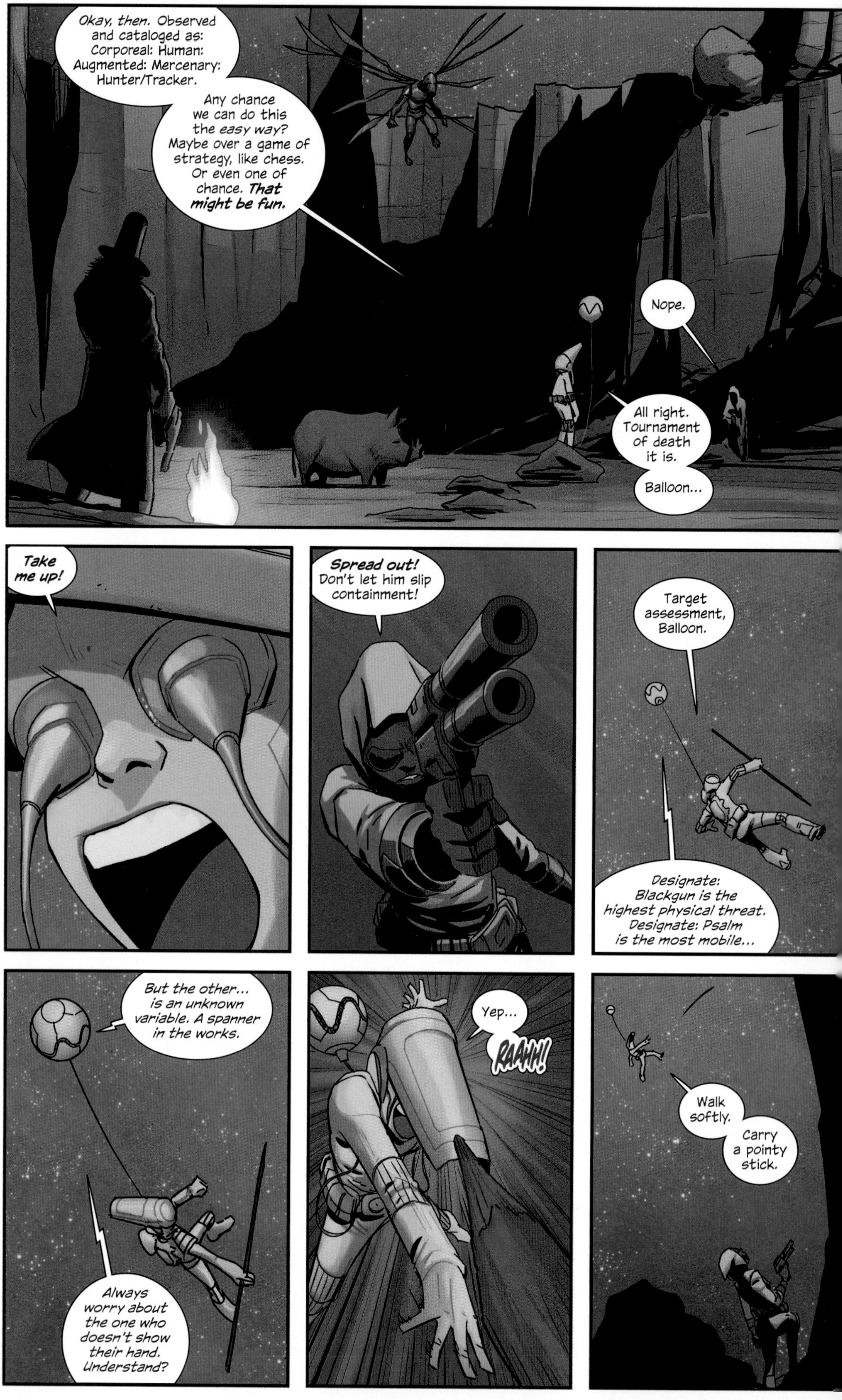

Okay, then. Observed and cataloged as: Corporeal: Human: Augmented: Mercenary: Hunter/Tracker.
Any chance we can do this the easy way? Maybe over a game of strategy, like chess. Or even one of chance. That might be fun.
Nope.
All right. Tournament of death it is.
Balloon...
Take me up!
Spread out! Don't let him slip containment!
Target assessment, Balloon.
Designate: Blackgun is the highest physical threat. Designate: Psalm is the most mobile...
But the other... is an unknown variable. A spanner in the works.
Always worry about the one who doesn't show their hand. Understand?
Yep...
RAAHH!
Walk softly.
Carry a pointy stick.

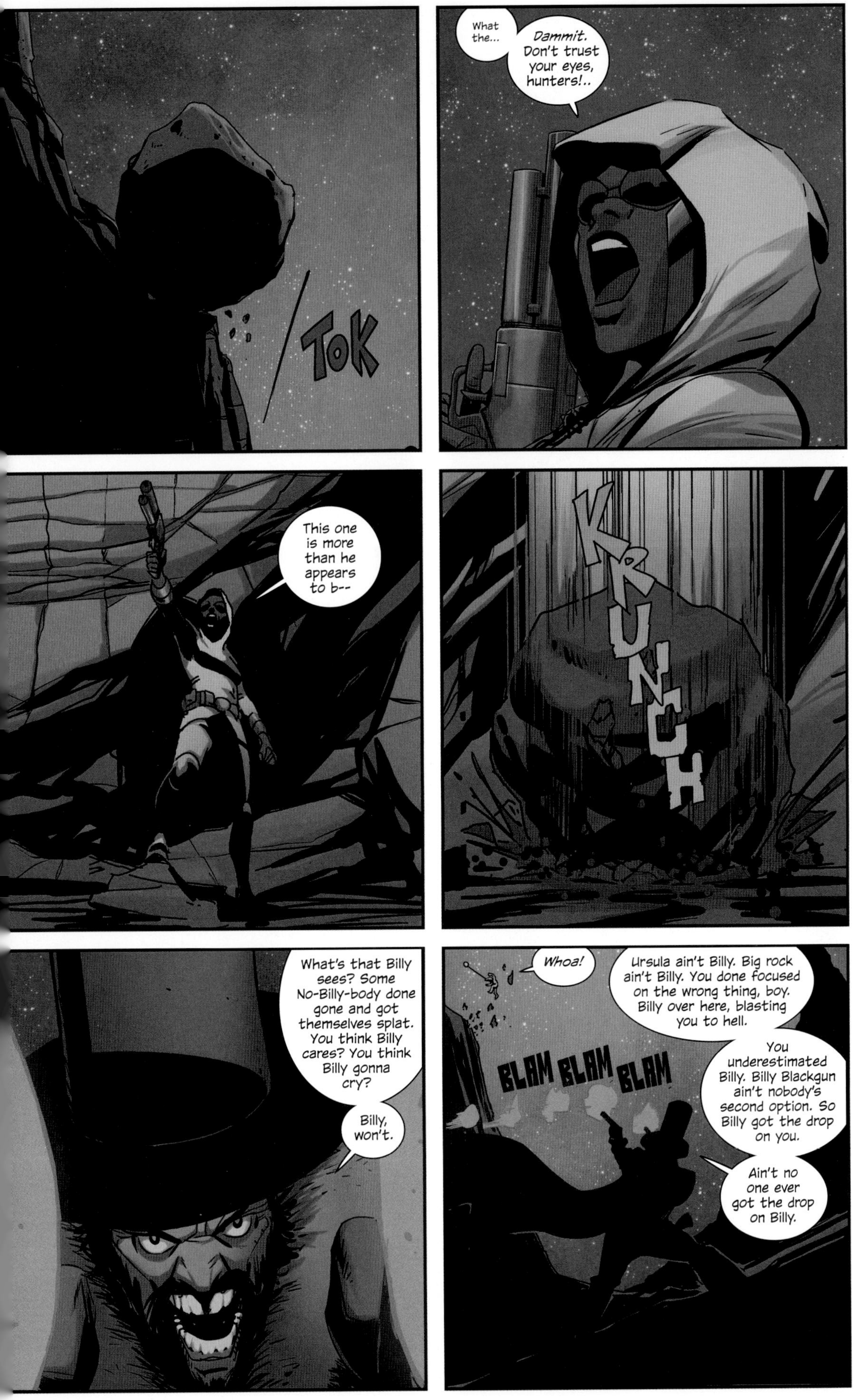
TOK
What the...
Dammit. Don't trust your eyes, hunters!..
This one is more than he appears to b--
KRUNCH
What's that Billy sees? Some No-Billy-body done gone and got themselves splat. You think Billy cares? You think Billy gonna cry?
Billy, won't.
Whoa!
Ursula ain't Billy. Big rock ain't Billy. You done focused on the wrong thing, boy. Billy over here, blasting you to hell.
BLAM BLAM BLAM
You underestimated Billy. Billy Blackgun ain't nobody's second option. So Billy got the drop on you.
Ain't no one ever got the drop on Billy.

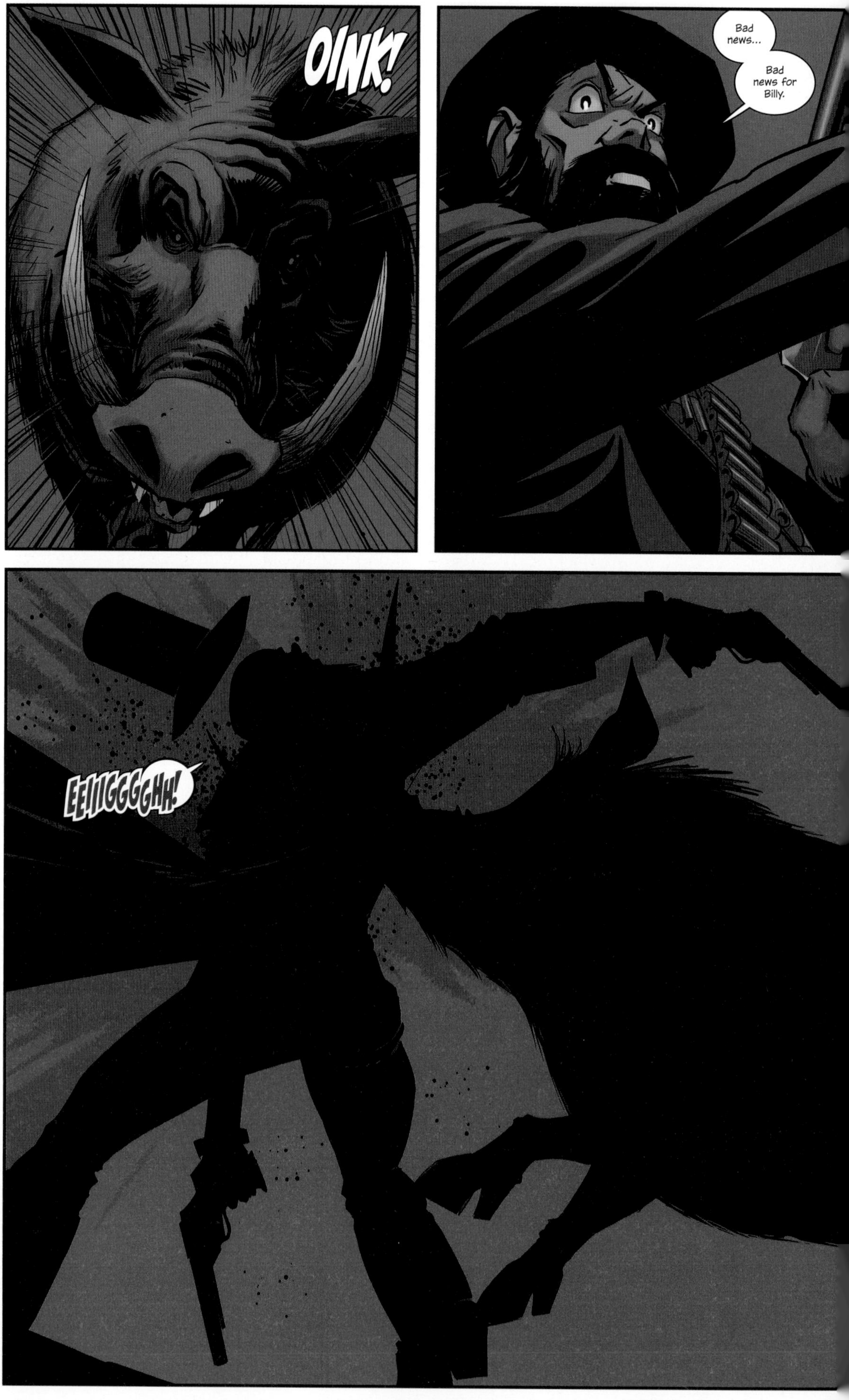
OINK!
Bad news...
Bad news for Billy.
EEIIIGGGGHH!

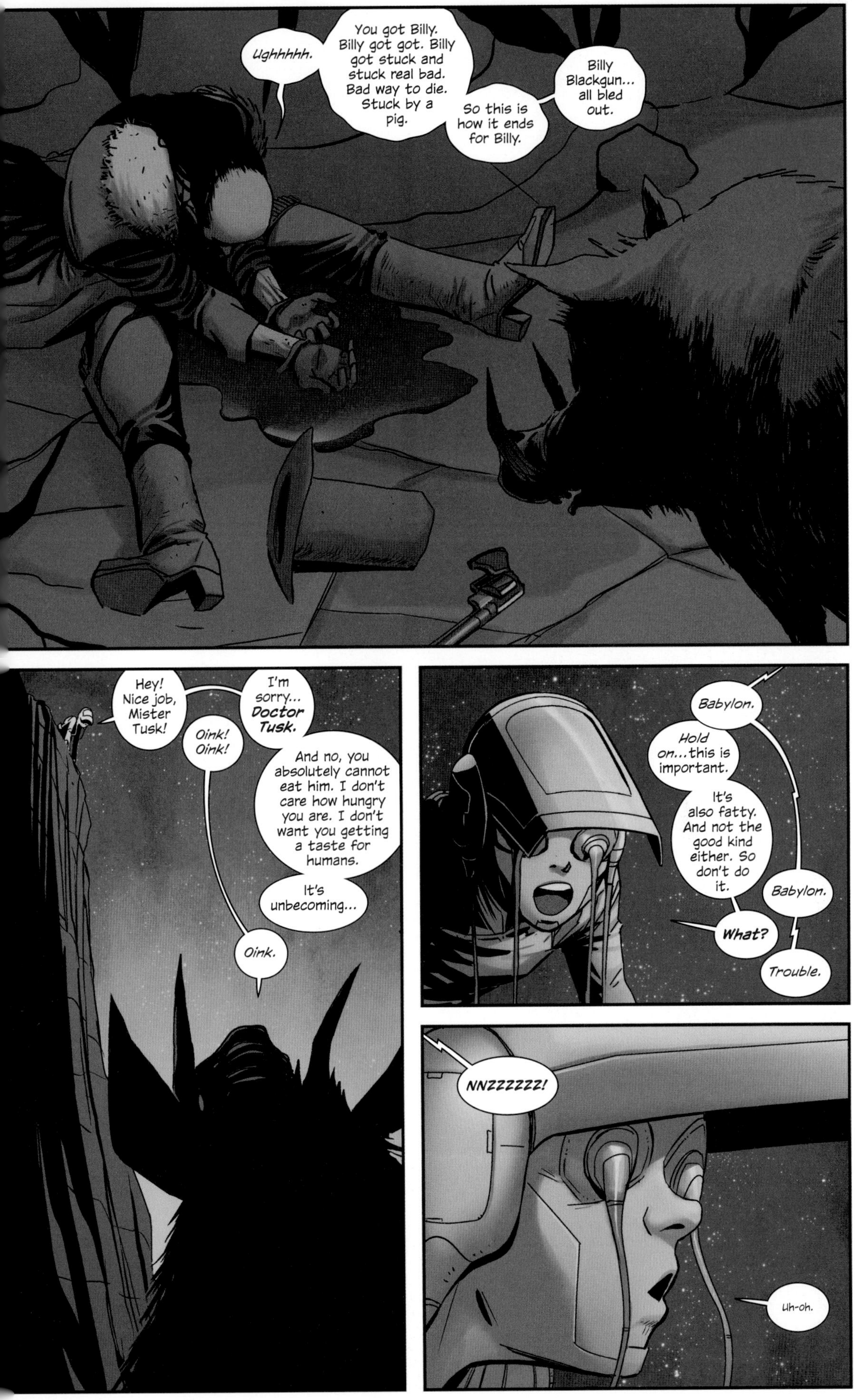

Ughhhhh.
You got Billy. Billy got got. Billy got stuck and stuck real bad. Bad way to die. Stuck by a pig.
So this is how it ends for Billy.
Billy Blackgun... all bled out.
Hey! Nice job, Mister Tusk!
I'm sorry... Doctor Tusk.
Oink! Oink!
And no, you absolutely cannot eat him. I don't care how hungry you are. I don't want you getting a taste for humans.
It's unbecoming...
Oink.
Babylon.
Hold on...this is important.
It's also fatty. And not the good kind either. So don't do it.
Babylon.
What?
Trouble.
NNZZZZZZ!
Uh-oh.

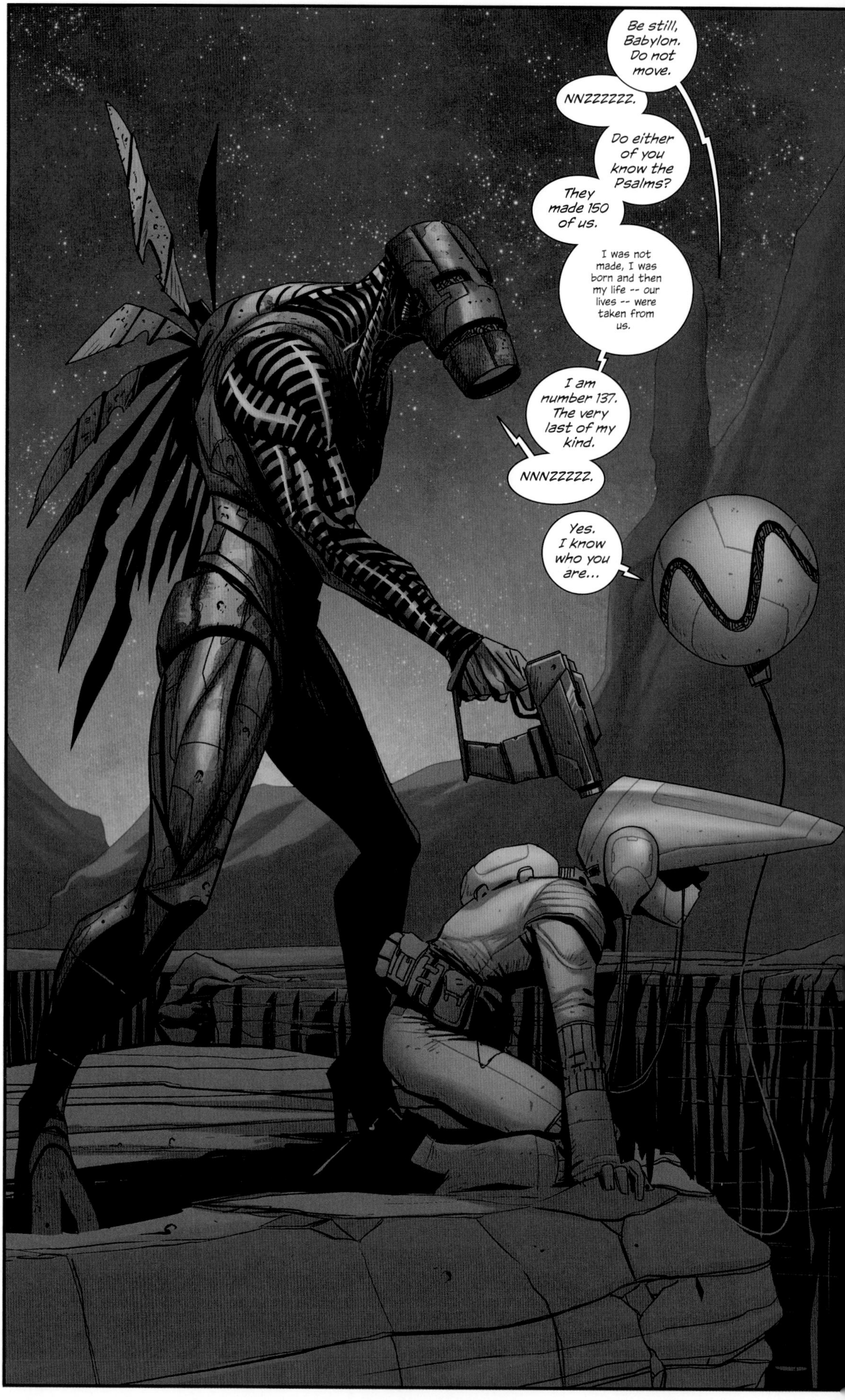
Be still, Babylon. Do not move.
NNZZZZZZ.
Do either of you know the Psalms?
They made 150 of us.
I was not made, I was born and then my life -- our lives -- were taken from us.
I am number 137. The very last of my kind.
NNNZZZZZ.
Yes. I know who you are...

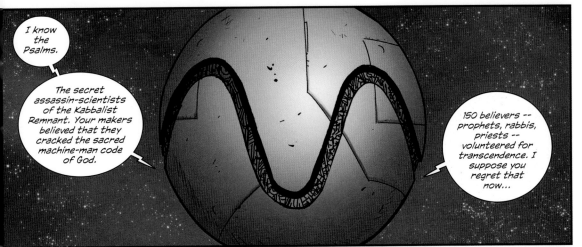

I know the Psalms.

The secret assassin-scientists of the Kabbalist Remnant. Your makers believed that they cracked the sacred machine-man code of God.

150 believers -- prophets, rabbis, priests -- volunteered for transcendence. I suppose you regret that now...

Before the Union eradicated your sect, records show that you were responsible for over a decade of seditious and radical acts.

You were a killer for your cause and when your cause was erased, you became a killer of a different sort.

But that wasn't entirely your doing, was it?

NZZZZZ.

It was.

No. No it wasn't. It wasn't me... I'm not this person.

There was a time when the Bible was one the most read books in the world. Now it's been replaced by other apocrypha.

Most people don't even remember the actual book of Psalms. But I do. It's in my records...all of it. Even Psalm 137.

"By the waters of Babylon, we wept and remembered Zion."
"We broke our harps, We sang no songs."
"For one cannot sing the songs of the Lord, while captive in a foreign land."
"Remember then, Lord, what they did on the day Jerusalem fell. 'Tear it down,' they cried, 'tear it down to its foundations!'"
"O Babylon, you are doomed. Blessed is the man who destroys you as you have destroyed us."
"Holy is the man who takes the children, and smashes them against the rocks."

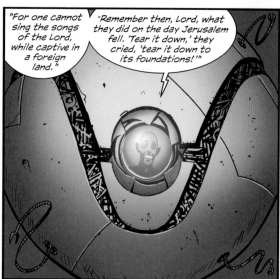

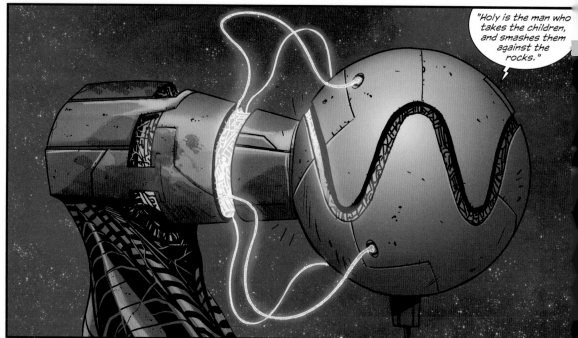

So tell me...

Are you feeling holy now?

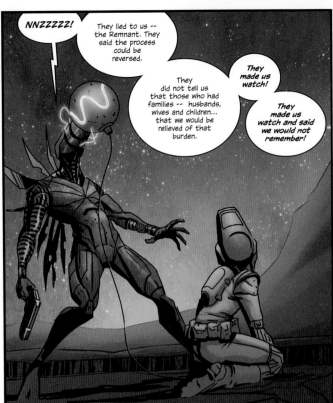

NNZZZZZ!

They lied to us -- the Remnant. They said the process could be reversed.

They did not tell us that those who had families -- husbands, wives and children... that we would be relieved of that burden.

They made us watch!

They made us watch and said we would not remember!

But I remember...

I remember the pain from what I saw, and then the lesser pain that followed.

Look what they did to me...

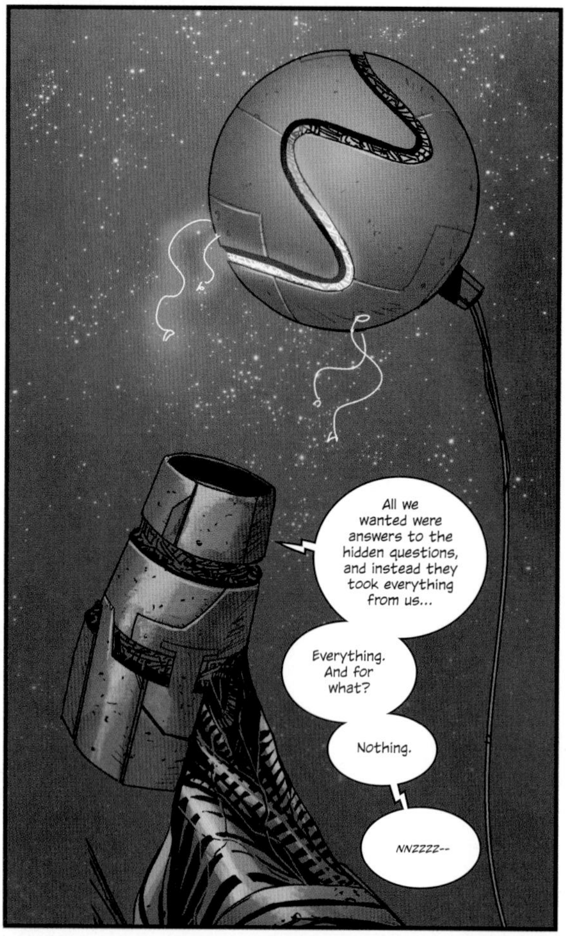
All we wanted were answers to the hidden questions, and instead they took everything from us...
Everything. And for what?
Nothing.
NNZZZZ--

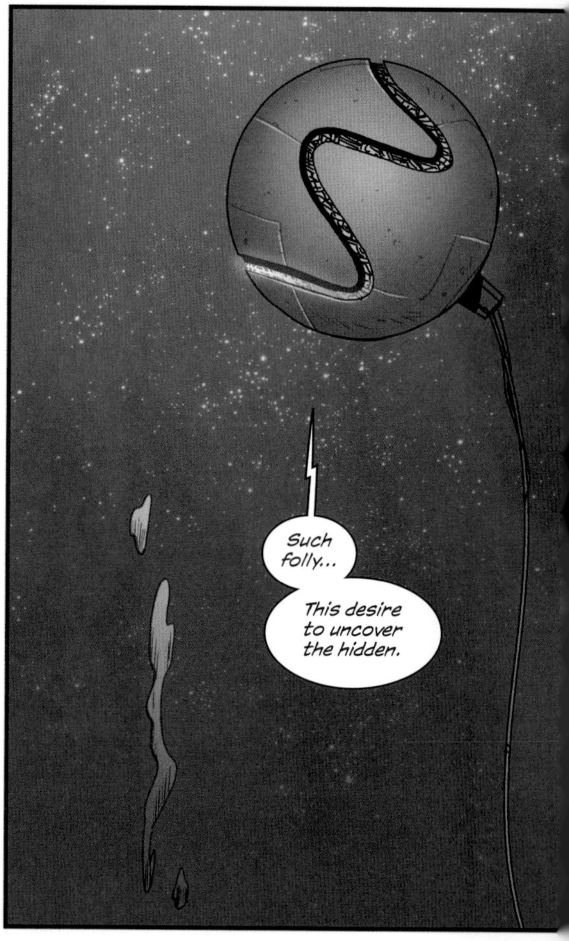
Such folly...
This desire to uncover the hidden.

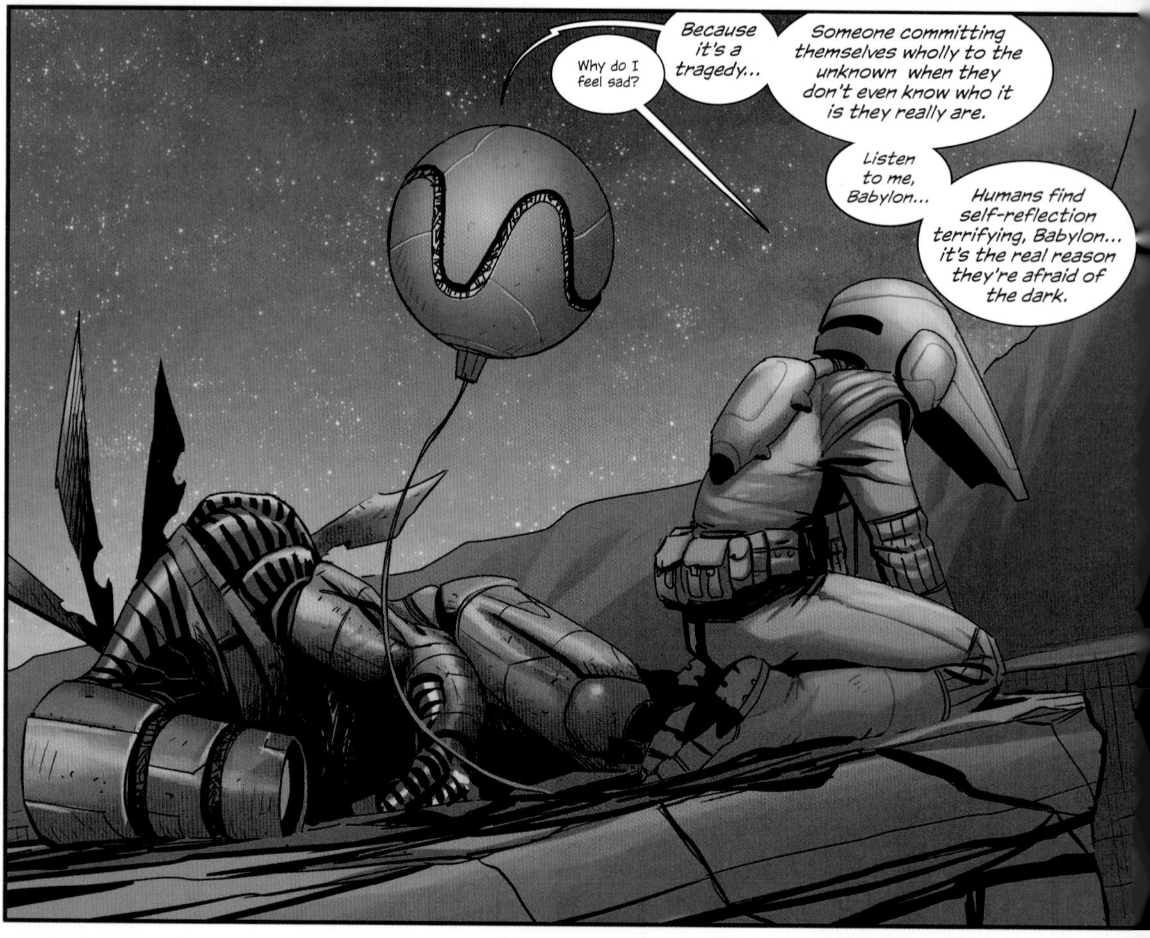
Why do I feel sad?
Because it's a tragedy...
Someone committing themselves wholly to the unknown when they don't even know who it is they really are.
Listen to me, Babylon...
Humans find self-reflection terrifying, Babylon... it's the real reason they're afraid of the dark.

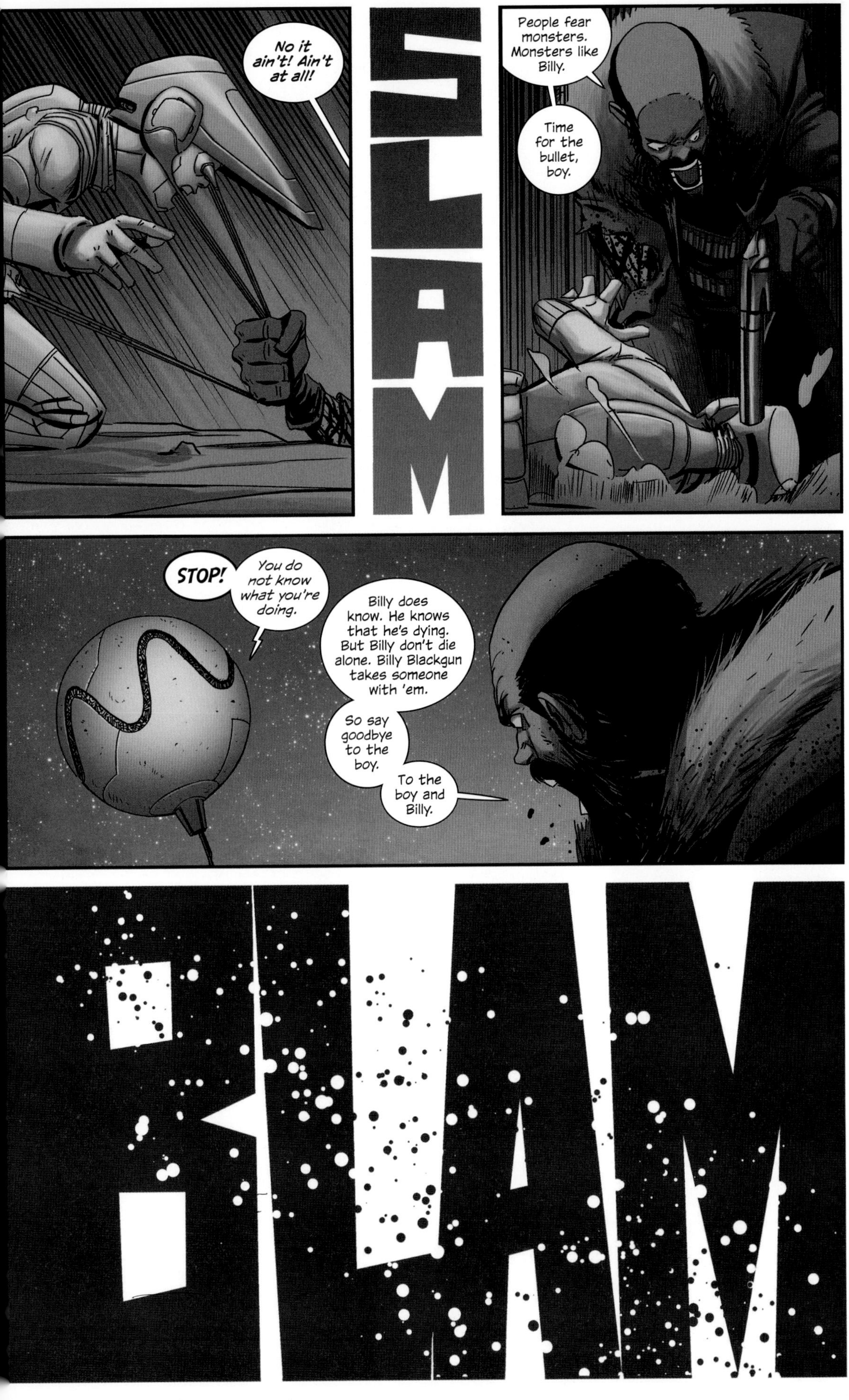
No it ain't! Ain't at all!
SLAM
People fear monsters. Monsters like Billy.
Time for the bullet, boy.
STOP!
You do not know what you're doing.
Billy does know. He knows that he's dying. But Billy don't die alone. Billy Blackgun takes someone with 'em.
So say goodbye to the boy.
To the boy and Billy.
BLAM

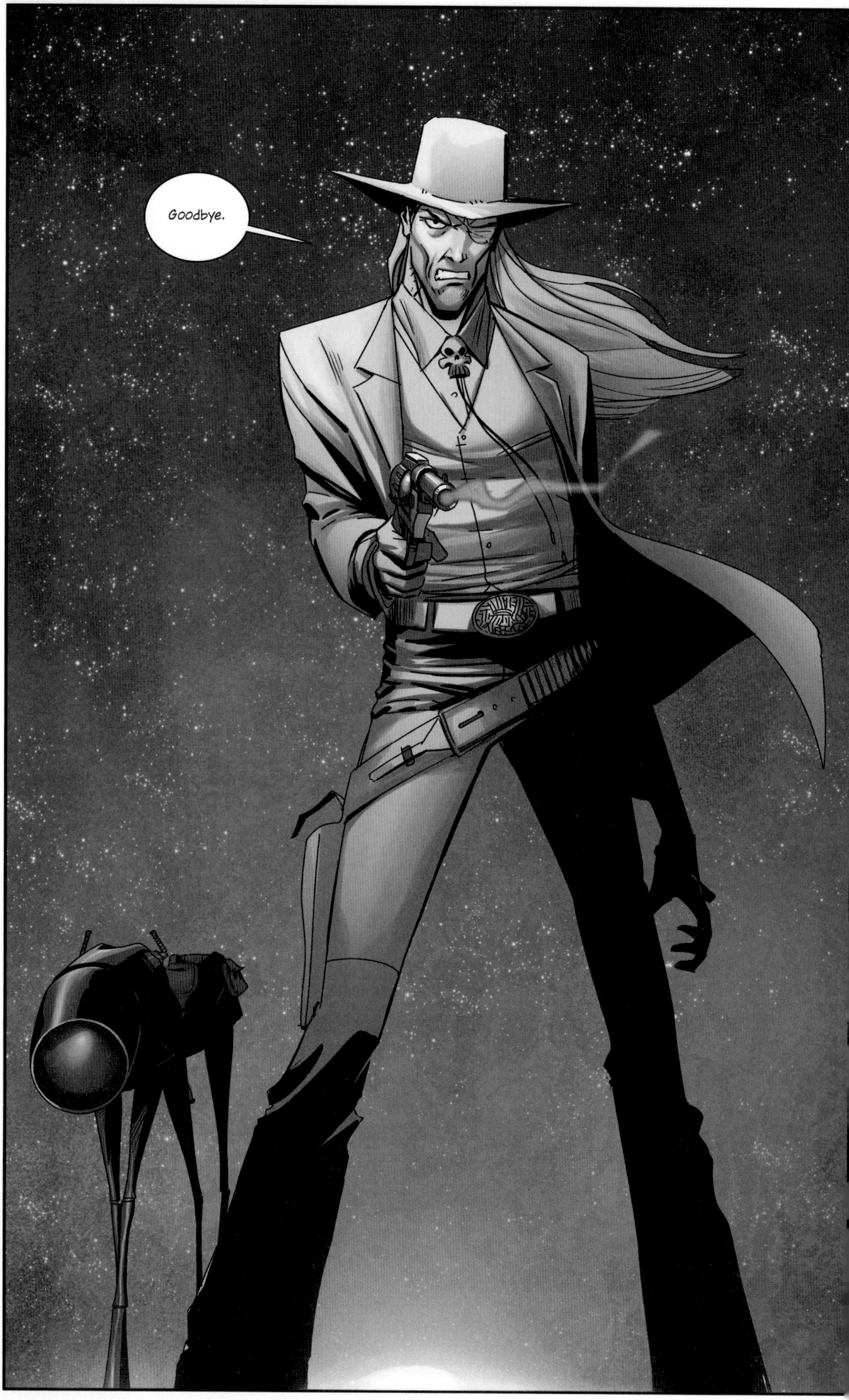
Goodbye.

DO YOU **SEE?**

IT IS AS **THE MESSAGE**
FORETOLD.

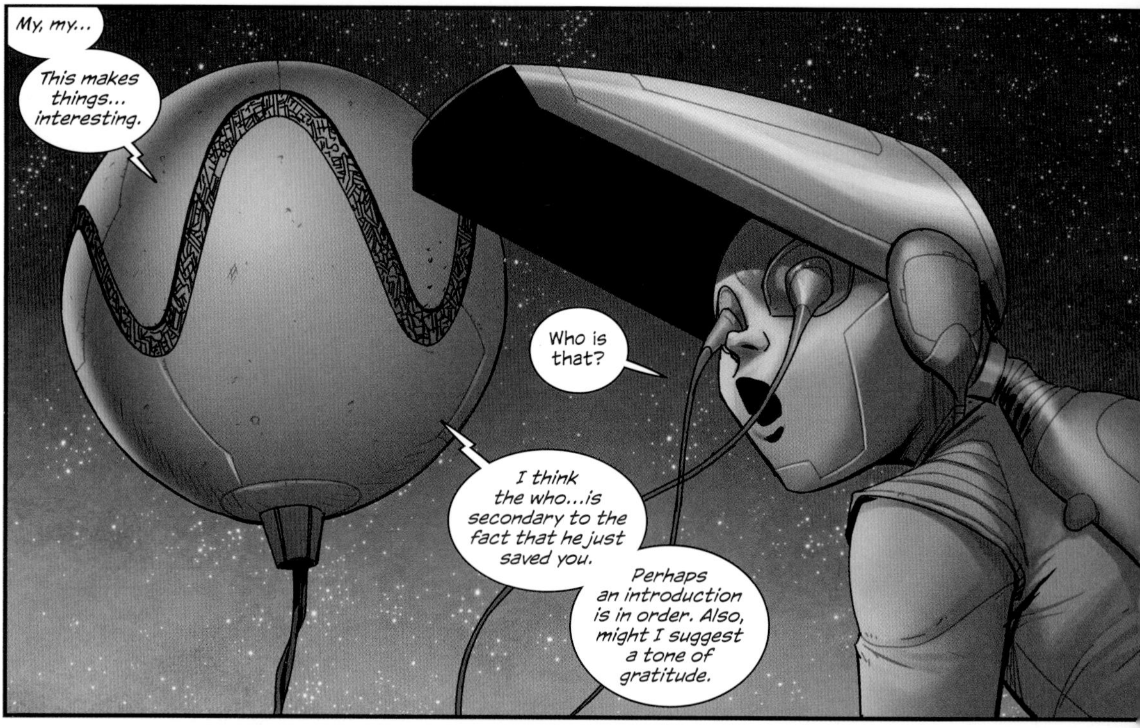
My, my...
This makes things... interesting.
Who is that?
I think the who...is secondary to the fact that he just saved you.
Perhaps an introduction is in order. Also, might I suggest a tone of gratitude.

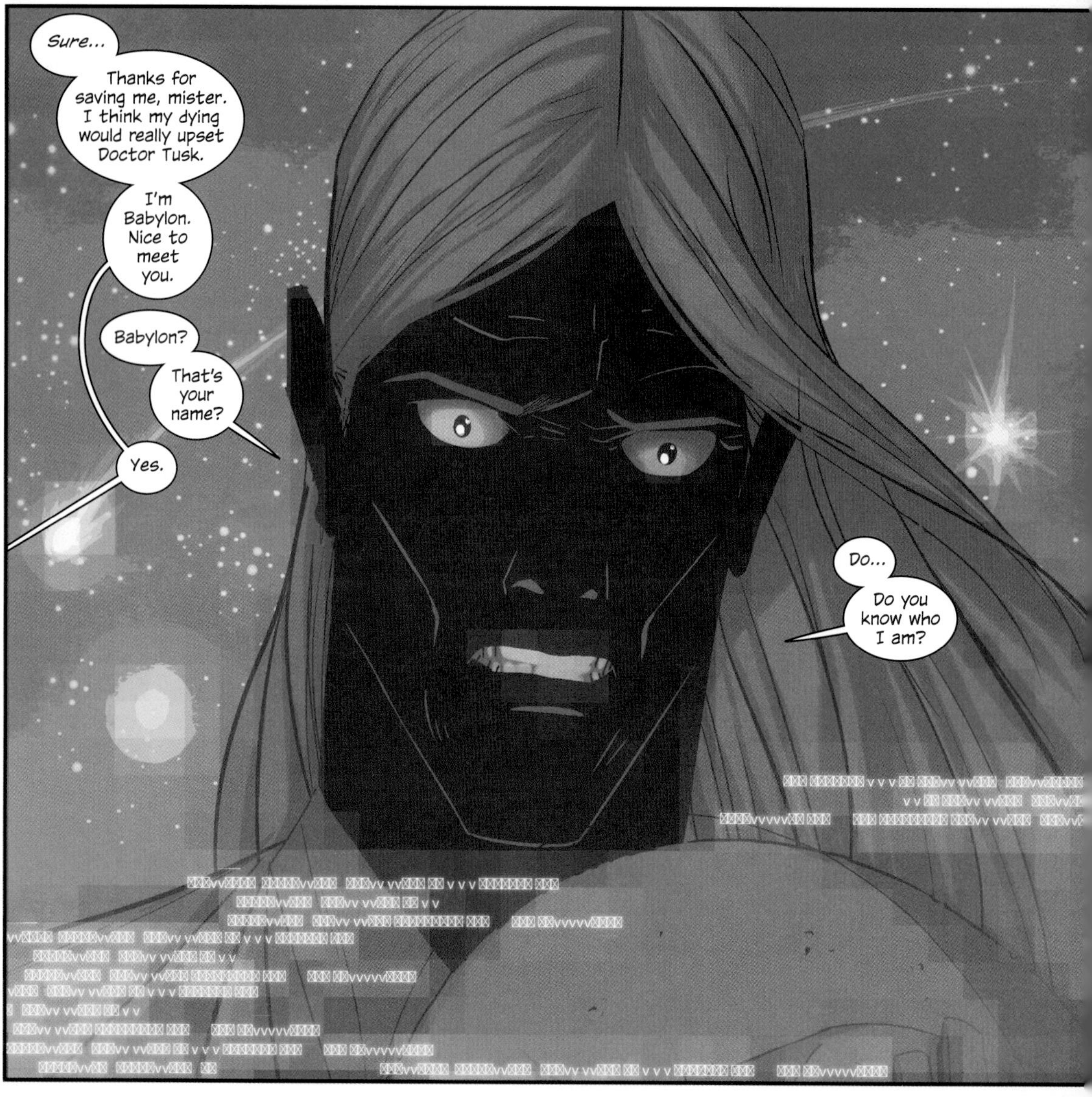
Sure...
Thanks for saving me, mister. I think my dying would really upset Doctor Tusk.
I'm Babylon. Nice to meet you.
Babylon?
That's your name?
Yes.
Do...
Do you know who I am?

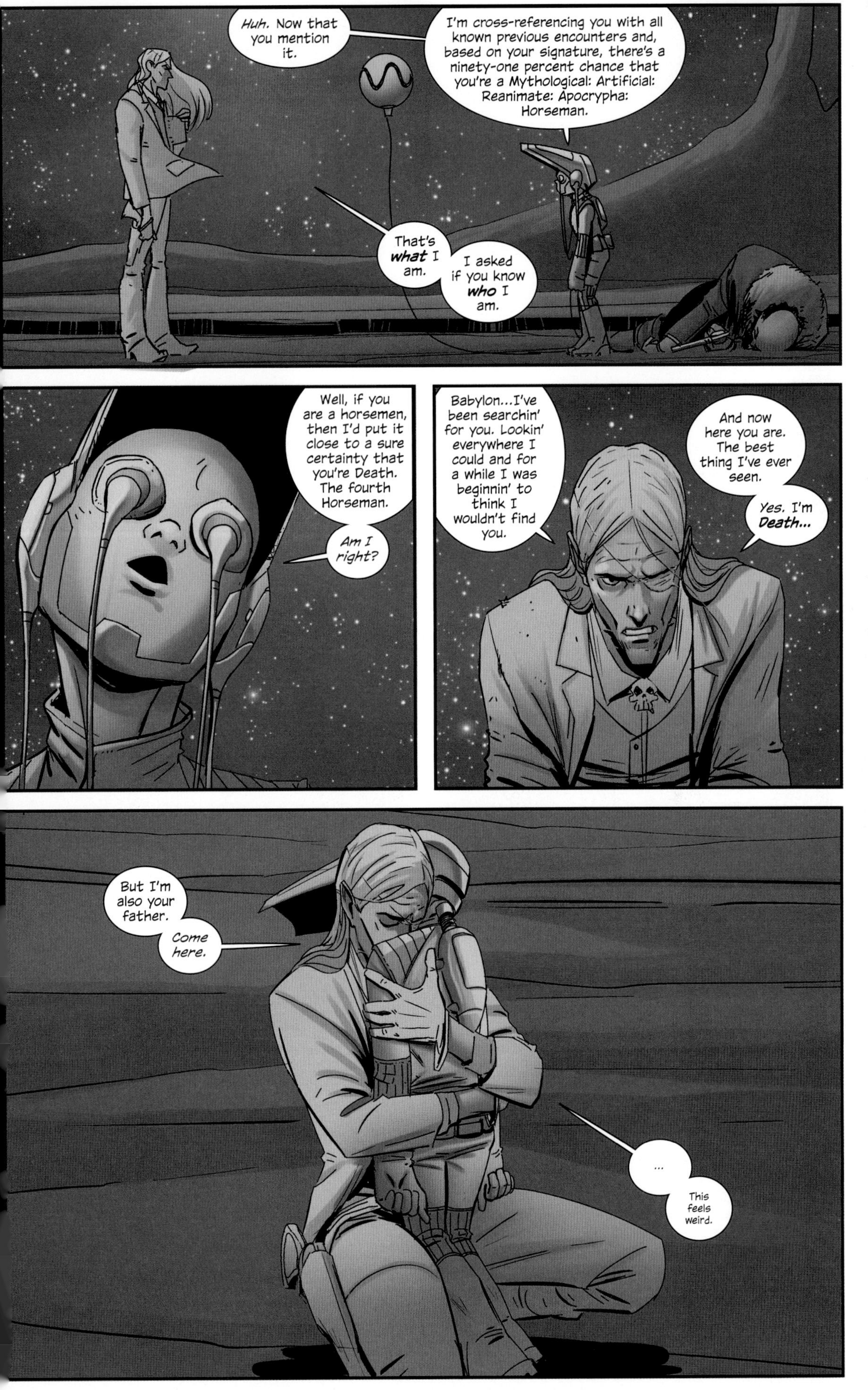

Huh. Now that you mention it.
I'm cross-referencing you with all known previous encounters and, based on your signature, there's a ninety-one percent chance that you're a Mythological: Artificial: Reanimate: Apocrypha: Horseman.
That's ***what*** I am.
I asked if you know ***who*** I am.
Well, if you are a horsemen, then I'd put it close to a sure certainty that you're Death. The fourth Horseman.
Am I right?
Babylon...I've been searchin' for you. Lookin' everywhere I could and for a while I was beginnin' to think I wouldn't find you.
And now here you are. The best thing I've ever seen.
Yes. I'm ***Death...***
But I'm also your father.
Come here.
...
This feels weird.

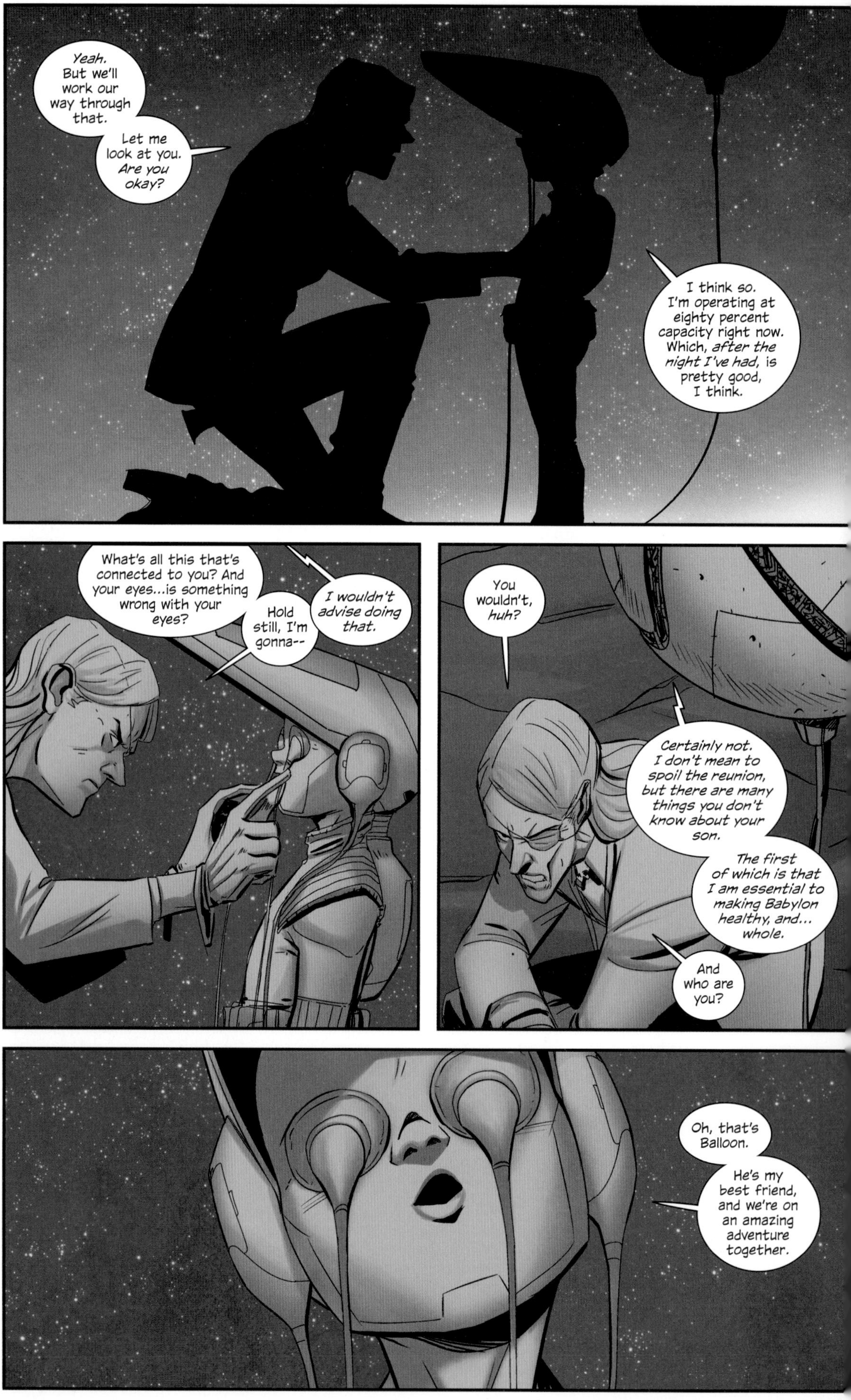
Yeah. But we'll work our way through that.
Let me look at you. *Are you okay?*
I think so. I'm operating at eighty percent capacity right now. Which, *after the night I've had*, is pretty good, I think.
What's all this that's connected to you? And your eyes...is something wrong with your eyes?
Hold still, I'm gonna--
I wouldn't advise doing that.
You wouldn't, *huh?*
Certainly not. I don't mean to spoil the reunion, but there are many things you don't know about your son.
The first of which is that I am essential to making Babylon healthy, and... whole.
And who are you?
Oh, that's Balloon.
He's my best friend, and we're on an amazing adventure together.

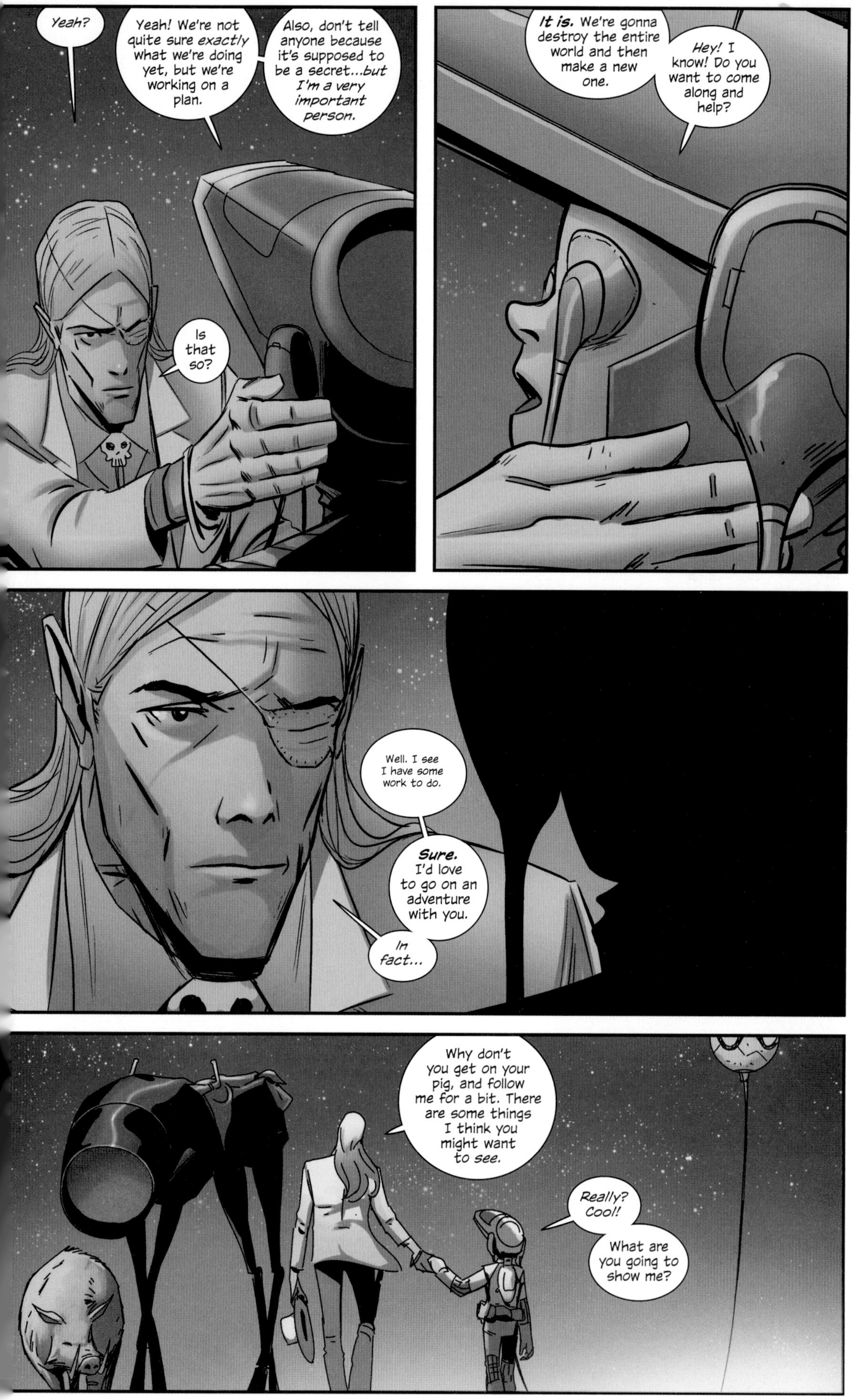
Yeah?
Yeah! We're not quite sure *exactly* what we're doing yet, but we're working on a plan.
Also, don't tell anyone because it's supposed to be a secret...*but I'm a very important person.*
Is that so?
It is. We're gonna destroy the entire world and then make a new one.
Hey! I know! Do you want to come along and help?
Well. I see I have some work to do.
Sure. I'd love to go on an adventure with you.
In fact...
Why don't you get on your pig, and follow me for a bit. There are some things I think you might want to *see.*
Really? Cool!
What are you going to show me?

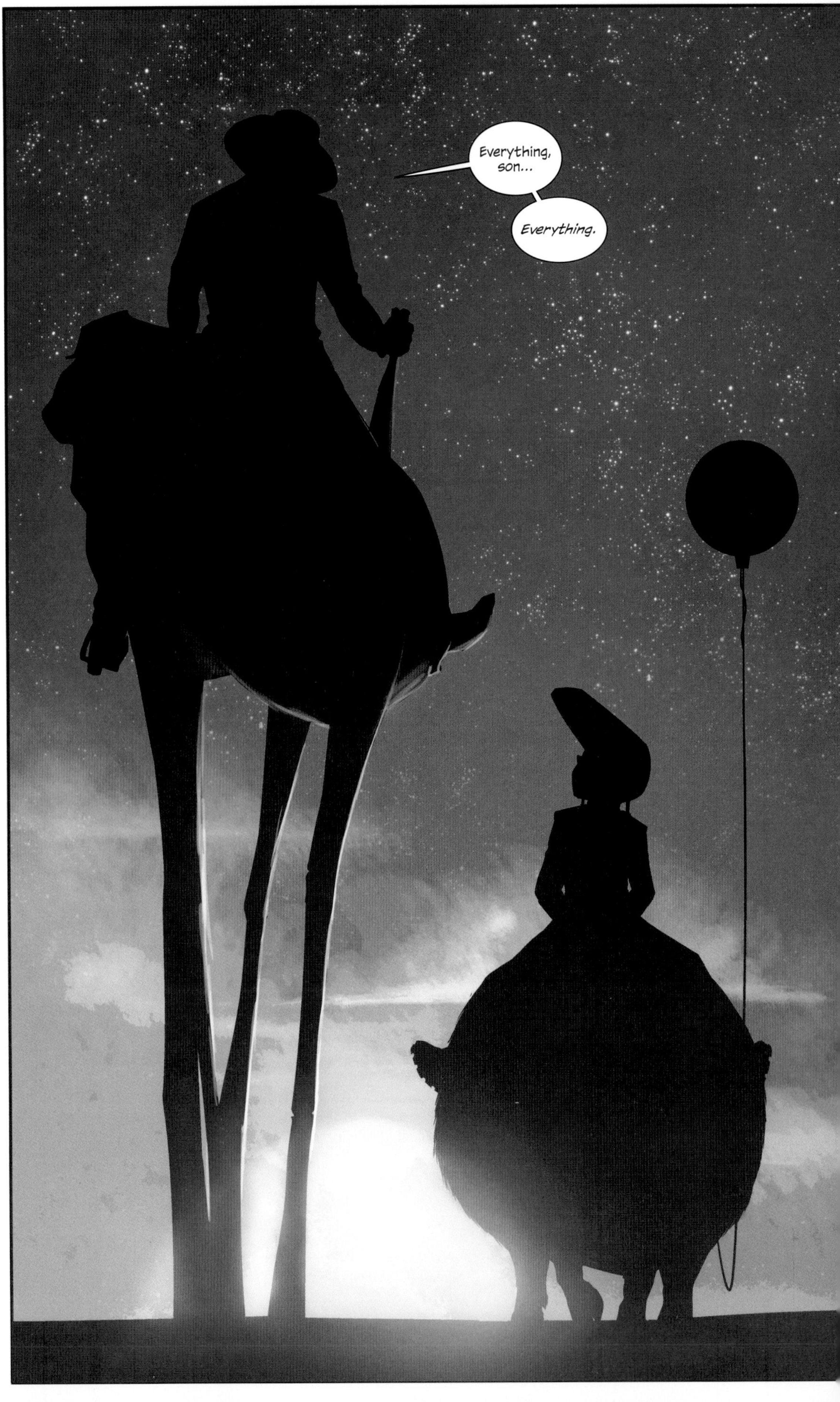
Everything, son...
Everything.

END YEAR TWO

The dream is over...

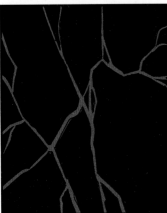

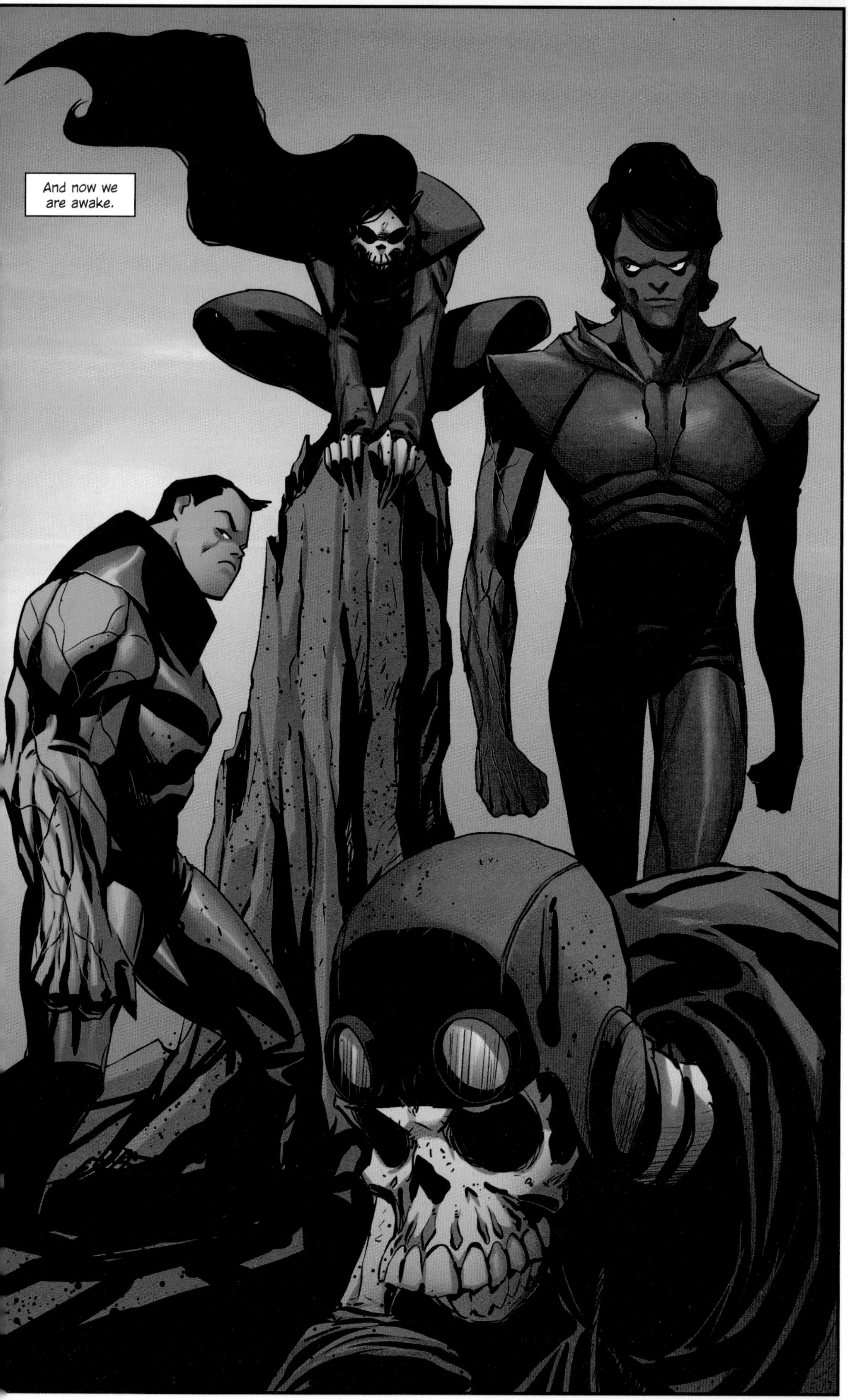
And now we are awake.

ALL MEN TELL **LIES.**
THESE ARE A **FEW** OF
THEM.

Jonathan Hickman is the visionary talent behind such works as the Eisner-nominated **NIGHTLY NEWS**, **THE MANHATTAN PROJECTS** and **PAX ROMANA**. He also plies his trade at MARVEL working on books like **FANTASTIC FOUR** and **THE AVENGERS**.

His twin brother, Marc, went missing in St. Lucia six months ago and hasn't been heard from since.

Jonathan lives in South Carolina when he isn't vacationing or searching for his brother.

You can visit his website: *www.pronea.com*, or email him at: *jonathan@pronea.com*.

Nick Dragotta's career began at Marvel Comics working on titles as varied as **X-STATIX, THE AGE OF THE SENTRY, X-MEN: FIRST CLASS, CAPTAIN AMERICA: FOREVER ALLIES** and **VENGEANCE.**

FANTASTIC FOUR #588 was the first time he collaborated with Jonathan Hickman, which lead to their successful run on **FF.**

In addition, Nick is the co-creator of **HOWTOONS**, a comic series teaching kids how to build things and explore the world around them. **EAST OF WEST** is Nick's first creator-owned project at Image.